James Lawrence Onderdonk

Idaho

Facts And Statistics

James Lawrence Onderdonk

Idaho
Facts And Statistics

ISBN/EAN: 9783744725620

Printed in Europe, USA, Canada, Australia, Japan

Cover: Foto ©Andreas Hilbeck / pixelio.de

More available books at **www.hansebooks.com**

IDAHO

FACTS AND STATISTICS

CONCERNING ITS

Mining, Farming, Stock-Raising, Lumbering, and Other Resources and Industries:

TOGETHER WITH NOTES ON THE
CLIMATE, SCENERY, GAME, and MINERAL SPRINGS.

INFORMATION FOR THE HOME-SEEKER, CAPITALIST, PROSPECTOR, AND TRAVELER.

BY

JAMES L. UNDERDONK,

TERRITORIAL CONTROLLER.

SAN FRANCISCO, CAL.:
A. L. BANCROFT & COMPANY, BOOK AND JOB PRINTERS.
1885.

CONTENTS.

CHAPTER I.—HISTORICAL.

	PAGE.
Organization—Origin of the Name—First Discoverers—Indian Depredations—Development	9

CHAPTER II.—DESCRIPTIVE.

Mountains—Rivers—Valleys—Climate—Natural Scenery—Shoshone Falls—Lakes 22

CHAPTER III.—NATIVE TREES, PLANTS, AND ANIMALS.

Timber—Wild Fruits—Grasses—Wild Flowers—Quadrupeds—Birds—Fishes 29

CHAPTER IV.—MINING.

Discovery of Gold—Oro Fino—Florence—Boisé Basin—Owyhee—Rocky Bar—Salmon River—Yankee Fork—Wood River—Cœur d'Alene—Snake River Placers—Iron—Copper—Coal—Marble—Mica—Sulphur—Idaho's Yield—Minerals at Present Mined—Minerals Known to Exist, but not Mined 33

CHAPTER V.—FARMING AND STOCK-RAISING.

Classes of Soil—Irrigation—Fruit—Grain—Unoccupied Lands—Advantages for Stock-raising—Idaho Cattle—Reclamation of Desert Lands. 47

CHAPTER VI.—COUNTIES OF IDAHO.

Ada—Alturas—Bear Lake—Boisé—Cassia—Custer—Idaho—Kootenai—Lemhi—Nez Percé—Oneida—Owyhee—Shoshone—Washington.... 54

CHAPTER VII.—IDAHO INDIANS.

Kootenais—Salish Family, Cœur d'Alenes and Pend d'Oreilles—Sahaptin Family, Nez Percés—Their Origin, Customs, and Laws—Lemhi Indians, Shoshones, Bannocks, and Sheepeaters — Shoshones or Snakes, Original Territory, Customs and Characteristics—Territory of the Bannocks—Sheepeaters—Fort Hall—Advancement in Civilization of Indians—Sign-language.................................. 133

CHAPTER VIII.—MISCELLANEOUS.

Schools—Churches—Societies—Newspapers—U. S. Land-offices—Railroads—Wages—Idaho Altitudes................................ 139

INTRODUCTORY.

It is within the memory of men still living when prominent statesmen declared that no scheme could be more visionary than that of an internal commerce between the Hudson and the Columbia. It was solemnly declared in the halls of Congress that "the God of nature had interposed obstacles to this connection which neither the enterprise nor the science of this or any other age could overcome." Less than two generations have passed away since these utterances were made, yet enterprise and science have virtually leveled these apparently insuperable obstacles. The spirit of "manifest destiny" long since determined to recognize no limit short of the Pacific Ocean, and is already erecting new empires in the far North-west. The trapper's trail has been followed by the emigrant's wagon, and both have been overtaken by the modern railway. Boisé City, Idaho, is now within easier reach of Washington City than was Boston two generations ago. So swift have been the changes, so rapid the developments, that there is a constantly increasing demand for the latest information concerning this newly opened section. It is in order to meet this demand, and to dispel much of the misapprehension now existing, that the following pages have been written.

We have endeavored to avoid the exaggeration and misrepresentation which have too often characterized works of this kind, it being our aim to set forth as concisely as possible plain facts and statistics regarding the resources of this Territory. Many of the articles descriptive of the different localities were prepared by actual residents of the sections; and as in many instances they were written under the direction of the commissioners of the respective counties, they may in a great degree be regarded as official.

The writer desires hereby to express his appreciation of assistance rendered by several gentlemen, whose contributions on the different localities will be found in their proper places, duly credited. He also acknowledges his obligations to Messrs. Robert E. Strahorn, W. W. Elliott, W. A. Goulder, H. S. Hampton, C. L. Rood, H. J. Burleigh, A. Leland, Edward Hammond, and others; also to the editorial press generally of the Territory, and to the *Salt Lake Tribune*, whose labors in advertising the resources of the Far West are especially deserving of commendation.

Idaho is pre-eminently a country of the present and the future. From where the picturesque lakes of Cœur d'Alene and Pend d'Oreille bask in the wooded mountains of the extreme north, to where the cattle feed upon a thousand hills in the south, her vast territory is now open for exploration. Responsive to the pick of the prospector, her hills are yielding up their treasures, which have lain hidden since the dawn of time. Her long-silent valleys are making to the husbandman a due return for his faithful and arduous toil. Within the past few months long-separated sections have been united by iron bands, and long-estranged communities brought into easy contact. The solitudes of ages are rapidly giving way to the demands of commerce and agriculture. This mountain-locked Territory, now rendered easily accessible, offers unsurpassed advantages to the home-seeker, the prospector, and the capitalist, and extends a cordial welcome to all who with sturdy wills and willing hands may seek to share her bounties. There is land enough for all who may choose to come. Her fertile fields and inexhaustible mines, her extensive forests and unoccupied pasture-lands, her rushing rivers and her placid lakes, invite energy and enterprise to develop the resources which nature has so lavishly bestowed.

Boisé City, December, 1884.

IDAHO.

Let others sigh of orange-groves,
　Where warmer sunbeams shine,
The lofty mountains freedom loves,
　And freedom's choice is mine.
I sigh not for a southern clime
　Where tropic roses blow;
Give me the pine-clad hills sublime,
　The hills of Idaho.

Here many a crystal streamlet clear
　Flows from its mountain home,
And on its banks the peaceful deer
　Are free, and fearless roam;
And beautiful in evening still
　To mark the sunset glow
Rest on some distant snow-crowned hill
　That towers in Idaho.

Though commerce rears no cities proud,
　Though wealth has here no shrine,
Though fashion draws no servile crowd,
　A prouder boast is thine.
Thy sons are fearless, free, and bold,
　Thy daughters pure as snow,
For honor, truth, and beauty hold
　The homes of Idaho.

And I do love thee, mountain land,
　Though not a son of thine.
For me thy scenes have something grand
　In every rugged line.
For I was born among the hills,
　And reared where tempests blow.
And thus my soul with rapture thrills
　To hail thee, Idaho.

O may thy children ever be
　To one another true,
And blessed with peace and harmony,
　Their upward path pursue,
Till, linked unto thy sister states,
　Thy star with theirs shall glow,
And tell what glory yet awaits
　The youthful Idaho.

　　　　　　　　—Cameron McDonald.

CHAPTER I.—HISTORICAL.

ORGANIZATION.

There seems to be some confusion in the minds of historical writers as to the time and manner in which the United States acquired possession of what is now Idaho Territory. The majority of writers and text-books assign it as a portion of the vast area included in the Louisiana purchase. This, however, is hardly correct. What was generically known as the "Oregon Country" was not included in that purchase. The facts are thus succinctly set forth in Mr. Blaine's "Twenty Years of Congress:" "The Louisiana purchase did not extend beyond the main range of the Rocky Mountains, and our title to that large area which is included in the State of Oregon and in the Territories of Washington and Idaho rests upon a different foundation, or rather upon a series of claims, each of which was strong under the law of nations. We claimed it, first, by right of original discovery of the Columbia River by an American navigator in 1792; second, by an original exploration in 1805; third, by original settlement in 1810, by the enterprising company of which John Jacob Astor was the head; and lastly and principally, by the transfer of the Spanish title in 1819, many years after the Louisiana purchase was accomplished. It is not, however, probable that we should have been able to maintain our title to Oregon if we had not secured the intervening country. It was certainly our purchase of Louisiana that enabled us to secure the Spanish title to the shores of the Pacific, and without that title we could hardly have maintained our claim. As against England, our title seemed to us to be perfect; but as against Spain, our case was not so strong. The purchase of Louisiana may, therefore, be fairly said to have carried with it and secured to us our possession of Oregon."

Oregon originally embraced all of the area claimed by the United States on the Pacific Coast from latitude 42° to 54° 40′ N. It was jointly occupied by Great Britain and the United States until 1846, when Great Britain renounced all claim to the region south of the 49th parallel. The Territory of Washington was created March 2, 1853, embracing all that region lying between the Pacific and the summit of the Rocky Mountains, and north of the Columbia River and the 46th parallel. When Oregon was admitted as a State, February 14, 1859, the region between what was established as its eastern boundary line, and the Rocky Mountains, and north of the 42d parallel, was added to Washington, which then comprised an area of 193,071 square miles, including the present Territory of Idaho and parts of Montana and Wyoming.

Idaho was created by the Act of March 3, 1863, from parts of Dakota, Nebraska, and Washington Territories. As originally constituted it embraced 326,373 square miles, including all the present Territory of Montana and a large portion of Wyoming. In 1868 Idaho was reduced to its present dimensions, extending from the British Possessions on the north to Utah and Nevada on the south; from Montana and Wyoming on the east to Oregon and Washington on the west, having a length from north to south of four hundred and ten miles, and a width from east to west varying from 60 to 257 miles.

ORIGIN OF THE NAME.

Idaho is generally supposed to be a corruption of an Indian word meaning "Gem of the Mountains." This, however, is disputed. The poet Joaquin Miller writes as follows on the subject:

"The distinction of naming Idaho certainly belongs to my old friend Colonel Craig (since deceased) of Craig's Mountain, Nez Percé County. As for some fellow naming it in Congress—bah! The name was familiar in 5,000 men's mouths as they wallowed through the snow in '61, on their way to Oro Fino mines long before Congress, or any man of Congress, had even heard of the new discovery.

"The facts are these: I was riding pony-express at the time rumors reached us through the Nez Percé Indians that gold was to be found on the head waters and tributaries of the Salmon River. I had lived with the Indians; and Colonel Craig, who had spent most of his life with them, often talked with me about possible discoveries in the mountains to the right, as we rode to Oro Fino, and of what the Indians said of the then unknown region. Gallop your horse, as I have a hundred times, against the rising sun. As you climb the Sweetwater Mountains, far away to your right, you will see the name of Idaho written on the mountain top—at least, you will see a peculiar and beautiful light at sunrise, a sort of diadem on two grand clusters of mountains that bear away under the clouds fifty miles distant. I called Colonel Craig's attention to this peculiar and beautifully arched light. 'That,' said he, 'is what the Indians call E-dah-hoe, which means the light, or diadem on the line of the mountains. That was the first time I ever heard the name. Later, in September, '61, when I rode into the newly discovered camp to establish an express office, I took with me an Indian from Lapwai. We followed an Indian trail, crossed Craig's Mountains, then Camas Prairie, and had all the time E-dah-hoe Mount for our objective point.

"On my return to Lewiston I wrote a letter containing a brief account of our trip and of the mines, and it was published in one of the Oregon papers, which one I have now forgotten. In that account I often mentioned E-dah-hoe, but spelt it Idaho, leaving the pronunciation unmarked by any diacritical signs. So that, perhaps, I may have been the first to give it its present spelling, but I certainly did not originate the word."

A writer in the *New West*, apparently well informed, declares that Idaho is not a Nez Percé word, adding: "The mountains that Joaquin Miller speaks of may be named with a somewhat similar appellation, but most likely the whole story grows out of the fertile imagination of the poet. Idaho Springs, in Colorado, were known long before Idaho Territory was organized. The various Territories at their organization should have been given some appropriate local name. Colorado was named after the river of that name, though it is not within its boundaries. It should have been called Idaho. It was the name first placed in the bill organizing it, but which was afterward changed."

William H. Wallace, the delegate to Congress from Washington Territory, who introduced the bill making a new territory out of the eastern portion of Washington, pleased with the beauty of the name of Idaho, suggested it as an appropriate one.

Ex-senator Nesmith of Oregon gives still another account: "The bill first passed the House of Representatives designating the present Territory of Idaho as 'Montana,' when it came up for consideration in the Senate on the 3d of March, 1863. Senator Wilson of Massachusetts moved to strike out the word 'Montana' and insert 'Idaho.' Mr. Harding of Oregon said: 'I think the name "Idaho" is preferable to "Montana."' Idaho in English signifies 'the Gem of the Mountains.' I heard others suggest that it meant in the Indian tongue 'Shining Mountains,' all of which are synonymous. I do not know from which of the Indian tongues the two words 'Ida-ho' come. I think, however, if you will pursue the inquiry among those familiar with the Nez Percé, Shoshone, and Flat Head tribes, that you will find the origin of the two words as I have given it above."

FIRST DISCOVERERS.

Probably the first white men that ever visited Idaho, so far as any authentic record shows, were the party that accompanied Lewis and Clarke in their exploring expedition in 1805-6. They had passed along Snake River, named by them the Lewis Fork, to its junction with the Columbia. The river farther north was named, in honor of the other leader of the expedition, Clarke's Fork.

On the 18th of August, 1805, the party were encamped near the junction of Horse Plain and Red Rock Creeks, in what is now Montana. Clarke set out with eleven men for a Shoshone village near where Fort Lemhi has since been built in what is now Lemhi County, Idaho. Clarke was to be joined here by Lewis, who brought forward the remainder of the party and the baggage. They expected to proceed thence to the "navigable waters flowing into the Columbia."

They arrived at the Lemhi on the 20th. There they learned that the stream near which they were encamped was joined ten miles below by a branch from the south-west. The Indian name of this "branch" was Sahaptim; the modern name is Salmon. In the afternoon of the same day the party set out for Sahaptim River. On the 21st another village was reached, where a fish weir was constructed. That evening they encamped on Salmon River, near where Salmon City now stands. Finding that the river was not navigable, they procured horses from the Indians. By the 30th twenty-nine animals had been procured, on which baggage and goods were packed, and the first pack-train controlled by white men on Salmon River set out to explore the way to the Columbia. Keeping on the north side of the river, they traveled for about fifty miles, encamping on a stream they called Fish Creek, ten miles from its junction with the Salmon River, September 1st. On the 13th of September the company emerged from the mountains in which rise the waters of the Lolo branch, and on the 20th reached a village of the Nez Percés not far from the south fork of the Clearwater River. It is an interesting fact, as showing the effect of change wrought by time and civilization, that the prairies, described at the time as barren and producing little more than a bearded grass about three inches high and a prickly pear of several varieties, have turned out to be of rich fertile soil, now covered with fields of waving grain. No white settlers were found, and no settlements were attempted to be made. Traces of white men were detected, however, as Lewis and Clarke write: "Those strangers who visit the Columbia for the purpose of trade or hunting must be either English or Americans. The Indians inform us that they speak the same language that we do, and indeed, the few words which the Indians have learned from the sailors, such as musket, powder, shot, knife, file, heave the lead, damned rascal, and other phrases of that description, evidently show that the visitors speak the English language."

Lewis and Clarke returned through Idaho in the following year. Early in June they reached the Salmon River, called by them the Sommanah. They first ascended the creek on the south side of the Clearwater, twenty miles, thence over a high, rough country to the Salmon. No fish appearing in the Clearwater by the 10th, the camp was transferred to Quamash Flats, now known as Camas Prairie in Idaho County. On the 16th, though the snow was still several feet deep, they renewed their journey, passing over into Montana to the head waters of the Missouri, and finally reached St. Louis September 23d, thus ending their journey of nine thousand miles. The accounts of their explorations naturally aroused an interest in the Far West. One of the results was the formation of the Missouri Fur Company, which established a post at Fort Henry on Snake River in 1810, but which was soon afterward abandoned. In 1811 Wilson P. Hunt and a party of sixty belonging to the Pacific Fur Company arrived at Fort Henry, whence they moved down Snake River. Leaving Fort Henry on the 19th of October they proceeded down the river in fifteen canoes. One of the party, named Miller, had joined some hunters and gone south as far as Bear River, had been very successful in negotiating with the natives for peltries, but had been subsequently robbed of everything by the Arrapahoes. Hunt's party proceeded down Snake River, but encountered many perils. At last it was determined to separate into two detachments, Hunt with his guide and eighteen men to take the right bank, and Crooks with the remainder to take the left. They little knew of the dangers and distance to be traveled before reaching the Columbia; more than a thousand miles of unexplored wilderness lay between them and Fort Astoria; over this region wandered hostile and savage tribes of unknown numbers. The pack of each man was reduced to twenty pounds, including seven and a half pounds of food. Through that dreary month of November, 1811, the two parties remained separated, and it was not until nearly a month had elapsed when Hunt's party one morning while breaking camp heard the voices of their late companions calling across the river for food. "A vague and almost superstitious terror," says Washington Irving, "had infected the minds of Mr. Hunt's followers, enfeebled and rendered imaginative of horrors by the dismal scenes through which they had passed. They regarded the haggard crew, hovering like specters of famine on the opposite bank, with indefinite feelings of awe and apprehension, as if something desperate and dangerous was to be feared from them." A boat was hastily made of sticks, over which was stretched the skin of a horse eaten the previous night, by means of which a little meat was carried over to them. One of Crooks' party, almost demented from hunger, declared he could not wait for the food to be cooked, and leaped into the canoe to be conveyed back to Hunt's party. As they neared the opposite bank, the thought of food so soon to be obtained acting upon his enfeebled brain drove him frantic with joy. Springing up, he danced with delight, but his motions upset the frail canoe. He was carried away by the swift current and drowned.

They were now about five hundred miles by river from Henry River. Several of the party, including John Day, were so ill that it was found necessary for the rest to leave them and push on. By the 15th of December they reached the site of old Fort Boisé. They were still in two parties—one on each side of the river. "With great difficulty," says H. H. Bancroft, "the river being full of floating ice, and the men half starved and half frozen, weak and dispirited, Hunt crossed with his party to the other side, and joining their old comrades on the 24th of December, they started, pursuing a north-westerly course, over mountains, plains, and valleys, buying food from the natives, picking up and carrying the exhausted, who would throw themselves upon the ground, declaring they could die but could not proceed an inch further; and stopping on New Year's Day, 1812, for the Canadians to have their dance, and feast on dog and horse meat, though some of them could not stand."

The next expedition of any importance was that of Captain Bonneville, who, in 1834, with one hundred men, camped on Port Neuf River, in eastern Idaho.

In the same year Nathaniel J. Wyeth, with a party of sixty men, started across the continent and established Fort Hall as a trading post near Snake River.

This was probably the first permanent settlement in eastern Idaho.

On the 11th of June, Wyeth and his party encamped on a branch of the Blackfoot, near Port Neuf; the 12th on Ross' Fork and the 14th on Snake River. The fort was permanently located on the east bank of the Snake River, a little north of the Port Neuf. "The post became famous," says Bancroft, "and performed good service during the several great overland emigrations. The emigrant trail was made to pass by it; it was near to the Great Salt Lake; was central and valuable in scores of ways. From this point in time radiated roads in every direction; to Missouri, to California, to Utah, to Oregon, and to British Columbia. In 1865, Angus McDonald valued the fort and lands belonging to it at $1,000,000. It was near the old war ground of the Blackfeet, Snake, and Crows, and prevented many a massacre. It was several times attacked and nearly burned, but stood to its duty nobly." Wyeth and his party crossed the Snake on the 6th of August and explored the region for miles around. Crossing the mountains they encamped on Malade River. On the 13th Camas Prairie was reached. Two days later they reached Boisé River, "crammed with salmon." On the 23d they crossed Snake River, leaving Idaho behind them, camping on the rich plains of Malheur.

In 1836, Wyeth was forced to sell Fort Hall to the Hudson's Bay Company. The latter company had already erected, probably in 1835, what is known as old Fort Boisé near the mouth of the Boisé River. The original structure fell down about 1847 or '48, but was rebuilt a short distance north. The new building continued to be occupied by the Hudson Bay Company until the United States acquired undisputed title to the land.

According to the published account by Mr. W. H. Gray, the first mission in Idaho was established in 1836 at Lapwai, twelve miles from the present town of Lewiston. A printing press with type was presented in 1839 by the missionaries of the Sandwich Islands to the Presbyterian missionaries of Oregon, and it reached Lapwai that year, where E. O. Hall put it in operation to print books in the Nez Percé language. Messrs. Rogers and Spalding soon learned to set type, and they printed small books in the Nez Percé language that were used in their school.

"That old press and type are now stored in the State Capitol of Oregon, and the building used for that primitive printing office is yet standing, though somewhat modernized, near the Lapwai Mission in Idaho. This was the first printing office on the Pacific Coast of America north of Mexico. Thus Idaho has the honor of having the first printing press on the coast."

The Roman Catholic missionaries seem to have been in the main more successful with the Indians than the Protestants, and in some instances have sustained their missions to the present day. Father De Smet in his *Letters*, published at Philadelphia in 1843, is responsible for the following statement: "The Jesuits De Smet, Mengarini, Point, and others had since 1840 made several missionary tours through the Columbia countries, in the course of which they baptized some thousands of Indians; they also erected a church at a place near the Kallerspelm Lake (Pend d'Oreille), on Clarke's River, where the Blessed Virgin appeared in person to a little Indian boy, whose youth, piety, and sincerity, say the good fathers, joined to the nature of the fact which he related, forbade us to doubt the truth of his statement."

The Cœur d'Alene Mission was established in 1853. The building is still in existence at the edge of the Indian Reservation, on the Cœur d'Alene River, about sixteen miles from the lake, where the steamboats make their upper landing. It is in charge of Father Joset, but has been virtually abandoned for the "New Mission."

INDIAN DEPREDATIONS.

One of the greatest obstacles to the development of Idaho previous to 1878 was the presence of predatory bands of Indians, who long regarded the mountain ranges and prairies of Idaho as their peculiar property. In another chapter space will be devoted to a description of the different tribes and their reservations. For the present it is our intention to refer to some of the depredations committed by the savages simply as tending to show with what the pioneers of Idaho had to contend in making the Territory a place safe as well as suitable for a civilized people to inhabit. From earliest times when Captain Pierce first led his band toward the unknown Golconda, which afterward developed into the great Oro Fino mining region, the Indians have disputed the approach of the whites. Step by step the dauntless pioneer has fought his way into the heart of the mountains. The most cruel, the most treacherous kind of warfare that human deviltry could suggest has been brought to bear to thwart his efforts. It was enough to make the stoutest heart quail and the most enthusiastic ardor cool.

But the same spirit which animated the early settlers in the eastern colonies two hundred years ago, and which, transmitted from sire to son, made American civilization possible, actuated the pioneers of the Far West in our own day. The men that blazed the trails through the wilderness and carved out new empires less than a generation since, were composed of the same stuff that has made American grit proverbial throughout the world.

The same opposition to the development of the mines of North Idaho was repeated for many years, wherever new discoveries were made. The first party that entered Boisé Basin, in 1863, were the victims of the blood-thirsty savages, and the death of Grimes disheartened the rest, for the time being, from further prospecting in that neighborhood. Subsequently a party were assembled on the Payette River, at a place known as Picket Corral. The savages, consisting of Shoshones and Bannocks, were swarming in the surrounding mountains. A company was organized under Capt. Standifer, and succeeded in effectually subduing the Indians. It was a long and fierce contest, and many of the survivors, broken down in health and property, never recovered and have never been reimbursed. Owyhee County likewise suffered for years. In July, 1864, an engagement took place between Indians and volunteers, about eighty miles south of Silver City on the Owyhee River. They were in a canyon, the walls of which averaged 200 or 300 feet in height. The fight commenced about 2 o'clock P. M. and lasted until midnight, and resulted in thirty-six Indians being killed and an unknown number wounded. But two of the whites were killed. A memorable encounter occurred near Battle Creek, in Oneida County, between United States trooops, under the command of Gen. P. E. Connor, and a large number of Indians. The following description was prepared expressly for this work, by Hon. Alexander Stalker, of Franklin, who was an eye-witness: The first settlement of South-eastern Idaho was made on the 14th of April, 1860, by thirteen families, subsequently augmented by others through the remaining spring and summer months to perhaps sixty families. The Territory of Idaho was not created by Act of Congress until nearly three years afterward. This portion of Idaho was infested by renegade Indians, they having been expelled from tribal relations because of their unmanageable and atrocious natures. The most blood-thirsty and ferocious of this class were the acknowledged leaders, the most notable of whom were Bear Hunter, Lehi, and Sagwitch, who, when not prowling around the settlements stealing horses and cattle, occasionally killing some one in the canyons or fields, were depredating upon the unfortunate emigrants on their way to Oregon and California; not infrequently were we subjected to dole out of our scanty store such exactions as their wants or caprice might suggest. What expostulation could not avert we were compelled to grant, keeping up an appearance of friendship totally at variance with our feelings. A sense of our insecurity made it necessary for us to corral and stand guard over our stock every night for nearly three years.

This condition of things culminated in the memorable battle of Battle Creek, in the winter of 1863, between a detatchment of California volunteers commanded by General P. Edward Connor, consisting of about fifty men, and a band of Indians of about one hundred and seventy-five, under Bear Hunter, Lehi, and Sagwitch. Of the above number seventy-five might have been squaws and papooses; the fighting number was about one hundred.

They were encamped by a stream running through a deep ravine and emptying into Bear River, eleven miles north-east of Franklin. The Indians were fully aware of the intention of General Connor to chastise them; the time of his leaving Salt Lake City; the number of troops in his command; their every movement up to the time of their appearance on the battle-field. So confident were the Indians of victory, that they did not even consider it necessary to remove their families to places of safety, as is customary with them in their warfare. Illustrative of this fact, as the infantry came in at the south-east corner of our fort (at that time Franklin consisted of four equal sides, forming a square, with openings at each corner) Bear Hunter went out at the north-east corner; some one remarked, as he was going out, that the soldiers would use him up; he very significantly replied: "Maybe so."

The day on which the battle was fought was one of the coldest incident to the hard winters in this high northern latitude.

The infantry and baggage wagons filed into Franklin on the afternoon preceding the battle. The cavalry came up in the night, and were on the battle-field early in the morning. Major McGarry led the charge. The Indians, under cover of the banks of the ravine, placed the troops at great disadvantage. As the volunteers advanced the Indians opened fire, killing fourteen volunteers and wounding six or eight more. General Connor, finding the Indians unassailable from that point, hastily ordered a flank movement, and charging from the head of the ravine, drove the Indians precipitately before them, ending in an indiscriminate slaughter, few escaping; some jumped into Bear River and were drowned. Sagwitch—incredible as it may seem—though severely wounded, floated down Bear River under the ice, made for the shore, and traveled some fifteen or twenty miles to Pocotello's camp in Malade Valley. Although badly frozen he lived, but was a confirmed cripple.

The number of Indians generally supposed to have lost their lives in the battle was one hundred and sixty-five. This ended the career of perhaps the worst Indians that ever infested this Western country.

Immediately after the battle the dead and those of the wounded who were unable to ride on horseback, belonging to General Connor's command, were brought into Franklin in wagons. Some of the wounded were taken to the school-house, others to private houses, receiving such kind care and attention as our scanty means afforded. On the following day the wounded were taken on sleds to Salt Lake City, some of whom died on the way; and although the campaign was short and decisive, there were few of the command that were not more or less disabled from wounds received in battle or from frost-bite or exposure. It would be useless and unprofitable to give an accurate account of every Indian engagement in Idaho. This chapter, however, would be incomplete without some reference to the Nez Percé war of 1877.

"The Nez Percé Indians," says A. F. Parker, "are one of the greatest nations of the Pacific Coast, and in intelligence, industry, loyalty to the whites, and for conforming to the methods of civilization they have demonstrated themselves to be the most enlightened tribe on the continent. The nation has been divided into two distinct tribes, known as Treaty and Non-treaty Indians. The Treaty Indians originally secured possession of their reservation by treaty of June 11, 1855. A new treaty was made June 9, 1863, reducing the area of the reservation, and upon the expiration of that treaty a new one was made August 13, 1868, which has expired, but still continues in force.

"The Reservation or Treaty Indians have ever been fast friends to the whites, and have proved their loyalty in the series of wars through which the country has passed in its march to civilization. The most notable instances of their friendship were displayed in the ill-fated Steptoe expedition, when they saved the command from massacre, and in offering shelter to the whites who fled to Lapwai after the Whitman massacre on the Walla Walla River.

"The Non-treaties resided in the Wallowa Valley in Oregon. They had never accepted government bounty, and refused to live on the reservation, although close relations were always maintained between the two tribes.

"In 1877, after a series of collisions with white settlers, the order came from Washington to eject the Non-treaties from the Wallowa, and to place them on the reservation in Idaho. Councils were held at Lapwai to apportion lands to the various chiefs of the Non-treaties, and it was thought that all arrangements for their peaceable transfer to the reservation had been made, when they startled the country by a series of murders and atrocities upon solitary settlers, which inaugurated the Nez Percé war of 1877. The settlements on Camas Prairie and Salmon River were raided, and Indian vengeance, summary and swift, was visited upon the heads of the innocent and unarmed settlers and their families. Neither age nor sex was spared in this merciless crusade."

Joseph, chief of the Non-treaty Nez Percés, and his band are now safe in Indian Territory. Lieut. C. E. S. Woods, who was a participant in the war, writes that he has been informed by an Indian that Joseph wished to surrender rather than leave the country or bring further misery on his people, but that in council he was overruled by the older chiefs, Ap-push-na-hite (Looking-glass), White Bird, and Too-hul-hul-suit; and Joseph would not desert the common cause. According to this informant Joseph's last appeal was to call a council in the dale, and passionately condemn the proposed retreat from Idaho. "What are we fighting for?" he asked; "is it for our lives? No! It is for this land where the bones of our fathers are buried. I do not want to take my women among strangers; I do not want to die in a strange land. Some of you tried to say once that I was afraid of the whites. Stay here with me now and you shall have plenty of fighting. We will put our women behind us in these mountains, and die on our land fighting for them. I would rather do that than run I know not where." But the retreat being decided on, he led his caravan, two thousand horses and more, women, children, old men and old women, the wounded, palsied, and blind, by a seemingly impassable trail, interlaced with fallen trees, through the ruggedest mountains to the Bitter Root Valley, where (a fact unprecedented in Indian warfare) he made a treaty of forbearance with the inhabitants, passing by settlements containing banks and stores, and near farms rich with stock, but taking nothing and hurting no one. So he pushed on; he crossed the Rocky Mountains twice, the Yellowstone and Missouri Rivers, and was within one day's march of Canada when he was taken.

A writer in the *Nez Percé News*, of Lewiston, thus sums up the whole affair:

"We are not a hard-hearted people in northern Idaho, but we have rights which not even the United States government can infringe with impunity, and when these rights are trodden upon we are bound to kick. In 1877 northern Idaho experienced the horrors of an Indian war. This war was not sought by our people. In this instance ninety soldiers were required to transport 300 Indians—who had never accepted government bounty—upon an Indian reservation maintained at government expense. * * * * *

"The experiment was not a success. The fair fertile fields of northern Idaho were the scenes of savage warfare, and were baptized in blood. Our best citizens found their homes laid low by the desolating torch; their wives, mothers, sisters, daughters, murdered in the malignant ferocity of savage wrath; women and children outraged while living and mutilated when dead; defenseless friends slain by treachery; kinsmen killed in bloody battle; the fruit of years of industry wantonly destroyed in barbarous glee; what provender the Indians left taken sometimes by force, to subsist the pursuing troops; citizen volunteers abandoning property, risking life, enduring hunger and thirst and deprivation, everywhere to the front, harassing the enemy in flank and rear, and engaging him in open fight in full sight of apathetic troops wearing United States livery, but indifferent to the result of the bloody conflict waging under their eyes—rapine, murder, carnage, stalking hand in hand with fierce and strategic foemen through the land, leaving in their wake a broad trail of desolation whose scars can be seen upon the face of the country to this day. All these dreadful scenes and many more were participated in by the people of northern Idaho without hope or promise of reward.

"The Indians were removed to the Indian Territory, where they have since been maintained in luxury and idleness at the expense of the government. After their removal our citizens devoted themselves once more to the peaceful pursuits of industry and agriculture. Six years of practical effort and fair industry have rebuilt the places laid waste by war, and made the face of the country more beautiful and productive than ever. The scars of war have been covered by the fruits of peace, until Camas Prairie is now the garden spot of the territory."

The Bannock Indians, originally comprising a very numerous tribe of widely scattered bands or families, claimed and roamed over the extensive region traversed by the upper and central sections of Snake River and its tributaries. These Indians had subsisted from time immemorial by the peaceful pursuits of hunting, fishing, and root-digging; though they managed to make their presence felt by their skill in the art of stealing and in occasional attacks upon helpless immigrant trains. With the discovery of gold in the mountain region drained by the Boisé River and its tributaries came a heterogeneous crowd of gold-hunters, whose advent was soon followed by frequent collisions with the Indians, resulting from the innate propensity of the red man to seize and appropriate horses and other property which chanced to be left in his way unguarded. The first attempts at permanent settlement by the whites made it necessary for the General Government to interfere between the whites and Indians, when the Bannocks with their tribes were subjected to the time-honored but much-criticised governmental policy of being collected upon reservations and placed under the care of Indian agents. The section of country set apart for the Bannocks is known as the Fort Hall Indian Reservation. Using this nominal home as a rendezvous upon which to meet and receive annuities and to consume government rations while they lasted, the Bannocks passed the greater part of each year in roaming over the Snake River plains and among the towns and settlements in the Boisé and other valleys. Among the favorite summer resorts of the Bannocks was the section now forming a part of Alturas County, known by the somewhat general appellation of "Camas Prairie." Here during several weeks of the summer months those Indians would meet and pitch their tepees or lodges, and while the men searched the mountains in quest of game the women would engage in digging the nutritious bulb which formed the root of the camas plant which grew in unlimited abundance on the damper portions of the prairie. Up to the summer of 1878 these Indians and the few whites who occupied the prairie and neighboring plains as a summer range for their stock got along without any serious collisions, though the Indians were known to be somewhat restive under this "joint occupancy," claiming that the prairie was a portion of their ancient domain which they had never ceded to the government by treaty, and that the presence of the whites with their herds of cattle and swine was fast destroying the camas plant, whose yield of roots formed an important and essential item among their limited sources of subsistence.

During the Nez Percé war of the preceding year, 1877, the Bannocks gave what was then considered a substantial proof of friendship for the whites by furnishing a company of active young warriors to act as couriers, guides, and scouts to the whites in the field in pursuit of Chief Joseph and his band of hostile Nez Percés, who were then making their way out of northern Idaho and across Montana. The leader of these Bannock scouts was a somewhat noted young warrior, known as Buffalo Horn, who had served in the same capacity under Generals Custer and Miles and other distinguished officers of the United States Army, in campaigns against the Sioux and other hostile tribes in Montana. After the surrender of Joseph at Bear's Paw Mountain, near the British line, late in the autumn of 1877, Buffalo Horn and his company of scouts returned to the Fort Hall reservation, where they passed the winter. The month of June, 1878, found the Bannock Indians in considerable force camped at their old haunts in Camas Prairie, while Buffalo Horn and a few of his braves were passing the time in Boisé City, making frequent visits to the officers and troops at Boisé Barracks. The young chief seemed excessively proud of the record he had made in the army, and no one suspected his want of friendship and loyalty to the whites. At length he disappeared from the neighborhood of Boisé City, and very soon there came rumors of threatened trouble between the whites and Indians on Camas Prairie, the Indians becoming daily more haughty and insolent, claiming the whole prairie and insisting that the whites should leave it.

About the 31st of May two white men arrived at Boisé City on foaming steeds, reporting that the Bannocks had become openly hostile, that they were strongly encamped to the number of several hundred in a natural fortress of lava rocks, near the prairie, from whence a party had issued on the preceding day and made a murderous assault on two white men who were peaceably herding their cattle in the prairie. It was thought that these white men would die of the wounds received, and that the Indians would soon begin their depredations upon the neighboring settlements. The news caused intense excitement in Boisé City, and within an hour's time Col. R. F. Bernard, in command of troop G of the 1st Cavalry, was on the way with his command to the scene of the trouble. Major Patrick Collins, then commanding Fort Boisé, promptly telegraphed General Howard at Fort Vancouver, and the latter hastened preparations to meet the threatened danger.

It soon became known that the Bannocks, under the promptings and counsel of Buffalo Horn, had been receiving emissaries from other tribes, notably the Piutes on the south, and the Umatillas and other tribes near and along the Columbia River, with a view to a general uprising. The situation assumed a formidable and dangerous aspect, and seemed fully to warrant the very serious apprehensions that were entertained. In the mean time the Indians, learning of the approach of the cavalry, called a hasty council, and while Buffalo Horn urged "war undisguised, relentless war," against the whites as the only course left open to them, the greater number of the Indians present chose discretion as the better part of valor, and began to beat a retreat toward the reservation. Buffalo Horn, at the head of about eighty warriors, decided to take the war-path, but disdaining to await the arrival of the troops, fled across the Snake River plains, crossed the river at Glenn's Ferry, and proceeded toward Silver City, in Owyhee County, destroying property and killing several white men who chanced to fall in their way.

On arriving at the lava-beds Colonel Bernard found them deserted, and soon after learning the course of the hostiles, hastened by forced marches diagonally across the plain, with a hope of intercepting the Indians in their progress through the country. The Indians, however, were in no humor to be overtaken. They fled rapidly across the Bruneau Valley, and gaining the mountains south of Silver City, met there a check at the hands of a company of citizens, who had been warned of their approach. The skirmish which took place in the Silver City Mountains, though it resulted in the defeat of the citizens and the death of a few of their number, was not without important fruit, as it took from the Indians their able and desperate leader, Buffalo Horn, who was found among the slain. Following this encounter, the Indians passed into eastern Oregon, and traversing the Stein Mountain country, the home of the Piutes, gathered a few allies as they went, and then hastened to the Malheur Reservation, where they were further re-enforced by the Piutes of the reservation. Bernard was in hot pursuit, and with the acquisition of three other companies pressed forward, overtaking the Indians on Silver Creek, where they had gathered in largely increased numbers. The evident plan of the Indians was to gain the Columbia River, where they had arranged to be joined by the Umatillas and other tribes on either side of the great river, when they intended to sweep backwards upon their track, carrying death and desolation in their path through eastern Oregon and Idaho. The plan failed through the extensive preparations that had been promptly made to meet them, and by the failure of the Umatillas and other tribes to take part in the insane undertaking. From the Umatilla Reservation, where their last open fight was made, the Bannocks, in the vain hope that the Umatillas, who were idle though deeply interested spectators of the battle, would be excited by their prowess to join them, the Bannock Indian war of 1878 soon degenerated into a disorderly retreat of demoralized and scattered bands of Indians, whose only remaining purpose was to regain by different routes the reservations from which they had set forth in the spring. In this they succeeded, after causing much trouble and loss to the settlers on their route of march, and entailing a heavy expense upon the government. Considering the large number of Indians engaged in these raids, and the scattered and helpless condition of the settlers, the number of deaths and casualties of all kinds was not very great. Perhaps 100 white persons in all met death at the hands of these fiends.

Lemhi County continued to be troubled more or less by Indians until 1878. The latest massacre in that section was that of five teamsters at Birch Creek. The Indians, after first getting drunk, fired the train and killed the men. In the autumn of 1878 another freighting outfit, under the charge of Jesse McCaleb, was attacked on Lost River while on the way to Challis. A skirmish ensued, resulting in the death of Mr. McCaleb. The loss by the Indians has never been ascertained. Mr. McCaleb was a leading business man of the Territory, a partner of Colonel George L. Shoup, and had made an honorable record in the Territorial legislature.

During the Bannock war, about thirty of the Sheep Eater and Miser Indians escaped from the troops and secreted themselves among the Salmon River Mountains, from whence they raided remote and unprotected settlements, murdering several citizens in the spring of 1879. They were captured by General Howard late in the fall and taken to Fort Vancouver.

This brief and imperfect summary of Indian troubles is given in order to explain one of the causes which, up to within a few years, retarded the development of Idaho, and prevented her limitless resources from receiving the recognition from the outside world to which they were entitled.

The last Indian wars in Idaho are over. The remnants of the tribes have been either "converted" to the happy hunting grounds or removed to places of safety on the reservations. The construction of railroads offering quick and ready transportation of troops in case of emergency—but more especially the extensive immigration during the past five years—precludes the possibility of any Indian wars in the future. Idaho to-day is as safe from apprehension of Indian trouble as any Eastern State.

DEVELOPMENT.

The first mining excitement which resulted in permanent settlement was the Oro Fino stampede of 1861 and 1862. One of the results was the founding of the town of Lewiston, at the junction of the Snake and Clearwater Rivers, which soon became a distributing point for the mines for hundreds of miles. From Oro Fino and Pierce City parties prospected in all directions, and Warrens and Florence were soon after discovered. Passing southward, Boisé Basin was discovered in 1863, and the Owyhee country soon after. From that date the settlement of southern Idaho may be said to have fairly begun. The discovery of gold and settlement of Boisé Valley led to the removal of the capital from Lewiston to Boisé City on the 24th day of December, 1864.

The Leesburg and Lemhi sections were opened up in 1867, when eastern Idaho began to be thoroughly explored, resulting finally in the discovery of the great Wood River galena belt. A more detailed description of the mineral development of Idaho will be found in the chapter on mining.

While the mineral resources of the Territory have been thus developing for the past score of years, the farmers, stock-growers, and lumbermen have been contributing to the growth and permanent settlement of the country. Since 1870 the Territory has increased fourfold in population. From a scattered population of less than 15,000 in that year, it increased to more than double that number in 1880, and has again more than doubled within the past four years.

There are at the present writing about 820 miles of railroad in Idaho, as follows:

Utah & Northern, Franklin to Monida	208 miles.
Oregon Short Line, Main Line, border to Burnt River	452 "
" " Wood River Branch	70 "
Northern Pacific	90 "
Total	820 "

The Utah and Northern skirts the eastern portion of the Territory, with Ogden, Utah, and Garrison, Montana, where it joins the Northern Pacific, as its terminal points. It is a narrow-gauge road, 454 miles in length. It enters Idaho at Franklin, near the upper end of Cache Valley, running through Oneida County for over 200 miles. At Pocatello it forms a junction with the Oregon Short Line, passing through Fort Hall Indian Reservation and a part of Snake River Valley; thence across sage-brush plains capable some day of a high degree of cultivation, until it begins the ascent of the Rocky Mountain range, leaving the Territory at Monida, which derives its name from the first three letters of the two Territories upon whose dividing line it is situated. This line has an immense traffic, not only with Montana, but with eastern and central Idaho. Its immense business makes it without doubt the most important narrow-gauge road in the world. It connects with stage lines in Idaho as follows: At Oxford for Clifton and Weston; at McCammon for Malad; at Blackfoot for Challis, Bonanza, and the Salmon River mines; and at Beaver Cañon for Yellowstone Park, at Red Rock, Montana, for Salmon City and Lemhi Valley.

The Oregon Short Line, standard gauge, is a branch of the Union Pacific, leaving the main line at Granger, Wyoming, passing through the southern and central portions of Idaho, including Bear Lake, Oneida, Alturas, Ada, and Washington counties. The distance from Granger to Huntington, Oregon, near the mouth of Burnt River, its western terminus, is 537 miles. After entering Idaho from the east it traverses the Bear River and Bear Lake Valley, in which are situated some of the finest farming lands in the west; thence through the town of Soda Springs, already a famous resort for westerners (see article on Oneida County), along Bear and Port Neuf Rivers for seventy miles. The scenery in the Port Neuf Cañon is much admired for its beauty. Leaving the Utah and Northern at Pocatello, it continues in a north-westerly course, crossing Snake River at American Falls, and for a number of miles passing over great lava-beds, until it reaches the town of Shoshone, where the Wood River Branch leaves it for Ketchum, seventy miles to the north. Continuing its course northwestward, at Kuna it connects with stage lines for Boisé City, fifteen miles north; after crossing Boisé River at Caldwell, it enters Washington County near Weiser, and after crossing the Snake a fourth time, it effects a junction with the Oregon Railway and Navigation Company's line at Huntington.

On the first of December, 1884, a through line was established by this road, connecting Omaha and Portland. It is claimed that this is the shortest route from the east to Puget Sound. The distance from Chicago to Portland by this line is about 2,200 miles; to Puget Sound 2,350 miles, being from 150 to 200 miles shorter than any other route. Vast areas of wheat, timber, and mineral land are thus rendered easily accessible, and a new empire opened up for thousands of home-seekers.

"The possibilities of the Oregon Short Line," says the Portland *Oregonian*, "are not to be exaggerated even at this early day. In the long-neglected Territory of Idaho its line is over two hundred miles southward parallel to the Northern Pacific; and for 160 miles of that distance, say from Weiser to the Malade or Wood River, it runs through one continuous belt of fruit-growing country, which is 445 miles nearer to Chicago than the fruit-producing counties of California. It surpasses California in peaches, nectarines, and pears, equals her in plums and apricots, and falls below her only in grapes and figs. The difference in distance will enable some shrewd man to lay down Idaho fruit in Chicago one day fresher than California fruit can be possibly placed there. It gives Oregon flour the 'top hand' in the mines of southern Idaho and northern Utah. The Short Line recrosses the Snake just above the mouth of the Weiser, and runs again through Baker County, Oregon, for a distance of about fifty miles, through a region fairly productive in grain and abounding in fruits of the greatest abundance and highest flavor. Just below old Fort Boisé it again crosses Snake River at a little town called St. Paul, and continues through Idaho until it reaches the Utah frontier. On the Port Neuf River, not far from Pocatello, it crosses that crooked stream not less than nine times in six miles, for the sake of a short and straight line with low grades. Then look how it reduces the expense of mining low-grade ores, by giving cheaper transportation to the furnaces located in densely timbered sections. Its locomotives burn coal brought all the way from Evanston, in Wyoming Territory, while those of the O. R. & N. burn coal brought from Tacoma by rail."

The Northern Pacific crosses Kootenai County in what is known as the "Pan-Handle" of Idaho. The northernmost point of the road is reached at Lake Pend d'Oreille, where the road crosses a trestle bridge 8,400 feet in length. This road, besides furnishing an outlet for the apparently inexhaustible timber of north Idaho, passes through some of the most superb lake and mountain scenery in the Territory. Thompson's Falls, Belknap, Trout Creek, Rathdrum, and Spokane Falls, all stations on this road, are distributing points for the Cœur d'Alene mining region. The Northern Pacific has nearly 2,000,000 acres of land in northern Idaho.

The Boisé City branch of the Oregon Short Line from Caldwell has been begun and is expected to be completed in the spring of 1885. The road-bed for the branch of the Northern Pacific from Colfax to Moscow in Nez Percé County has been graded and is ready for the rails. Other roads or branches are in contemplation, such as a branch of the Central Pacific from Kelton to Wood River; of the Utah and Northern from Camas to Birch Creek, and of the Oregon Short Line down Snake River.

A little over six years ago there was not a mile of railroad in Idaho. The development of the Territory since that period has been immense. Immigration has been stimulated, new and unexplored sections have been opened up to the world, and the limitless resources of Idaho are rapidly becoming known. While it is possible that individual communities may have suffered from the temporary derangement of affairs caused by the advent of railroads, the Territory at large has been the gainer. New towns are constantly springing up, new enterprises are being fostered, new roads built; outside capital is seeking investment within her borders, and stretches of what a few years ago seemed a barren desert are now being made to bloom with the happy homes of a thrifty people.

As an indication of the material growth of the Territory, I subjoin a table showing the assessed valuation taken from the official assessment rolls for the past seven years:

1878	$4,520,800.50	1882	$ 9,339,071.05
1879	5,926,149.00	1883	13,938,412.31
1880	6,408,089.14	1884	15,497,598.34
1881	8,066,365.75		

The figures given for 1884 include only what is known as the "original assessment rolls" for this year, and will doubtless be considerably increased by the "subsequent assessment rolls" to be reported in January. The assessed valuation is probably much less than a half of the actual valuation, and does not include unpatented mining property, or the proceeds of the mines, which are not taxed.

The following table shows the census returns of the population by counties for 1880. The figures for 1884 are estimated from such data as are accessible in the shape of poll-tax payers, property tax payers, popular vote, and school population, besides returns from the official assessment rolls.

	POPULATION.		ASSESSMENT ROLL.	
COUNTIES.	1880.	1884.	1880.	1884.
Ada	4,674	8,500	$1,325,152 00	$2,409,914 00
Alturas	1,693	13,000	371,591 00	3,015,336 61
Bear Lake	3,237	3,500	148,479 00	449,597 00
Boisé	3,213	3,000	713,527 00	635,000 00
Cassia	1,315	3,500	304,388 00	602,996 00
Custer*		2,000		640,598 00
Idaho	2,031	3,000	532,908 00	636,425 00
Kootenai†	318	1,500		544,133 98
Lemhi	2,230	2,000	500,000 00	518,730 00
Nez Percé	3,965	8,000	864,737 00	2,050,546 00
Oneida	6,972	12,000	878,722 00	2,380,862 00
Owyhee	1,467	1,500	542,896 00	871,921 00
Shoshone	467	2,500	45,646 00	113,555 00
Washington	877	3,000	180,043 00	627,978 75
Total	32,611	67,000	$6,408,089 00	$15,497,598 34

* Organized out of Lemhi County in 1882.   † Organized 1882.

Within the past four years the territorial tax has been reduced from 75 cents to 25 cents on the $100, and will probably be reduced still further during the coming winter. The only indebtedness is $69,000 worth of outstanding bonds, $22,000 of which matures in December, 1885, and the balance in December, 1891. In January, 1885, there will be over $80,000 in the territorial treasury, so that the Territory is practically out of debt. As the question of taxation is one of direct personal interest to every citizen, the above showing is worthy of consideration.

CHAPTER II.—DESCRIPTIVE.

There are in Idaho over 55,000,000 acres, classified as follows: 12,000,000 acres capable of cultivation; 25,000,000 acres of pasture and grazing lands; the remainder being forest, mountainous, or mineral. The average elevation is about 4,700 feet, being from 2,000 to 3,000 feet less than that of Wyoming, Utah, Nevada, or Colorado. The highest peaks range from 9,000 to 13,000 feet in height. The lowest altitude is at Lewiston, where the Clearwater joins the Snake at an elevation of 680 feet.

MOUNTAINS.

Professor F. V. Hayden, in his "Geological Survey of the Territories," in referring to the surface of a large portion of Idaho, describes it as literally crumpled or rolled up in one continuous series of mountain ranges, fold after fold. Perhaps even better examples of these remarkable folds may be found in the country drained by Salmon River and its branches, where lofty ranges of mountains, for the most part covered with limestones and quartzites of the carboniferous age, wall in all the little streams. None of our published maps convey any idea of the almost innumerable ranges. We might say that from longitude 110° to 118°, a distance of over five hundred miles, there is a range of mountains, on an average, every ten to twenty miles. Sometimes the distance across the range in a straight line, from the bed of a stream in one valley to the bed of the stream in the valley beyond the range, is not more than five to eight miles, while it is seldom more than twenty miles. "From these statements," says the Professor, "which we believe to be correct, the reader may form some conception of the vast amount of labor yet to be performed to explore, analyze, and locate on a suitable scale these hundreds of ranges of mountains, each one of which is worthy of a name."

Though the foregoing may be somewhat exaggerated, Idaho is in reality a mountain territory. It is from the interior of her mountains that her chief source of her wealth is derived. It is her mountain sides that afford the nutritious grasses that sustain hundreds of thousands of her cattle, and it is her intermountain vales that furnish the soil of her farms and ranches.

In the north are the Cœur d'Alene and Bitter Root Mountains, a portion of the latter range, together with the crest of the Rocky Mountains, forming the dividing line between Idaho and Montana. Spurs from the main range of the Rockies ramify into all sections of the Territory. The Sawtooth, Salmon River, Wood River, Boisé, and other ranges are the scenes of active mining operations in central Idaho; while the Wahsatch and Owyhee Mountains are among the more important in the south-eastern and south-western portions, respectively.

RIVERS.

With the exception of a comparatively small portion of south-eastern Idaho, whose waters flow into the basin of Great Salt Lake, the river system of Idaho is entirely tributary to the valley of the great Columbia River. There are three important rivers in Idaho which empty directly into the Columbia, namely, the Spokane, Clarke's Fork, and the Snake.

The first named is the outlet of Lake Cœur d'Alene, and flows through a portion of Kootenai County, near the Washington line.

Clarke's Fork, also in north Idaho, is fed by a number of streams, empties into Pend d'Oreille Lake, and under the name of Pend d'Oreille River pours its waters into the Columbia.

The sources of the Snake River are in the Rocky Mountains in north-western Wyoming, near the head waters of the Yellowstone and Madison rivers, at an elevation of 8,000 feet. The main feeder flows north-west to the junction of Lewis Fork, the outlet of Shoshone and Lewis lakes; thence south through Jackson Lake, and again north-west to the junction of Henry's Fork. From this point it describes a curve of more than 350 miles through southern Idaho, flowing south-west and then north-west, and strikes the Oregon line in about latitude 44° 40'. Thence it flows northerly between Idaho on the east and Oregon and Washington on the west for about 200 miles, when it takes a sharp turn to the west again for about 150 miles through Washington to where it joins the Columbia. Its total length is nearly 1,000 miles. At present it is not navigated above Lewiston.

The Snake River, deriving its volume from the melting of the mountain snows, is said to be a direct gauge of the annual advance of the sun. In June and July it is a tremendous torrent, carrying a full half of the Columbia. From the middle of July it constantly shrinks, reaching its minimum in midwinter. At the lowest, it is a river equal to the Sacramento or Connecticut. An enthusiastic writer thus describes its course: "Springing from perpetual snows amidst the dizzy heights and towering summits of the Rocky Mountains, the Snake follows a tortuous course to the Columbia, nearly a thousand miles, through regions so vast in extent, so varied in character, and so notable in appearance as to admit of no parallel in the cosmography of our possessions. Draining the waters of the most extensive area of grazing, agricultural, and mineral lands on the Pacific slope, it embraces in its sources, which are legion, portions of Montana, Wyoming, and Utah, absorbs the rivers of Idaho, and finds affluents that rise in the pine forests of Oregon's Blue Mountains. Grouped in silent majesty, grand cloud-piercing peaks watch its departure westward. Dazzling ice-bound pinnacles mark its way. Now dashing over precipices, rolling through the gloom of dense forests, now skirting the rugged mountains of the wild Teton range, gathering strength as it runs; now coursing by grass-clad hills or through cheerless tracts where burning lava once flowed, making tremendous jumps, rushing headlong and foaming through deep, dark, narrow canons with upright walls a thousand feet high, winding in its course—the mad stream hurls its waters two hundred feet into the air in one mighty, despairing, awful leap over the Shoshone Falls."

Some of the streams, of which Big and Little Lost Rivers are notable examples, apparently sink into the sage-brush plains, but in reality doubtless have subterranean outlets underneath the lava into the Snake or some of its tributaries.

A bird's-eye view of the territory would represent a vast, wedge-shaped plateau, rising from an elevation less than 700 feet in the extreme west, to over 10,000 feet in the extreme east. Over this rugged surface countless streams are flowing as tributaries to one of the three rivers named. In its long serpentine course through the Territory, the Snake absorbs the waters of such streams as the Clearwater, Salmon, Payette, Boisé, Owyhee, Bruneau, Wood, and other streams. Of these the largest is the Salmon, which, rising in the Sawtooth range, after a long circuitous course, receiving numberless tributaries, and forcing the very mountains asunder, finally empties into the Snake not many miles above Lewiston. The immense water power of Idaho is one of its great resources, affording as it does ample facilities for irrigating, mining, and manufacturing purposes

VALLEYS.

There are within the Territory 13,200 square miles of valley lands situated at an elevation less than 3,000 feet, 10,000 square miles between 3,000 and 4,000 feet, 22,000 square miles between 4,000 and 5,000 feet, and 19,200 square miles between 5,000 and 6,000 feet.

We are indebted to Robert E. Strahorn, Esq., for the following list of the most prominent of the valleys of Idaho:

Name and Location of Valley.	Length.	Breadth.
South Fork of Snake River, Eastern Idaho	30 miles	2 to 4 miles
Salt River Valley, Eastern Idaho	20 "	1 to 2 "
Bear River Valley, Eastern Idaho	40 "	3 to 5 "
Snake Valley, North Fork, Eastern Idaho	60 "	2 to 10 "
Blackfoot Valley, Eastern Idaho	20 "	2 to 5 "

Name and Location of Valley.	Length.	Breadth.
Round Valley, Eastern Idaho	30 miles	8 to 12 miles
Wood River Valley, Central Idaho	50 "	1 to 2 "
Camas Prairie, Central Idaho	80 "	18 to 25 "
Boisé Valley, Western Idaho	60 "	2 to 6 "
Payette Valley, Western Idaho	75 "	2 to 15 "
Weiser Valley, Western Idaho	40 "	2 to 5 "
Lemhi Valley, North-eastern Idaho	70 "	3 to 6 "
Pah-Simari Valley, North-eastern Idaho	25 "	1 to 5 "
Northern Camas Prairie, North Idaho	30 "	20 to 25 "
Potlach Valley, North Idaho	25 "	10 to 15 "
Palouse Valley, North Idaho	20 "	5 to 10 "
St. Joseph Valley, North Idaho	15 "	5 to 10 "

The valleys mentioned above are not all that are suitable for settlement. I could name over a score or more in addition, where the opportunities are fully as advantageous as in these. Beautiful little vales, cozy parks hidden among the hills—these are innumerable; while sheep ranches, cattle ranges, dairy farms, poultry ranches, and apiaries could be established in a thousand localities, and will be as soon as the advantages that await the settlers in Idaho are more fully known.

In the northern part of the Territory there are over a million acres of land open to settlement under the homestead and pre-emption laws, all of which have been surveyed.

It will be observed that the valleys generally are narrow. The soil is rich, however, and the flat bottom-lands or undulating plateaus are capable of producing abundantly. Probably not one twentieth part of the arable valley lands is occupied.

What is known as the great Snake River Basin is a broad, nearly level plain, from seventy-five to one hundred miles in width and one hundred and fifty to two hundred miles in length, surrounded on all sides by mountain ranges. According to Professor Hayden, this basin follows the course of Snake River, and is really an expansion of the valley, and it at first extends from the north-east to the south-west, bends around west, and then continues north-westerly toward Boisé City. The mountains on either side form a series of more or less lofty ranges, some of the more prominent summits rising to a height of 10,000 feet. These ranges appear to the eye, from any one point of view, to trend about north and south, but the trend of the aggregate ranges is plainly a little west of north and east of south. Between these ranges are valleys of greater or less breadth, varying from one to five miles in width, oftentimes of great beauty and fertility, through which wind some of the numerous branches which flow into Snake River. The great basin is entirely covered with a bed of basalt of quite modern date, and this basalt has set to a greater or less distance up the valleys of all these streams. It extends up the Port Neuf Valley thirty or forty miles. The American Falls are formed by the descent of Snake River over the basalt. The Professor is of the belief that this vast basin has been worn out of the mountain ranges by erosion; that the three buttes and other fragments of ranges scattered over the plains serve as monuments in proof of this statement. This basin was also the bed of a lake which probably originated during the Pliocene period. In the immediate vicinity of this basin no Tertiary beds of older date than the Pliocene have been discovered, and underneath the basaltic crust there is a considerable thickness of the deposit. The effusion of the basalt was one of the latest events, and must have merged well on to our present period.

CLIMATE.

The superb climate of Idaho is one of its chief attractions. With its varying altitudes almost any desired temperature may be obtained.

In the valleys snow rarely falls to any great depth, while on the other hand some of its peaks are crowned with eternal snow.

Idaho is sufficiently near to the Pacific Ocean to be affected by its warm currents. "By reference to any map whereon these ocean currents are set down, it will be seen that the great Japan current (Kuro Sivo)—that mighty stream of warm water—bears directly against the western shores of America. The temperature of the winds blowing over it is of course affected by its heat, and they carry their modifying influences inland to Idaho. Meeting the obstruction of the great natural wall of the Bitter Root and Rocky Mountains, these 'Chinook' winds are deflected along their western bases and pass southward beyond the limits of the Territory. It is not claimed for Idaho that its climate is as warm as that of the same latitude in Europe, but that it is not is due, not to its geographical location, but to its topography and surroundings. Over 400 miles in length from north to south, the Territory is crossed by numerous mountain ranges or spurs, many of whose peaks tower up beyond the line of perpetual congelation."

Fort Lapwai, in latitude 46° 32', and at an altitude of 2,000 feet, has about the same average temperature as Nebraska, 400 miles farther south, and is warmer than Wisconsin or Michigan. Boisé City, in latitude 43° 37', at an elevation of 2,800 feet, has a mean temperature of about 51°; 12° below zero is exceptionally cold, and 105° above zero exceptionally warm. It should be borne in mind, however, that there is a difference in effect equal to about 20° between the temperature of a dry rarified atmosphere, like that of Idaho, and the moist, penetrating atmosphere of the Atlantic coast; that is, a temperature of 105° in Idaho is not felt to any greater extent than that of 85° in New York; or 12° below zero in Idaho is not felt more perceptibly than 8° above zero on the Atlantic coast. Perhaps the best idea of the climate of the Territory is given in the following extract taken from official sources:

The influence of climate upon agriculture, stock-raising, or mere personal comfort is sufficiently important, but its effect upon health is paramount to every other consideration. According to the official report of the Surgeon-General of the United States army, the percentages of deaths from disease to each 1,000 soldiers in the different military districts of the Union are as follows, the result having been the average of four years:

Localities.	Deaths each year from Disease.
Atlantic coast, out of each 1,000 men	17.83
Arizona, " " " "	12.11
Pennsylvania and Michigan, " "	6.05
New Mexico, out of each " "	7.77
California, " " " "	6.88
Montana, " " " "	5.62
Dakota, " " " "	4.76
Wyoming, " " " "	4.71
Idaho, " " " "	4.66

The Gulf States make a worse showing than the Atlantic States, and Idaho shows the smallest ratio of mortality of any locality in the Union. It will be noted that the troops of the United States army are subjected to exactly the same condition and surroundings and have the same habits everywhere more nearly than any other class of people. Their food, clothing, medical attendance, and places of abode are nearer identically the same wherever they go; consequently comparing the ratio of mortality among them in these different regions enables us to obtain a more correct estimate of the actual healthfulness of each region that could possibly be obtained in any other way.

But the most striking illustration of the general healthfulness of Idaho is afforded by the mortality statistics taken in connection with the national census of 1870 (those of 1880 are not yet available). According to them the death-rate in Idaho *was less than in any other State or Territory*, as will be seen from the following table, giving the exact figures of the census. The percentage of deaths to population was, in—

Idaho	0.33	Colorado	0.94
Alabama	1.08	Connecticut	1.26
Arizona	2.61	Dakota	0.71
Arkansas	1.26	Delaware	1.25
California	1.61	District of Columbia	1.53

Florida	1.21	New York	1.58
Georgia	1.15	Nebraska	0.81
Illinois	1.33	Nevada	1.45
Indiana	1.03	North Carolina	0.98
Iowa	0.81	Ohio	1.11
Kansas	1.25	Oregon	0.69
Kentucky	1.09	Pennsylvania	1.49
Louisiana	2.00	Rhode Island	1.26
Maine	1.23	South Carolina	1.05
Maryland	1.24	Tennessee	1.13
Massachusetts	1.77	Texas	1.37
Michigan	0.94	Utah	1.03
Minnesota	0.80	Vermont	1.07
Mississippi	1.11	Virginia	1.24
Missouri	1.63	Washington	0.93
Montana	0.90	West Virginia	0.91
New Hampshire	1.35	Wisconsin	0.94
New Jersey	1.17	Wyoming	0.81
New Mexico	1.23		

The average temperature of the four seasons may be summed up as follows: 52° in the spring, 73° in the summer, 53° in the autumn, and 34° in the winter. One reason of an agreeable climate is the difference in the atmospheric moisture, which has a great influence upon comfort in hot weather. The air is so dry that the perspiration is carried away rapidly, leaving the body cool and refreshed. Sunstrokes and hydrophobia are unknown. Stock is seldom fed or sheltered, living through the winter on bunch-grass and white sage. According to the report of the U. S. Surveyor-General, the annual rain-fall south of the Snake River is about fifteen inches, increasing gradually north of that point. The summer is always dry, from June to September, and often till October, insuring to the farmer a harvest and threshing season for securing his grain. Peach-trees thrive well and bear profusely, and corn is raised and matured as far north as Spokane Valley.

Like all other portions of the Pacific Coast, a few hundred feet of increased altitude gives much lower temperature, so that people need only go a few miles during the warmest weather to enjoy the pure cold mountain air. In the valleys, however, the nights are sufficiently cool during the summer to insure refreshing sleep.

With a climate to suit the most exacting taste, shown by official statistics to be the most healthful in the world, where epidemic and endemic diseases are almost unknown, whose dry and antiseptic qualities preclude many of the diseases incident to the most moist regions of the Eastern States, it is no wonder that the people of Idaho feel a pride in what has been so lavishly bestowed by nature.

NATURAL SCENERY.

The character of the country through which the railway traveler passes in southern and eastern Idaho is adapted to repel rather than attract. The vast stretches of lava fields and sage-brush plains become monotonous in the extreme; yet amid Idaho's placid lakes, rushing rivers, and rugged mountains, may be found many a romantic scene. Rocks piled mountain high, cañons a thousand feet deep, through which streams rush and roar and foam, cataracts leaping from rock to rock, tossing their spray aloft, somber forest scenes beneath towering trees, where foliage is so dense as to leave a twilight dimness at mid-day—these are some of the characteristics of the landscapes of picturesque Idaho. Chief among all, however, are the great Shoshone Falls of Snake River.

"The three great falls of America," says Clarence King, "Niagara, Shoshone, and Yosemite, all happily bearing Indian names, are as characteristicly different as possible. There seems little left for a cataract to express."

The Shoshone Falls have been called the Niagara of the West. The title is not a fortunate one, as these falls have a scenery peculiarly their own. They are higher than Niagara, though during most of the year there is less volume of water. Probably the best description is that written by Mr. King himself, from which we make copious extracts without further apology. "A few miles in front the smooth surface of the plain was broken by a rugged zigzag line of black, which marked the further wall of the Snake Canyon. A dull, throbbing sound greeted us. Its pulsations were deep, and seemed to proceed from the ground beneath our feet. Leaving the cavalry to bring up the wagon, my friend and I galloped on, and were quickly upon the edge of the cañon wall.

"We looked down into a broad, circular excavation, three quarters of a mile in diameter, and nearly 700 feet deep. East and north, over the edges of the cañon, we looked across miles and miles of the Snake Plain, far on to the blue boundary mountains. The wall of the gorge opposite us, like the cliff at our feet, sank in perpendicular bluffs, nearly to the level of the river, the broad excavation being covered by rough piles of black lava and rounded domes of trachyte rock. A horizon as level as the sea; a circling wall, whose sharp edges were here and there battlemented in huge, fortress-like masses; a broad river, smooth and unruffled, flowing quietly in the middle of the scene, and then plunging into a labyrinth of rocks, tumbling over a precipice 200 feet high, and moving westward in a still, deep current, to disappear behind a black promontory.

"It is a strange, savage scene—a monotony of pale blue sky, olive and gray stretches of desert, frowning walls of jetty lava, deep beryl-green river stretches, reflecting here and there the intense solemnity of the cliffs, and in the center a dazzling sheet of foam. In the early morning light the shadows of the cliffs were cast over half the basin, defining themselves in sharp outline here and there on the river. Upon the foam of the cataract one point of the rock cast a cobalt-blue shadow. Where the river flowed around the western promontory, it was wholly in shadow and of a deep sea-green. A scanty growth of coniferous trees fringed the brink of the lower cliffs overhanging the river. Dead barrenness is the whole sentiment of the scene. The mere suggestion of trees clinging here and there along the walls serves rather to heighten than to relieve the forbidding gloom of the place. Nor does the flashing whiteness where the river tears itself among the rocky islands, or rolls in spray down the cliff, brighten the aspect. In contrast with its brilliancy the rocks seem darker and more wild.

"The descent of 400 feet from our standpoint to the level of the river above the falls has to be made by a narrow winding path among rough ledges of lava. We were obliged to leave our wagon at the summit, and pack down the camp equipment and photographic apparatus upon carefully led mules. By mid-day we were comfortably camped on the margin of the left bank, just above the brink of the falls. My tent was pitched upon the edge of the cliff directly overhanging the rapids. From my door I looked over the cataract, and whenever the veil of mist was blown aside could see for a mile down the river.

"The lower half of the cañon is excavated in a gray porphyritic trachyte. It is over this material that the Snake falls. Above the brink the whole breadth of the river is broken by a dozen small trachyte islands, which the water has carved into fantastic forms: rounding some into low domes, sharpening others into mere pillars, and now and then wearing into deep caves. At the very brink of the fall a few twisted evergreens cling with their roots to the rock, and lean over the abyss of foam with something of that air of fatal fascination which is apt to take possession of men. Under the influence of the cool shadow of cliffs and pine, and constant percolating of surface waters, a rare fertility is developed in the ravines opening upon the cañon shore. A luxuriance of ferns and mosses, an almost tropical wealth of green leaves and velvety carpeting line the banks. There are no rocks at the base of the fall. The sheet of foam plunges almost vertically into a dark beryl-green lake-like expanse of river.

"Immense volumes of foam roll up from the cataract base, and whirling about in eddying winds, rise often a thousand feet in the air. When the wind blows down the cañon a gray mist obscures the river for half a mile, and when, as is usually the case in the afternoon, the breezes blow eastward, the foam cloud curls over the brink of the fall and hangs like a veil over the upper river.

On what condition depends the height to which the foam cloud rises from the base of the fall it is apparently impossible to determine. Without the slightest wind the cloud of spray often rises several hundred feet above the cañon wall, and again, with apparently the same conditions of river and atmosphere, it hardly reaches the brink. Incessant roar, re-enforced by a thousand echoes, fills the cañon. Out of this monotone from time to time rise strange wild sounds, and now and then may be heard a slow, measured beat, not unlike the recurring fall of breakers. From the white front of the cataract the eye constantly wanders up to the black, foaming parapet of lava. Angular bastions rise sharply from the general level of the wall, and here and there isolated blocks, profiling upon their sky line, strikingly recall barbette batteries. To goad one's imagination up to the point of perpetually seeing resemblances of everything else in the forms of rock is the most vulgar vice of travelers; to refuse to see the architectural suggestions upon Snake Cañon, however, is to administer a flat snub to one's fancy. The whole edge of the cañon is deeply cleft in vertical crevices. The actual brink is usually formed of irregular blocks and prisms of lava, poised upon their ends in an unstable equilibrium, ready to be tumbled over at the first leverage of the frost. Hardly an hour passes without the boom of one of those rock masses falling upon the ragged *débris* piles below.

"Night is the true time to appreciate the full force of the scene. I lay and watched it many hours. The broken rim of the basin profiled itself upon a mass of drifting clouds, when torn openings revealed gleams of pale moonlight and bits of remote sky trembling with misty stars. Intervals of light and blank darkness hurriedly followed each other. For a moment the black gorge would be crowded with forms. Tall cliffs, ramparts of lava, the rugged outlines of islands huddled together on the cataract's brink, faintly luminous foam breaking over black rapids, the swift white leap of the river, and a ghostly, formless mist through which the cañon walls and far reach of the lower river were veiled and unveiled again and again. A moment of this strange picture, and then a rush of black shadow, when nothing could be seen but the breaks in the clouds, the basin rim, and a vague white center in the general darkness. * * *

"To the left of the island half the river plunges off an overhanging lip, and falls about 150 feet, the whole volume reaching the surface of the basin many feet from the wall. The other half has worn away the edge, and descends in a tumbling cascade at an angle of about forty-five degrees. The river at this point has not yet worn through the fields of basaltic lava which form the upper 400 feet of the plain. Between the two falls it cuts through the remaining beds of basalt, and has eroded its channel 100 feet into underlying porphyritic trachyte. The trachyte erodes far more easily than basalt, and its resultant forms are quite unlike those of the black lava. The trachyte islands and walls are excavated here and there in deep caves, leaving island masses in the forms of mounds and towers. In general, spherical outlines predominate, while the erosion of the basalt results always in sharp perpendicular cliffs, with deeply inclined talus of ragged *débris*.

"The cliffs around the upper cataract are inferior to those of the Shoshone. While the level of the upper plain remains nearly the same, the river constantly deepens the channel in its westward course. In returning from the upper fall, I attempted to climb along the very edge of the cliff, in order to study carefully the habits of the basalt, but I found myself in a labyrinth of side crevices, which were cut into the plain from a hundred to a thousand feet back from the main wall. These recesses were usually in the form of an amphitheater, with black walls 200 feet high, and a bottom filled with immense fragments of basalt rudely piled together."

These falls are easily accessible by a stage line from the town of Shoshone on the Oregon Short Line, only twenty miles distant. A hotel is to be built shortly, with ample accommodations.

LAKES.

Scattered among the mountain ranges are countless lakes of every description. Kootenai is *par excellence* the lake county of Idaho. Within her boundaries are Cœur d'Alene, Pend d'Oreille, Kanisku, Cocolalla, and numerous smaller lakes and mountain tarns.

Though nearly every county in the Territory can boast of its ponds and lakes, the principal body of water in southern Idaho is Bear Lake, which gives its name to the extreme south-eastern county, and which is described in the article on that county. Cœur d'Alene Lake is about thirty miles long, with a width varying from two to four miles. A daily line of steamers plies its waters from Fort Cœur d'Alene to the old Mission. Its waters are clear and cool, and abound in fish. The banks are mountainous, covered with timber. Cœur d'Alene, St. Joseph's, and St. Mary's rivers flow into it, and the Spokane is its outlet. As the greater portion of it is surrounded by an Indian reservation, but little signs of civilization are visible, excepting at the military post, which occupies the lower end of the lake, and where a commodious hotel offers accommodations for visitors and tourists.

Lake Pend d'Oreille is doubtless one of the most beautiful sheets of water in the United States. It is of irregular shape, about sixty miles in length, and of a width varying from three to fifteen miles. It is in reality a widening of Clarke's Fork, and winds its picturesque way among the wood-covered mountains, which rise up from its shores in a never-ceasing panorama of beautiful surprises. An excellent view is had from the car windows of the Northern Pacific, which crosses a neck of the lake upon a trestle bridge 8,400 feet long. There are two steamers on the lake at present. If unsurpassed natural scenery, abundance of fish in the lake, and plenty of game in the surrounding forests can offer any attractions, Pend d'Oreille must within a few years become one of the most noted resorts in the North-west.

Kanisku Lake, in the northern part of the county, is about twenty miles long, and half as wide. This and others are situated in wild and still unexplored regions. Lake Waha is a favorite resort for the people of Lewiston. It is a small sheet of water not two miles long, and about half a mile wide. Its banks are precipitous, and covered with timber. One of its chief claims to popularity is its abundance of trout. An enthusiastic writer, in referring to Waha, says: "Nothing we have ever seen can exceed the tranquil beauty of this sylvan, this idyllic scene, with its mountain solitudes, unbroken by a discordant sound, and its wealth of charming landscapes and xanthic skies."

The Payette Lake is one of the sources of Payette River. It is situated in Boisé County, and is rapidly becoming a favorite resort for the people of Boisé City and neighborhood. It is ten miles long, and about half as wide. It is surrounded by mountains, and is famous for its trout, red fish, and white fish. Its depth is unknown. It has been sounded to a depth of half a mile without striking bottom.

Among the most beautiful of the smaller lakes is Tahoma, situated in the Sawtooth Mountains, at an elevation of 8,000 feet. It is about fifty miles from Hailey, and is reached by a good wagon road from the Sawtooth mining camps. With the exception of the narrow, level space traversed by the road, the lake is mountain-locked, the peaks on one side rising a thousand feet above the surface of the water. These peaks are covered with evergreen timber, pine, spruce, and fir, while on the other side a mass of granite crags rises 1,500 feet. The lake has been sounded to a depth of 1,000 feet without striking bottom. It is supposed to be 1,500 feet deep, but this is merely an estimate.

Other lakes and objects of natural scenery will be referred to in their proper places in articles on the respective counties.

CHAP. III.—NATIVE TREES, PLANTS, AND ANIMALS.

TIMBER.

The railroad traveler crossing southern and eastern Idaho, after traversing the vast extent of sage-brush plains, would hardly imagine that within the Territory were immense reaches of timber, in many places so thick as to exclude the light of the sun. In Boisé, Lemhi, Custer, and Alturas counties are extensive forests. The upper waters of the Boisé River and its tributaries, including the South Fork, are heavily timbered. The amount of merchantable timber in that section is estimated from fifty to sixty million feet, exclusive of the South Fork, which is claimed to be more heavily timbered than either of the other tributaries. These forests extend thirty or forty miles into the mountains, and consist of white pine, fir, and cottonwood in abundance. The tributaries of the upper Salmon also abound with the same kind of timber. On Salmon and Craig's mountains, in Idaho County, an extensive body of excellent timber is found, reaching from the Snake River, near the mouth of the Salmon River, to and across the North Fork of the Clearwater, some sixty miles. It is estimated that this belt is from five to ten miles in width, and consists of white and yellow pine, red and yellow fir, and white cedar. This timber is of large growth, and valuable for lumbering purposes. Spruce and tamarack are found on the Lolo Creek, a tributary of the Clearwater. Yew trees one foot in diameter are found on the mountains, also mountain mahogany of small size. Silver birch is found on the upper part of the Clearwater. White-pine logs five feet in diameter and 100 feet in length, without a knot, have been rafted down the Clearwater, furnishing the finest quality of lumber for finishing purposes.

The greatest timber regions are in Shoshone and Kootenai counties. The Pend d'Oreille forests extend in all directions from the lake, covering an area over a hundred miles square. Gigantic monarchs of the forest lift their heads aloft at a height over two hundred feet. Bull pine, white pine, tamarack, and fir predominate. Cedars attain marvelous height and thickness. From many of the trees the Spanish moss hangs in long, graceful festoons, adding a pleasing variety to the otherwise somber scene. "This superb forest of the Pend d'Oreille," writes E. V. Smalley in the *Century* magazine, " is a vast lumber preserve for future generations. The pineries of Michigan and Minnesota look like open parks compared with it. Nowhere else in the United States, save on the western slopes of the western mountains in Washington Territory, can be found such a prodigious amount of timber to the acre."

The following list of Idaho trees is from Mr. Elliott's history. The maximum observed height and diameter are given. It is probably true that some species here ranked as trees are never really arboreous, and that others which have been entitled as shrubs should be classed as trees.

	Feet in Height.	In. in Diam.
Rhamnus Purshiana, Chittim wood. Bearberry. Bark decoction a violent cathartic	40	8
Acer Circinatum, Vine Maple; bushy, beautiful	25	8
Acer Macrophyllum, Large-leaved Maple	70	40
Prunus (cerasus) emarginata, varmollis, Wild Cherry	50	8
Prunus (cerasus) demissa, Choke Cherry	35	7
Nuttalia cerasiformis, Seamberry, Squawberry	20	3
Cercocarpus ledifolius, Mountain Mahogany	25	4
Cratægus Douglasii, Blackhaw	20	..
Cratægus rivularis	20	..
Amalanchier Canadensis, Serviceberry	20	4
Cornus Nuttallii, Dogwood; very showy in flower	50	10
Sambucus Glauca, Elder	40	20
Arbutus Menziesii, Laurel, Madrona; very beautiful; wood takes good polish; hard	50	36
Umbelluria (Oreodaphne) Californica, Myrtle; tree beautiful; wood well adapted to cabinet work	100	50
Quercus densiflora; resembles the Eastern chestnut oak. Southern half of Idaho	60	12
Quercus Garryana, White Oak; habitat all parts of Idaho	90	40
Castanopsis Chrysophilla, Chinquapin	60	12
Alnus rhombifolia, Alder	80	36
Salix lasiandra, Willow	50	13
Populus tremuloides, Quaking Asp	30	8
Populus trichocarpa, known as balm	90	72

	Feet in Height.	In. in Diam.
Taxus brevifolia, Yew. The most durable timber in Idaho....	..	..
Juniperus occidentalis, Juniper.............................	50	24
Cupressus (Chamæcyparis) Lawsoniana, Port Orford Cedar. One of our most valuable trees, but of very limited habitat.	200	72
Abies concolor, frequently called White Fir in California. Found in the mountains.................................	..	..
Abies grandis, White Fir. This tree is the ordinary white fir of all our valleys.......................................	200	60
Abies nobilis, the Noble Fir. Inhabits all our mountain regions at an elevation of from 3,000 to 5,000 feet................	200	72
Abies amabilis, Lovely Fir. This is also a mountain tree, with nearly the same habitat as the preceding, though very distinct from it..	100	36
Abies subalpina. Grows at an elevation of 3,000 to 6,000 feet..	60	24
Abies Douglasii, our most common fir........................	300	144
Abies Mertensiana, Hemlock.................................	150	40
Abies Pattoniana, Mountain Hemlock........................	100	40
Abies Engelmanni, a small mountain tree.....................	50	12
Abies Sitchensis, Tideland Spruce. Frequently known among botanists as *Abies Menziesii*............................	200	..
Larix Lyrallii, Larch. A small tree on the eastern slope......	..	..
Pinus contorta, Black Pine, Jack Pine........................	70	86
Pinus albicaulis...	60	24
Pinus Lambertana, Sugar Pine. Found on the mountain tops.	250	100
Pinus monticola, Silver Pine. Resembles the sugar pine......	150	40
Pinus ponderosa, the common pine in the valley..............	175	60
Pinus tuberculata, a small tree, and found in patches in the mountains...	50	12

In the above list the scientific name is printed in Italics, and is, with few exceptions, followed by the popular name in Roman.

In Kootenai County, in the neighborhood of the Northern Pacific Railroad, is a region of magnificent timber, many of the trees being from seven to ten feet in diameter, and of great height. The varieties are red fir, white pine, white cedar, hemlock, tamarack, and larch.

WILD FRUITS.

Grapes, blackberries, huckleberries, gooseberries, raspberries, salmonberries, and strawberries grow wild in profusion on the mountain sides and foothills. The camas, which gives a name to several prairies in the Territory, is found in all sections. It is a bulb which is prized highly by the Indians for food.

GRASSES.

In central Idaho there are not less than thirteen different species of indigenous and nutritious grasses, all differing in leaf, height, root, and seed top, and which retain vigorous vitality throughout the coldest winters. "There are," says Mr. Miller, "several species of flowering certeluisia, or greasewood, and from two or three times as many more of wild desert thyme, or sage brush, all very valuable for medicinal properties, and in many localities almost indispensable for fuel, together with several species of wild grasses. Some varieties of the sage are eaten with avidity by cattle, sheep, horses, mules, and wild game, such as elk, deer, bear, rabbit, sage-hens, crows, hawks, grouse, and others, during the winter season."

WILD FLOWERS.

Wild flowers grow in profusion, not only in the cañons and the valleys, but along the mountain sides. In early summer the surface is resplendent with gay tints. Among the more common may be mentioned the larkspur, columbine, harebell, lupine, primrose, aster, painted cup, gentian, daisy, buttercup, forget-me-not, and phlox. There are several species of violets and fragrant wild roses. Other beautiful varieties might be mentioned, which, however, would be of more interest to the botanist than the general reader.

NATIVE ANIMALS.

With the advancement of civilization many of the wilder animals have withdrawn farther into the mountain fastnesses. Buffalo, for instance, were once numerous in eastern Idaho, but have wholly disappeared. Still there is sufficient to satisfy the most ambitious hunter. Grizzly, black, and cinnamon bears are still numerous in the forests and mountains. The silver-tipped bear is more rare. The specimen exhibited at the New Orleans Exposition was captured among the mountains of Sawtooth range. The Ketchum *Keystone* thus chronicles the important event:

"On the 28th of August last, Mr. Schwartz of Sawtooth, an old bear-hunter, succeeded in trapping alive a huge Bruin of the silver-tipped species, and safely caged it after repeated efforts lasting through several days. This is the only bear of the kind ever caught in the country that any one is aware of. He is king of a rare species, and had become familiar to the people in that vicinity through his repeated raids and the immense footprints he left behind him, said to be little less than a bushel basket. He was known as 'Sawtooth Jack,' and was the recognized monarch of the Upper Salmon Valley. For three consecutive seasons every possible effort and strategy were exerted to capture 'Jack,' but he was aware that he was wanted and kept close watch for trap-signs. Salmon were scarce the past summer, and 'Jack' resorted to the slaughter-house offal for sustenance wherewith to keep his huge frame in good condition; and one dark night while fooling around the aforesaid butcher's corral, he 'put his foot in it.'

"When the people of Sawtooth and surrounding country heard that 'Jack' was entrapped, they turned out, to a man, woman, and child, and helped to cage him, after which they had a banquet and a torchlight procession.

"'Sawtooth Jack' is believed to be 27 years of age, and pulls down the hay scales to the 1,100 notch, and takes in a sheep for breakfast with great relish. He leaves a devoted wife and two small children to mourn him in his untimely taking off, with a long cold winter staring them in the face.

"'Jack' is on exhibition in Ketchum to-day (October 14th), and from here, in charge of Fritz Schwartz and his captor, goes to Hailey, Bullion, Bellevue, and other points below, and will also be exhibited at prominent places all the way down to New Orleans, where he will be assigned a prominent corner with the Idaho exhibit.

"Mr. Schwartz has a fortune in his 'catch.' Every person between Wood River and New Orleans should see the old 'Sawtooth' guerrilla and the first settler of the upper Salmon country."

The American elk is found now chiefly in the northern counties, but is rapidly disappearing. Antelope are still comparatively numerous throughout the Territory, as are also black-tail and white-tail deer.

It is beyond the province of this work to give an extensive or scientific treatise on the fauna of Idaho. It will be sufficient for our purpose to give, in addition to those already mentioned, simply a list of the more common native quadrupeds of the Territory, viz.: the Rocky Mountain sheep, California lion, yellow wolf, coyote, moose, wolverene, lynx or catamount, wildcat, fox (black, gray, silver, and cross), weasel, badger, marten, mink, large striped skunk, small spotted skunk, large gray, ground, pine, and flying sqirrel, chipmunk, otter, raccoon, woodchuck, gopher, mole, wood-mouse, "kangaroo rat," and jack rabbit.

The birds are those common throughout the north-west. Eagles (bald and golden) are abundant in the mountains, especially in the neighborhood of streams. Wild ducks, swans, geese, pelicans, and quail are plentiful in season. The burrowing owl, fish-hawk, and buzzard may be mentioned among the larger birds. In addition to these, are the usual varieties of woodpecker, raven, hawk, grouse, pigeon, meadow lark, magpie, red-winged blackbird, bluebird, robin, snipe, plover, curlew, sparrow, crossbill, linnet, oriole, California canary, swallow, two varieties of humming birds, and mallard and canvas-back ducks.

In nearly all the streams and lakes trout abound, frequently weighing over two pounds. Salmon run up the Columbia River into the Snake and its many tributaries, there spawn, and return late in the spring or early summer. Sturgeon of enormous size, frequently from 600 to 1,000 pounds in weight, are abundant in Snake River.

The Payette Lakes and Lake Tahoma are the homes of the red-fish. This is a large, beautiful fish, weighing from 2½ to 4 pounds, is of a bright red color, with head and fins of light brown, and is excellent eating. When the young fish are hatched, they seek the deeper waters of the lake, where they disappear, remaining until nearly full grown. A species known as bull-trout is found in Payette Lake; they are larger than the ordinary salmon-trout, and weigh from five to eleven pounds.

CHAPTER IV.—MINING.

Idaho is essentially a mining Territory. It was her mines that first stimulated immigration to within her borders, and it is to the results of the mines that her present prosperity is due in a great measure. Now that mining has been reduced to a legitimate occupation, there is less reckless speculation, perhaps, than of old, but more solid, substantial business. The days of stock gambling in mining properties are about over. Science, aided by practical experience, has taught the best methods of treating ores. Capitalists no longer purchase prospects for fabulous prices on the strength of picked specimens or the vicinity of rich claims. It is a fortunate circumstance for Idaho that mining for the past eight years has been for the most part a steady, productive industry, yielding rich returns to the patient and intelligent prospector, and it has not been necessary to rely on fictitious "booms."

As in the case of mining countries generally, the placer mines first attracted attention. The placers of Boisé Basin, Salmon River, and other localities had yielded rich returns. But it is within a comparatively brief period that quartz mining has become as general as at present in southern and central Idaho. Even now, in the best known mining regions there are hundreds of miles as yet unexplored.

The minerals of Idaho are gold, silver, copper, iron, lead, plumbago, quicksilver, coal, and others. There are also mountains of sulphur, productive salt springs, quarries of the finest marble and building stone, large deposits of mica, and various varieties of semi-precious stones. Her precious-metal belt is three hundred and fifty miles long, and from ten to one hundred and fifty miles wide.

DISCOVERY OF GOLD.

It is reported that gold was discovered by a French Canadian in Pend d'Oreille River, in 1852. Two years later General Lander found gold while exploring the route for a military road from the Columbia to Fort Bridger. The earliest discoveries of which we have any authentic record, however, were probably made by members of the party with that veteran pioneer and path-finder, Captain John Mullan, the originator of the now famous Mullan road, built nearly thirty years ago, from Fort Benton to Walla Walla, a distance of 624 miles. In a letter dated Washington, D. C., June 4, 1884, to Mr. A. F. Parker of Eagle City, he says:

"I am not at all surprised at the discovery of numerous rich gold deposits in your mountains, because both on the waters of the St. Joseph and the Cœur d'Alene, when there many years ago, I frequently noticed vast masses of quartz strewing the ground, particularly on the St. Joseph

River, and wide veins of quartz projecting at numerous points along the line of my road along the Cœur d'Alene, all of which indicated the presence of gold. Nay, more: I now recall quite vividly the fact that one of my herders and hunters, a man by the name of Moise, coming into camp one day with a handful of coarse gold, which he said he found on the waters of the north fork of the Cœur d'Alene while out hunting for our expedition. This was in 1858 or 1859. * * * The members of my expedition were composed very largely of old miners from California, and having had more or less experience in noticing the indication of mineral deposits, their universal verdict was that the entire country, from Cœur d'Alene Lake on toward and including the east slope of the Rocky Mountains, was one vast gold-bearing country, and I was always nervous as to the possible discovery of gold along the line of my road; and I am now frank to say that I did nothing to encourage its discovery at that time, for I feared that any rich discovery would lead to a general stampede of my men from my expedition, and thus destroy the probable consummation of my work during the time within which I desired to complete the same. I then regarded it as of the first importance to myself and to the public to open a base line from the plains of the Spokane on the west to the plains of the Missouri on the east, from which other lines could be subsequently opened, and by means of which the correct geography of the country could be delineated. My object at that time was to ascertain whether there was a practicable railroad line through the valleys, and if there existed any practicable pass in the main range of the Rocky Mountains through which, in connection with the proper approaches thereto, we could carry a wagon road, to be followed by a railroad line, and I did not hesitate to make all other considerations secondary or subordinate thereto, believing then, and knowing now, that if a railroad line was projected and completed through the valleys and the passes of the Rocky Mountains, between the forty-fifth and forty-eighth parallels of latitude, all other developments would naturally and necessarily soon follow."

A romantic tale is told of the discoveries which led to the Oro Fino excitement in 1860. Tradition relates that a Nez Percé Indian, in 1860, informed Captain E. D. Pierce that while himself and two companions were camping at night among the defiles of his native mountains, an apparition in the shape of a brilliant star suddenly burst forth from among the cliffs. They believed it to be the eye of the Great Spirit, and when daylight had given them sufficient courage they sought the spot, and found a glittering ball that looked like glass, embodied in the solid rock. The Indians believed it to be "great medicine," but could not get it from its resting-place. With his ardent imagination fired by such a tale, Captain Pierce organized a company, and with the hope of finding the "eye of their Manitou," explored the mountains in the country of the Nez Percés.

He was accompanied by W. F. Bassett, Thomas Walters, Jonathan Smith, and John and James Dodge. The Indians distrusted them, however, and refused to permit them to make further search. They would doubtless have had to leave the country had not a Nez Percé squaw come to their relief and piloted them through to the North Fork of the Clearwater and the Palouse country, cutting a trail for days through the small cedars, reaching a mountain meadow, where they stopped to rest. While there Bassett went to a stream and tried the soil for gold, finding about three cents in his first panful of dirt. This is said to be the discovery that resulted in the afterwards famous Oro Fino mines. After taking out about eighty dollars they returned to Walla Walla. Sergeant J. C. Smith of that place thereupon fitted out a party and started for the mines, reaching there in November, 1860. In the following March Smith made his way out on snow-shoes, taking with him $800 in gold-dust. This dust was shipped to Portland, where it caused a blaze of excitement.

During 1861 and 1862 the rush continued. Steamers arrived at Portland from San Francisco and Victoria loaded down with freight and passengers for the new gold-fields. New mining regions were constantly discovered. In the spring of 1861 Pierce City was founded, and named in honor of Captain Pierce. The Elk City mines were discovered early in 1861 by parties from Oro Fino. Florence was discovered in the following autumn. In August, 1862, James Warrens and others located claims in what was thereafter known as Warrens'

Diggings. These last-named are all in Idaho county, on the tributaries of the Salmon River. Warrens never caused the rush and excitement that attended the discovery of Florence. The latter, it was claimed, was found by a greenhorn, one of a party of seven hunters. The recklessness characteristic of new mining camps found full play here. Thirty men were killed in the first year; shooting and cutting were every-day matters. Prices were abnormal. Flour cost $1 per pound; bacon, $1.25; butter, $3; sugar, $1.25; gum boots per pair, $30; and other articles in proportion.

The Walla Walla *Statesman*, in chronicling the event, gives the following description of the discovery of the Salmon River mines in 1861: "S. F. Ledyard arrived last evening from the Salmon River mines, and from him it is learned that some 600 miners would winter there; that some 200 had gone to the south side of the river, where two streams head that empty into the Salmon, some thirty miles south-east of the present mining camp. Coarse gold is found, and as high $100 per day to the man has been taken out. The big mining claim of the old locality belongs to Mr. Weiser of Oregon, from where $2,680 were taken on the 20th, with rockers. On the 21st $3,360 were taken out with the same machines. Other claims were paying from two to five pounds a day. Flour has fallen to fifty cents per pound, and beef at from fifteen to twenty-five cents is to be found in abundance. Most of the mines are supplied till the first of June. Mr. Ledyard met between Slate Creek and Walla Walla, en route for the mines, 394 packs and 250 head of beef cattle."

The same journal on December 13, 1861, gives the following account of the new diggings: "The tide of emigration to Salmon River flows steadily onward. During the week past not less than 225 pack-animals, heavily laden with provisions, have left this city [Walla Walla] for the mines. If the mines are one half so rich as they are said to be, we may safely calculate that many of these trains will return as heavily laden with gold-dust as they are now with provisions.

"The late news from Salmon River seems to have given the gold fever to everybody in this immediate neighborhood. A number of persons from Florence City have arrived in this place during the week, and all bring the most extravagant reports as to the richness of the mines. A report in relation to a rich strike made by Mr. Bridges of Oregon City seems to come well authenticated. The first day he worked on his claim, near Baboon Gulch, he took 57 ounces; the second day he took 157 ounces; third day, 214 ounces; and the fourth day 200 ounces in two hours. One gentleman informs us that diggings have been found on the bars of the Salmon River which yield from twenty-five cents to $2.50 to the pan, and that on claims in the Salmon River diggings have been found where 'ounces' won't describe them, and where they say the gulches are 'full of gold.'

"The discoverer of Baboon Gulch arrived in this city yesterday, bringing with him sixty pounds of gold-dust; and Mr. Jacob Weiser is on his way in with a mule loaded with gold-dust."

Such glowing descriptions twenty-three years ago had their inevitable effects, while the more substantial argument was adduced in the fact that $1,750,000 in gold-dust were exported from this region that year. According to Mr. Elliott, during April, 1862, 3,000 persons left Portland, by steamer, for the mines, and by the last of May it was estimated that between 20,000 and 25,000 persons had reached or were on their way to and near the mines east of the Cascade Mountains. The yield accounted for, of gold, in 1862, in this region of country, reached $7,000,000, and several millions in addition to this were shipped through avenues not reported.

"Such," says the chronicler, "were the results following in a few short months upon the trail pioneered by E. D. Pierce, W. F. Bassett, and their little party of prospectors whom the Indians had driven out of the country, but to return to it again and again, first led by a squaw, then through the assistance of J. C. Smith, when pursued as trespassers by a company of United States cavalry. Enough has been given to show the reader the influence that awoke eastern Washington, Oregon, and Idaho from their sleep through the centuries, to a new era of activity and usefulness."

It was a strange throng that came pouring over the mountains of north Idaho in the days of 1862. On foot, horseback, or any other means that could be obtained, they pushed their way over swollen rivers, rugged mountains, and Indian-infested valleys. Lewiston, Lapwai, Oro Fino, Pierce City, Elk City, Florence—these were the magic names that fired the imaginations and stimulated the ardor of these dauntless pioneers.

One of the effects of the Florence excitement was the discovery of Boisé Basin, in Boisé County. A party of men left Florence in the fall of 1861, and in the following summer passed over into central Idaho. They came by the way of Oregon, crossing the Snake River by the mouth of the Boisé. They followed up Boisé River to the site of Boisé City. Under instructions from an Indian whom they there encountered, they struck out for the mountains north of Boisé River, and subsequently camped near where Centreville now stands. While prospecting on the creek, one of the party named Grimes was killed by Indians. The creek, which has become famous in the history of Idaho placer mining, has ever since been called Grimes Creek.

After the death of Grimes, his companions left the country for Walla Walla. Another party returned to the Basin in October, 1862. A stockade was built, and the place was styled "Fort Hog'em," a name which survives to this day, though Pioneerville is the appellation given on the maps. A writer in the *Idaho World* gives the following account of the discovery of Boisé Basin:

"A party of thirty-eight men, known as Turner's party, left Auburn, Oregon, in the spring of 1862, for Sinker Creek, in Owyhee County. It was reported that emigrants, in fishing along this creek, used gold nuggets, picked up on the creek, for sinkers—hence the name. Joseph Branstetter of this place was with Turner's party. Failing to find gold on Sinker Creek, Branstetter and seven others left the party and met Captain Grimes' party of eight men, between Sinker Creek and Owyhee River. Grimes' party and Branstetter and three others of his party, Colonel Dave Fogus one of the number, making twelve men all told, concluded to strike up into the mountains of this section. They crossed Snake River, eight miles above the Owyhee River, in skiffs made of willows. Snake River was then at high-water mark. The party struck Grimes Creek near Black's Ranch and followed up said creek, along which they first discovered gold, near where the town of Boston stood—two or three miles below Centreville. They obtained good prospects there—about a bit to the pan. The party proceeded up to Grimes Pass, near the head of Grimes Creek. One day, while all of the party were in camp, a shot was fired a short distance from the camp, the bullet passing over the men's heads. A few moments after a second shot was fired, the bullet cutting the hair over one of Mr. Branstetter's ears. Grimes, a Portuguese named Phillip, Mose Splann, and Wilson, Grimes' partner, then struck out from camp on the hunt of the Indian that did the shooting. Grimes got on the track of the Indian, on the hill above camp, and was following the tracks with his shot-gun in his hands when the fatal shot was fired. Splann was about fifty yards to Grimes' left, and the Portuguese a short distance behind. Grimes was within thirty steps of the Indian and about a hundred and fifty yards from the camp when he was shot. The Indian made his escape. Grimes was shot near the heart, and lived only long enough to tell Wilson to tell his wife, who was in Portland, how he came to his death. Grimes frequently made the remark that he would never reach home—that he was to be killed by Indians. The day before he was killed he remarked, while gazing at the picture of his only child, a daughter of a few years of age, that he would never see her again—that he had only a short time to live. His daughter, we are informed, is still living, and visited Boisé City a year ago. Grimes' remains were buried at Grimes Pass, where he was killed. Grimes was a young man, twenty-seven or twenty-eight years of age. The party consisted of four Portuguese and three other men, in addition to those mentioned, the names of two of whom Mr. Branstetter never knew, and the names of the others he has forgotten. Grimes was killed in August, 1862. A short time after his death the party left for Auburn, Oregon, and returned in October of the same year. There are now only two of the Grimes party known to be living, Colonel Fogus and Mr. Branstetter. That fall Branstetter and A. Saunders rocked out from $50 to $75 a day near Pioneerville, and packed the dirt 100 yards in sacks. A. D. Saunders and Marion Moore returned with the party in October. The party numbered ninety-three men. Jeff Standifer's party arrived from Florence about a week after the party of ninety-three got in from Auburn. W. B. Noble of this place was with the Standifer party. The above was related to us by Mr. Branstetter. He was the youngest man in Grimes' party; was twenty years of age when they reached Boisé Basin."

The mines on Granite Creek were discovered about the 1st of December by the party, who also located the site of Placerville, which contained about six cabins partly completed on the 14th day of that month.

Boisé Basin soon became known as the greatest placer country outside of California. By the 1st of January, 1863, over three thousand men had made their way into it. Centreville, Pioneerville, Placerville, Granite Creek, Idaho City (originally known as Bannock), sprung into existence, and by September of that year there were probably 2,500 men scattered through the Basin. Several million dollars had been taken out by the close of the season that year. In July, 1864, over 2,500 claims had been recorded in Banner district; in Centreville over 2,000, and in Placerville over 4,500.

Idaho City, or Bannock, became the metropolis of the Basin, and at one time could boast of a population, transient and permanent, estimated as high as from seven thousand to ten thousand. On the 18th of May, 1865, the town was completely destroyed by a disastrous fire, property to the extent of one and a quarter million of dollars lost, and seven thousand people left homeless and shelterless. The town was rebuilt during the same season, however, and though three times destroyed by fire, for many years retained its prestige as the leading mining town of Idaho.

The first ferry across Snake River was established in 1862. A number of persons from Placerville, twenty-seven in all, in the spring of 1863, visited what is now Owyhee County. They discovered Reynolds Creek, which was named in honor of one of their party. On the following day the men reached a stream, where they camped, panned the gravel, and obtained a hundred colors. The place was named Discovery Bar. Happy Camp, near the site of Ruby City, was discovered soon after. The creek was named after the leader of the expedition, and the district was called Carson, after another member of the party.

In July the first quartz lead was discovered by R. H. Wade, and named Whisky Gulch. In the following month the placers in the French District were discovered, and also the Oro Fino quartz ledge.

The celebrated Poorman mine was not discovered until October, 1865.

The mines of middle and south Boisé, in Alturas County, including Atlanta, Yuba, and Rocky Bar, were discovered in 1864, and are worked up to the present time.

Such in brief is the history of the mineral discoveries in Idaho prior to 1870. By that time the rush, the fever, the excitement attendant upon new discoveries, had quieted down. Many of those who had come into the Territory, carried along by the wave of excitement, left with the ebbing tide. The placer mines had been worked, though by no means exhausted. The rush had subsided and a reaction had set in. According to statistics, the yield of 1869 was less than that of any year before or since. Those who remained in Idaho, however, continued to prosper.

Idaho's present area is about 84,800 square miles. Dispersed over this immense surface, comprising a territory greater than that of New York, New Jersey, Massachusetts, and New Hampshire combined, there were in 1870, exclusive of tribal Indians, less than 15,000 inhabitants, including 4,274 Chinamen. Her settlements were scattered, frequently a hundred miles or more apart.

Situated far from the ordinary lines of through travel, only the most daring and hardy adventurers sought her mountain solitudes. The only means of communication were by tedious journeys by stage or team, or more frequently on horseback, over rough mountain trails, where natural obstacles were only enhanced by the oft-recurring presence of prowling bands of Indians, who so long resented the intrusion of the whites. The nearest railroad at this time was the Central Pacific through Utah and Nevada.

None of these drawbacks, however, could deter the pioneer and prospector. Great as these obstacles were, they shrunk into insignificance when confronted by the spirit of the gold-seekers. The discoveries of the past were regarded as but an earnest of the future. It was known that far up among her mountain fastnesses were other storehouses of precious metals that needed only enterprise and capital to develop their hidden treasures. From the remote and secluded mountains of "Far Idaho," as from an almost unknown and unseen source, the golden streams continued flowing. For years the placers of Boisé Basin and Salmon River, and the ledges of Owyhee, Rocky Bar, and Atlanta, continued yielding their riches, thus constantly adding to the national wealth.

No discoveries of new fields, and no stampedes of any importance, occurred, however, for several years. In the mean time the great work of prospecting the rugged mountains still went on. Far up among the snow-capped hills of north-eastern Idaho was an unknown region, still described on some maps as "unexplored country." Along the tributaries of the upper Salmon, in the neighborhood of Yankee Fork, Kinni-kinnick and Bay-horse creeks, in what is now Custer County, prior to 1877, solitary prospectors had located a few claims, and placers had been worked to advantage. Occasional visitors from that far-off land had exhibited among the mining men of Salt Lake City specimens of gold and silver ore, whose assay value could be expressed only in four figures. The Charles Dickens had been located in 1875. A thousand dollars had been crushed out in small hand-mortars in a day. During the first month, two men pounded out about $12,000. A few tons of ore were then sacked and shipped to Salt Lake City and to Swansea. The net results were $15,000, the highest grade sampling $3,700 per ton. A lot of twenty-three tons netted over $17,000. In 1878 a two-bed arrastra, with pan and settler, was built at a cost of $19,400, and started up late in August. By the first of November, by crushing two tons of quartz per day, the arrastra had produced bullion to the amount of $32,000. A well-known writer, speaking of the General Custer mine in the same district, says: "It is the only instance on record where a ledge so immense in wealth and size was already opened and developed when the eyes of prospector first looked upon it. Ore bodies are usually found beneath the surface, and miners consider themselves fortunate if, after long searching by shafts and tunnels, they strike a vein that insures them reasonable dividends over and above the cost of development. The Custer required no outlay of money to make it a paying mine. Its face was good for millions. Nature, in one of her philanthropic moods, did the prospecting and development. The outer wall of this great treasure-vault, through the wear and tear of ages, crumbled and slipped from the ore body for a distance of several hundred feet, leaving many thousands of tons of the very choicest rock lying against the mountain side, to be broken down at little expense."

The Montana mine on Mt. Estes has been pronounced by mining men to be the richest vein of quartz ever discovered, taking the whole vein matter from wall to wall. Some of the ledge matter is so rich that it has been worked in a mortar at the mine. A lot of 225 pounds yielded $1,800. The richest ore is so abundant that four to six men can take out $15,000 to $25,000 per month. Such were the reports from that section, and experience proved them to be well founded.

The completion of the Utah and Northern to Blackfoot, early in the spring of 1879 brought the Bay-horse district within 150 miles, and the Yankee Fork within 190 miles, of railroad communication. In the spring and summer of 1879, people rushed in by the hundreds, and Challis, Custer City, Bonanza, Clayton, Crystal City, and Ætna became prosperous mining camps. The Sawtooth and Wood River sections in Alturas County now began to attract attention, but were not thoroughly prospected till the following year. (See article on Alturas County). The editor of the Hailey *Times* gives the following terse statement, as the record of Wood River:

WOOD RIVER'S RECORD.

In 1878...Wild Indians
In 1880...Settled by the Whites
In 1881—yield of the mines..$1,250,000
In 1882—yield of the mines..2,500,000
In 1883—yield of the mines..3,500,000
In 1884—yield of the mines (estimated)..................................5,000,000

One of the most remarkable mining excitements in history was the great Cœur d'Alene stampede of 1884. Gold had been discovered in that country in former years, but no developments had ever been made, owing to the remoteness of the locality. In 1883 a man named Pritchard discovered and located the "Widow's Claim," which proved of more than average richness. Further discoveries were made, which were rapidly noised abroad. From the heart of the Cœur d'Alene Mountains, though distant only 40 miles from the Northern Pacific, came the most exaggerated accounts. The whole region was subjected to an artificial "boom," at a most inopportune time. In February of 1884, over the snows came trudging an eager multitude, who would hearken neither to the voice of reason nor the warnings of experience. The mails were flooded with fantastic descriptions of this latest El Dorado. Newspaper correspondents from all over the land came flocking thither, and contributed to give further publicity to a region already overadvertised. Circulars were sent broadcast all over the land, giving the most glowing accounts of nuggets of fabulous wealth, that could be had almost for the seeking. It was declared that old prospectors and miners, conversant with the history of the banner districts of California, Montana, and Colorado, would stand amazed at the new fields so unequaled in richness and extent; that $25 to $40 per man per day were being panned out in the gulches; that the fields being practically inexhaustible, rendered impossible any overcrowding of the district; that wherever the bed-rock had been uncovered, beautiful rich dust was being "scooped up" by the lucky owners; that no machinery or capital was required; that limitless quartz ledges were being struck "fairly glistening with free gold." The result was that in a few weeks, early in the spring of 1884, the forest land at the junction of Eagle and Pritchard Creeks became metamorphosed into a city of 5,000 restless inhabitants, all waiting for the snow to disappear. The effect of overadvertising soon became manifest in the reaction that took place after the summer had fairly set in. A hasty exodus followed, and hundreds left on foot, "packing their blankets" and cursing the country. The region was even more misrepresented by the unsuccessful adventurers, who, in spite of incontestable facts, declared there "was no gold in the country." Many of the claims got into litigation, which retarded their development. The July term of court at Eagle City settled the disputed titles, when the work of development was fairly begun, and since which time the region has been keeping up a steady output of gold. Business has settled down to a legitimate basis, new discoveries are being constantly made, and the country is being systematically opened up. The result proves it to be one of the finest fields now offered for the investment of capital.

SNAKE RIVER PLACERS.

The course of Snake River has already been described. From Eagle Rock, in north-eastern Idaho, for hundreds of miles down the river, the sands of the Snake are capable of furnishing remunerative employment to miners for generations to come.

The gold-bearing gravel lies in immense banks, or what were bars when the river was higher and larger than it now is. They extend along the river, with low channels, sometimes cutting them in two or crossing them. They vary, therefore, in width from a few feet to as many miles, and in thickness, from a few feet to two hundred.

At the request of the writer, Major N. H. Camp, superintendent of the United States assay office at Boisé City, has kindly furnished the following description of the Snake River gold-fields:

"It is popularly supposed that the occupation of a gold-miner is most favorably adapted to the development of those qualities called for by a bold and adventurous life, uncheered by the amenities of social civilization, untrammeled by its laws and intercourse between its members, unlubricated by the presence of fair woman. What wonder, then, that gold-seeking should be the chief interest of this lonely region! The character of its banks forbids the construction of towns, while the lack of navigation facilities prevents this great water way from ministering to the transportation needs of the neighboring stock-farms, sage prairies, or the supplying of the isolated mining camps. It is in such localities that gold delights to reward the pains taken by the lonesome prospector, and here does he find, not only the coveted treasure, but in such quantities as will reward his patient search at a minimum of expense. The only drawback is the extremely small size of the particles of gold; coarse gold is unknown on Snake River, but from Eagle Rock, in Oneida County, to the mouth of the river, gold can be found of such exactly similar metallurgical conditions, both as to fineness in grade (shape of grains being scalelike in form) and fineness in character of grains, that it might have come from either end of the river. On the affluents of this river gold is also found; but even within half a mile of its mouth, 'Boisé' gold sinks to an assay fineness of from 720 to 780, while that from the river under review will assay over 900 and even 990. The shape of the grains is noticeably a feature of Snake River gold, being so flat and scale-like that the precious metal is often seen floating on the surface of the water, while gold from any of the feeder streams assumes more the character of shot gold, is coarser, and much more easily harnessed to the service of man. Its extremely small size is also a distinguishing mark of this gold. The writer has seen a gold-pan full of the gold-bearing sands, which, in the hands of an experienced prospector, soon showed its bottom as if gilt by a practiced workman. Out of curiosity, an attempt was made to count the 'colors,' but when the sum of fourteen hundred was reached, the business was given up in disgust—*there were so many left to count!*

"Nor has Nature herself been niggardly in furnishing facilities to man for mining these rich deposits. From many a fissure in the cañon walls along the banks of this wonderful river fall 'springs'—some of which are the size of young rivers—as they are called. Issuing from one to two hundred feet above the level of the river, they only require to be conducted to the gravel bars to assume the duties of washing out gold. At other points rivers fall into the Snake, along whose banks it is only necessary to dig the necessary ditches, to convert the streams into the obedient and useful servants of mankind. In many cases, however, these ditches have to be blasted out of the lava rock, and the dams across the smaller streams are costly and tedious structures, making the enterprise, when completed, as dear to the heart as something attained only at great cost of time, labor, and capital, as in one instance where a miner for two years contented himself with the privations and solitude of his cabin, mining in a small way, but devoting all his savings and leisure to the construction of a ditch, despite the sneers and ridicule of his neighbors. The ditch was completed in the spring of 1884, and now he harvests $3,000 per month in virgin gold.

"Where springs gush from the cañon walls in sufficient volume to wash gravel for gold, the expense of a moderately profitable mining outfit, comprising say 400 yards of ditching, 72 feet of fluming, 36 feet of sluice-boxes, 12 feet of grizzlies (sheets of perforated iron), two amalgamating plates, a concentrating tank 3 by 6, and 24 feet of burlap tables — ought to be not less than $350 to $600; add the cost of one month's subsistence, $40, for two men, and the services of a laborer, and about the cost of a small mining establishment on this river is told. This outfit ought to pay for itself in three months, and yield a moderate profit—twelve to fifteen per cent. per annum in excess of working expenses. 'High bars' there are, too, prospecting rich, but until some inexpensive method is discovered of raising, and utilizing for mining purposes, the water of Snake River, these spots must remain closed to the avarice of man. A patent motor has been devised for raising water by using the force of the river current, but experiment has failed to demonstrate its economy, or to bring its price within the means of the moderately wealthy.

"But it is not only the production of fruits, and the golden results of placer mining, that the Broadway of Idaho relies on to attract to her borders those energies necessary in the development of a hitherto *terra incognita*. In the range of mountains through which our river cuts her way, forming here the western boundary of Washington County, are rich deposits of copper and silver, assays of which show from twenty-six to sixty-eight per cent. of copper, and from nine to one hundred and sixty-three ounces of silver per ton. This region is now brought into communication with the rest of the United States by the railroad system rendered available by the meeting of the Oregon Short Line and the Oregon Railway and Navigation Company's lines.

The Wood River country has proved an immense silver success; but it is predicted that the copper region of Western Idaho will largely exceed it in bringing material prosperity to those of limited means coming in to work the bowels of the earth for the riches to be extracted therefrom. To such, Idaho must look in large measure for the permanence of her prosperity, and it is with a view of attracting their attention to our Territory that this is written."

A. D. Foote, Esq., the well-known mining expert and engineer of the Idaho Mining and Irrigation Company, writes of the Snake River placers:

"I have spent a great deal of time and labor prospecting these placer fields, and confess that the results obtained are beyond my expectations. I sunk shafts where the gravel was not so loose as to prevent me, ran tunnels into the sides of bars where I could not sink shafts, dug numerous prospect holes, tried gravel in ant-hills, and also that which is brought to the surface by badgers or gophers, in order to get as nearly as possible an accurate idea of the quantity and value of these immense auriferous deposits of gravel. I took accurately measured half cubic yards of gravel, washed it with rocker and pan, saving black sand and gold. The results of several of these tests accompany this report. Some of them I assayed, and several I smelted. The results obtained by assays varied from a few cents to eighty cents per cubic yard of gravel; assays made from the same samples by different assayers varying largely, while the gold obtained by the pan would be about the same in each instance. It is difficult to account for this great variation in the results of assays; but I find it is the experience of every one who deals with black sand."

The Castle Creek Mining Company's property (office, No. 58 Broadway, New York) is situated on the south side of Snake River, about eighteen miles above the Silver City ferry. Its water supply is taken from Castle Creek and is very limited, except during a short time in the spring. It uses only one flume, essentially similar to one (described further on) used by Mr. Chesebro. Their bank of gravel is from fifteen to thirty feet thick. The water is simply run over the face of the bank without pressure, and carrying the gravel down into the sluice. The company employ three men and a superintendent. It has paid seventeen consecutive monthly dividends, of three thousand dollars each, and expects to continue them, there being no apparent reason why it should not, as the gravel and water are there in quantities sufficient to last a century at the company's present rate of working.

Mr. John R. Murphy has investigated this property thoroughly, and says that the cost of mining is two and one quarter cents per cubic yard. From measurements carefully made before and after several months' washing, the value of gold saved from a cubic yard of gravel was found to be twenty-seven cents.

The Holyoke Mining Company, at Bonanza Bar, is also a dividend-paying property, though working on a small scale because of a small supply of water. Carefully made measurements prove the value of its gravel to be twenty-one cents per cubic yard.

The Juniper Gold (placer) Mining Company, adjoining the Holyoke, is best described by the following extract:

"NEW YORK, February 6, 1883.
"JUNIPER GOLD MINING COMPANY, New York City.

"GENTLEMEN: In compliance with your request of the 2d inst., addressed to me by your secretary, requesting my views as to the character and value of your property on Snake River, I beg to submit the subjoined as covering the same. Respectfully yours, JOHN R. MURPHY.

"In the interest of a few of my friends who were desirous to invest in the property, provided they could be assured that it was possessed of such merit as was claimed for it, I went to the mines on Snake River, in Idaho Territory, in September last, and made a very thorough examination of the same, devoting over thirty days to it. I found the area of the gravel to be quite correct, but in depth and quantity I found it to be fully one fourth more than is claimed in the company's prospectus.

"The depth of the gravel beds I found by actual survey to be from 40 to 100 feet vertical; while the quantity in cubic yards I found to be fully fifteen per cent more than is claimed.

"The quantity of gold-bearing gravel comprising this property is all that could be desired, as it cannot all be worked out in seventy-five years, using say 4,000 inches of water, washing continuously.

"In the matter of value of a given quantity of the gravel, I have exercised the utmost care to ascertain how much it would pay to the cubic yard.

"After 200 tests by pan-washing, and several others by a system of concentration, making five assays of the concentrates, I satisfied myself that the gravel throughout this property will average forty-two cents to the cubic yard.

"This value may seem high when it is understood that in California gravel that will yield five to eight cents per cubic yard is considered safe and profitable; while that which goes from eight to twenty cents is considered extra valuable.

"One difficulty, however, has heretofore stood in the way of saving a high percentage of the gold—that is, its extreme granular fineness; but the experience of the past two years has enabled parties to devise means by which from seventy-five to eighty-five per cent of the gold contained is being saved.

"I have found the gold to be uniformly distributed throughout the whole mass of gravel, from bottom to top, there being no rich leads or pay streaks; it is of like value at grass roots as at bed-rock."

Mr. Murphy also says that his investigations on the Snake River prove conclusively that the gravel bars are richer on the lower part of the river than on the upper, and also that the gold is coarser in the lower bars.

Near Silver City Ferry, on the south side of Snake River, Mr. Chesebro of Boisé City owns a bar which he works for a few months every spring with water brought from Reynolds Creek. His water supply is very small, and is simply run down the face of the bar without being confined in any way. He works three men, and says he averages about ten dollars per man per day in gold. He thinks the gravel contains from fifteen to twenty-five cents per ton (two thirds of a cubic yard), but has made no tests to determine accurately. His gravel is precisely similar to that of this company. If there is any difference, judging from panning out in both localities, I should say that the first twelve miles above Boisé River, on the north side of the Snake, was somewhat richer than the Chesebro claim.

The cost of washing a cubic yard of gravel in the large hydraulic mines of California has been determined in several instances with great care, and averages about three and one half cents. From what I have already quoted of the mining experience on Snake River, it is certain that the Snake River bars can be washed more cheaply than the California mines. I wish to be absolutely safe in the following estimate, and shall allow four cents as the expense of mining a cubic yard.

I have determined the area of the placer lands controlled by the company, assisted partially by the government lines and the surveyed line of canal to be between thirty-five and forty-five thousand acres. It is difficult to determine them precisely without an extensive system of shafts to prove their limit on the northern edge. I am perfectly safe, however, in placing their area at thirty-five thousand acres. In regard to the thickness or depth of the gravel, I could only determine it by the thickness disclosed at the sides or faces of the bluffs. Often I could get on three sides, and there is no reason to suppose that a great flat plain, which shows stratified gravel seventy-five feet thick on three sides, is any less in the center. These bars run from twenty to one hundred and fifty feet thick, as seen from their sides, averaging at least fifty feet.

Supposing, however, that they are only twenty-seven feet thick, then each square foot of surface will give a cubic yard of gravel, or forty-three thousand five hundred and sixty cubic yards to the acre, and thirty-five thousand acres make a little over fifteen hundred million cubic yards of gravel.

As I have shown, several placer mines on the river yield from twenty to thirty cents in each cubic yard of gravel. Although this gravel is precisely like the gravel of those mines, I prefer to value it at twelve cents per cubic yard, and as I before said, allow the cost to be four cents for mining, leaving eight cents profit for the company on each cubic yard of its gravel. Fifteen hundred million cubic yards at eight cents per yard makes the enormous sum of one hundred and twenty million dollars, which is the profit to be realized from the company's placer lands at the low valuation and high cost of mining which I have used as a basis for my estimate. It is approximately a profit of thirty-five hundred dollars per acre.

The above profit will not appear so very large when the time necessary to obtain it is realized. There is a practical limit to the rapidity with which this gravel can be washed. By the system of washing which is described further on, the lands can be attacked at a number of different points at the same time. Say five points were taken, and four thousand inches of water used at each, or twenty thousand per day. For two hundred days in the year this would amount to four million inches.

An inch of water will in this loose gravel wash ten to twelve cubic yards; but as an elevator will have to be used for a portion of the gravel, it is perhaps as well to take the amount given by Hamilton Smith, Jr., as washed in the hard-bottomed gravel of the North Bloomfield mine, viz., five cubic yards. Four million inches will wash at this rate twenty million cubic yards, or approximately, five hundred acres; which at thirty-five hundred dollars per acre, would yield a yearly income of one million seven hundred and fifty thousand dollars, and require seventy years to exhaust the supply of gravel.

Before going further, it is perhaps best to explain some of the methods in use on the river for saving gold, and also the methods which will be used in washing in this particular locality.

Mr. Chesebro's method consists of a flume thirty feet long and three feet wide, in which is secured a perforated sheet of iron, three feet wide by sixteen long, four inches above the bottom of the flume. It is placed in the upper portion of the flume. The holes in it are about one quarter of an inch in diameter. At the upper end of the flume is fixed a wide-mouthed box, like a funnel lying horizontally, into which the water carries the gravel. In this case the water runs over the bank, and in its fall gathers headway enough to gradually bring the bank with it into the box; when the bank is washed away too far in one place, the direction of the water above the bank is changed, and another portion washed down. This portion of the work occupies two men. Water enough is thus passed into the flume to carry the gravel along it over the "grizzly." In passing over this the finer portion of the gravel and sand finds its way down through the "grizzly" into the space below, from which it is constantly drawn by a number of side flumes, or tables, set at right angles to the main flume. These are three feet wide and nine feet long. They are lined on the bottom with heavy canvas tacked down. This heavy canvas is of just sufficient roughness to catch the gold and heaviest black sand; the coarser and lighter material rolls over it and passes off as fine "tailings," while the still coarser material which has passed through the main flume is called the coarse tailings. At the head of the tables are gates on the main flume, which can be opened or closed when desired, and along one side of the table is a trough, just below the level of the table. After an hour's run the gate at the head of the table is closed, and the black sand and gold on the canvas carefully brushed into the trough, when the gate is opened and the next table cleared, and so on.

The black sand thus obtained is, in Mr. Chesebro's method, treated with a little cyanide of potassium, to clean the gold, and then run slowly through another flume, or trough, on the bottom of which are silver-plated copper plates covered with quicksilver. This collects the gold in the shape of amalgam, which is scraped off occasionally and retorted.

Mr. Chesebro himself says, and I agree with him, that there are far better ways of amalgamating the gold than the method he uses, especially on a large scale, where there is cheap water power. Two Cornishmen at work on the river near Glenn's Ferry have hit upon the idea in a crude and cheap way. They have built a small arrastra, run by water power, in which they put their black sand and quicksilver. An arrastra is simply a circular pit paved with stone, in which a large stone is dragged around on the pavement, as a horse goes around in a whim. It is the crude idea from which the amalgamating pan of the modern silver-mill is evolved. In working the black sand of these placers on a large scale, something similar to the amalgamating pan will be used, changing it sufficiently to adapt it to the different material and work required.

Placer mining in California has been seriously checked, if not ruined, by the accumulation of tailings in the rivers and on the lands below. In the case under consideration, there is no danger of anything of the kind happening, as the company proposes to send only a very small portion of its tailings into the river.

In addition to the Snake River gold-fields above described, the placers now receiving the most attention are those of Boisé Basin, Salmon River and its tributaries, and the Cœur d'Alene. The last named will be found described in the article on Shoshone County.

The precious metals are not the only minerals found in Idaho. Copper ores abound in different sections. The copper mines of Washington County now attract much attention. They will be found more fully described in the article on that county. Near Rocky Bar, in Alturas County, is a vein carrying fifty-six per cent pure iron. Other veins have been found near Wood River carrying a large percentage of iron. Near Challis, in Custer County, is said to be an immense body of micaceous iron, yielding fifty to sixty per cent of that metal. Near South Mountain, in Owyhee County, is the great Narragansett iron mine, showing an immense vein. There is a solid body of magnetic and specular iron, carrying as high as ninety-five to ninety-eight per cent pure iron. There is also a fifteen-foot vein of hematite near by, very rich in iron, carrying also $30 per ton gold. There are also valuable iron deposits in the neighborhood of Lewiston.

St. Charles mining district, in the eastern edge of Idaho, near the Oregon Short Line, is said to contain copper ore assaying sixty to eighty per cent., and native copper of great purity. The copper deposit can be traced for thirty-five miles. Along the south-western edge of Camas Prairie is an extensive network of copper veins, from one to six feet in thickness, their ores containing about forty per cent copper. Near Brownlee's Ferry, 120 miles north of Boisé City, are several large veins running sixty per cent. copper. There are many other copper deposits in Alturas and Custer counties.

The coal deposits have not been developed to any great extent. Near Goose Creek, in Cassia County, a species of coal has been found, and it is claimed that bituminous coal can be found in apparently inexhaustible quantities along Bear Lake. Coal mines have also been opened at Smith's Fork and on Twin Creeks. The Mammoth mine shows a vein seventy feet thick of clear coal, which with adjacent veins, separated by their veins of clay, will aggregate 200 feet in thickness. A good quality of lignite has been found near Boisé, bituminous at Horseshoe Bend, twenty miles from Boisé, also between the Payette and Weiser and at the Big Bend of Snake River. A good blacksmithing coal has been found on Sucker Creek, and some in north Idaho.

A description of an inexhaustible salt mine will be found in the article on Oneida County.

Marble has long been known to exist in the valley of the Snake. The marble bluffs in the vicinity of Bonanza Bar, sixteen miles below American Falls, have come into possession of the Union Pacific Railway Company, and it is said that there will be a track laid soon from the Oregon Short Line to the quarries. This marble has been known for years to be of good, marketable quality, but nothing was attempted towards its utilization until recently. The Union Pacific mineralogist and geologist some time ago took samples of the marble to Omaha, and it is found to be of a quality hardly second to the best Italian. The talk is that machinery will be put up for quarrying and sawing the marble and putting it in marketable shape. Large deposits of white and variegated marble are found along the Clearwater, and also in Kootenai and Cassia counties. Sandstone of superior quality is found in Nez Percé County. Granite and sandstone abound of the finest quality, white, pink, gray, and other shades, easily quarried and worked into any desirable shape.

Near Wieser River, in Washington County, are two ledges of mica, eight to ten feet wide each. Clear merchantable sheets four by six inches in size can be extracted in vast quantities. Deposits of mica are also found in Kootenai County near Lake Pend d'Oreille, and also near Lewiston in Nez Percé County.

The following reports of minerals mined and not mined in Idaho were prepared by Mr. Albert Williams, Jr., of the U. S. Geological Survey:

ORES, MINERALS, AND MINERAL SUBSTANCES OF INDUSTRIAL IMPORTANCE, WHICH ARE AT PRESENT MINED.

Mineralogical name.	Common name.	Remarks.
Anglesite (argentiferous)	Sulphate of lead	Wood River County; in surface ores of some of the argentiferous lead mines.
Argentite	Silver glance	Silver City, Owyhee County; Tahoma Mine, Atlanta, Alturas County; and elsewhere.
Arsenopyrite (auriferous)	Mispickel	Notably at Rocky Bar, Hardscrabble, Granite, Yuba, and Shaw's Mountain Districts; but frequent in many other localities.
Azurite	Blue carbonate of copper	Lemhi County, Alturas County.
Calcite	Limestone	Used as flux and burned for lime.
Cerargyrite	Horn silver, "chloride"	Many mines of Owyhee County; surface ore of Monarch Lode, Atlanta, Alturas County.
Cervantite	Antimony ocher	Small quanties in surface lead ores of Wood River country.
Cerussite (argentiferous)	Carbonate of lead, "carbonate"	Wood River and neighboring districts.
Chalcopyrite (auriferous)	Copper pyrites	In many gold mines.
	Clay (common brick)	Boisé City.
	Clay (fire)	Of poor quality; refractory furnace linings commonly brought from Santa Cruz, California.
Dufrenoysite	Sulpharsenide of lead	Crown Point Mine, Banner District.
Freibergite	Argentif. tetrahedrite	Columbia, Pilgrim, and other mines, Sawtooth Dist.
Galenite (argentiferous)	Galena	Important deposits in Wood River country, Alturas County, and in Lemhi County.
Gold, native	Gold	Deep placers in Boisé Basin, Boisé County; placer gold is found along many of the streams throughout the Territory, and in the Snake River; hydraulic mining in many scattered districts, quartz gold in Yankee Fork, Mount Estes, Granite, Rocky Bar, Bonaparta, Atlanta, Red Warrior, Cañon Creek, Shaw's Mountain, Silver City, Florence, Warrens, Wagontown, and other districts; crystallized specimens from Gold Hill mine; Granite District, Boisé County, particularly fine.
Hematite	Iron ore	Used as flux.
Limonite	Iron ore	Used as flux.
Malachite	Green carb. of copper	Lemhi County.
Marcasite	White pyrites	In some gold mines.
Proustite	Light ruby silver, arsenical ruby	Notably in Monarch and Buffalo mines, Atlanta; associated with pyrargyrite in Sawtooth and other districts.
Pyrargyrite	Dark ruby silver, antimonial ruby	Atlanta District, Monarch, Tahoma, Jessie Benton, Buffalo, and other mines; Sawtooth District; Smiley's Basin.
Pyrite (auriferous)	Iron sulphurets	In many gold mines, notably in Granite and Yuba Districts.
	Sandstone	Fine varieties of red and gray freestone near Boisé City.
Silver, native	Silver	Atlanta District.
Sphalerite	Zincblende	Auriferous at Bonaparte mine.
Stephanite	Brittle silver	Custer and unknown mines, Yankee Fork; also in Queen's River District, and reported elsewhere.
Stibnite	Sulphide of antimony	In argentiferous lead mines of Wood River.
Tetrahedrite	Fahlerz	Obscure, but probably frequent with antimonial and arsenical silver ores.

ORES, MINERALS, AND MINERAL SUBSTANCES OF INDUSTRIAL IMPORTANCE AND KNOWN OCCURRENCE, BUT WHICH ARE NOT AT PRESENT MINED.

Mineralogical name.	Common name.	Remarks.
Arsenopyrite (auriferous)...	Mispickel..................	In many mines which are unproductive because of the absence of proper reduction works.
Azurite............	Blue carbonate of copper	With other copper ores in many unworked deposits, as in Lemhi Custer, and Alturas counties.
Bismuthinite.....	Sulphate of bismuth.......	Reported.
Calcite.............	Marble...................	Reported.
Cerargyrite........	Horn silver................	
Cerussite...........	Carbonate of lead..........	
Chalcopyrite.......	Copper pyrites..............	
	Clays.......................	
Cuprite............	Copper oxide...............	
	Dolomite...................	
Erubescite.........	Variegated copper ore.....	
Galenite............	Galena.....................	Many unworked deposits.
Gold................	Gold........................	Many unworked deposits.
	Granite.....................	Principal country rock of central Idaho. Often a good building-stone, but unused.
Halite..............	Salt........................	In South-eastern Idaho.
Hematite...........	Iron ore....................	
Lignite.............	Coal........................	Owyhee, Ada, and Boisé counties.
Limonite...........	Iron ore....................	
Malachite..........	Green carbonate of copper..................	Many localities.
Marcasite..........	White pyrites..............	(See Arsenopyrite.)
Molybdenite.......	Sulphide of molybdenum	Reported.
Muscovite..........	Mica........................	Fine specimens of large sheets at Payette River and near Boisé City. Samples have been shipped.
Proustite..........	Light ruby silver...........	
Pyrargyrite........	Dark ruby silver............	
Pyrite (auriferous)...............	Iron sulphuret..............	
Pyrolusite.........	Manganese ore.............	Shaw's Mountain.
	Sandstone..................	
Sphalerite.........	Zincblende, "black jack"......................	Never worked except as accidental component of precious metal ores.
Stibnite............	Sulphide of antimony.....	(See remark on Sphalerite.)

At Soda Springs in Oneida County is a mountain of almost pure sulphur running to eighty-five per cent.

For a more detailed description of the different mining localities, the reader is referred to the articles on the respective counties. Alturas, Custer, Lemhi, and Shoshone counties are at present the scenes of most active mining operations. Owyhee and Idaho counties have been most productive in former years, and still continue to send forth their regular output of precious metals. Each of the last named has plenty of ledges that have never yet been developed. Washington and Kootenai counties are rapidly coming to the front as ore producers. The remaining counties being chiefly agricultural, their mining interests have as yet attracted comparatively little attention.

The following table shows the estimated production of the precious metals in Idaho since first discovery:

Year.	Amount Produced.	Year.	Amount Produced.
1862	$5,000,000 00	1874	$3,100,447 09
1863	7,448,400 91	1875	1,963,720 27
1864	9,019,704 30	1876	2,267,013 36
1865	12,914,364 25	1877	3,474,787 69
1866	10,001,850 44	1878	2,657,216 91
1867	7,388,064 31	1879	2,533,634 58
1868	3,030,213 56	1880	1,634,637 19
1869	1,613,453 63	1881	4,915,100 00
1870	2,239,190 61	1882	5,500,000 00
1871	2,219,937 94	1883	5,000,000 00
1872	2,675,192 00	1884 (estimated)	6,500,000 00
1873	3,653,605 15		

Total production of Idaho mines..................$106,790,530 14

CHAPTER V.—FARMING AND STOCK-RAISING.

While it is chiefly as a mining territory that Idaho is known to the outside world, yet it is not upon her mineral resources alone that she depends. In a region covered by such a vast area as is included within her boundaries, traversed by mountain ranges formed of rocks of all kinds and ages, there is necessarily a great variety of soil. For the sake of convenience, her soils have been divided into four classes, as follows:

1. Alkali Soil. This is of limited extent, producing greasewood, which cattle eat readily, particularly the young shoots. The cause of alkaline soils is now generally well understood. The rain which falls during the wet season penetrates deeply into the earth, where it gradually takes up such soluble salts as it encounters there. By capillary action this water always tends to diffuse itself throughout the loose materials which make up the overlying soils. As fast as it is evaporated at the surface, more water from below rises by capillary action to take its place. The water which may have accumulated beneath has gradually risen by percolation through the interstices of the unconsolidated materials of the soil, bringing with it whatever soluble salts it may have taken into solution during its sojourn beneath the surface. "There is no difficulty, however," says Captain C. E. Dutton of the United States Geological Survey, "in removing any quantity of these readily soluble salts from the soil, provided the leaching process be continued long enough; and it is usually found that lands which were originally highly alkaline become, when reclaimed from their alkalinity, among the most fertile."

2. Mountain Soil. This soil is exceedingly rich, especially in the wooded sections, where it is black, deep, and full of vegetable mold.

3. Plain and plateau soil, which contains all the elements for the successful growth of all the cereals, containing a great amount of vegetable mold.

4. Valley soil, which, according to Professor Butler, "cannot be excelled in any other State or Territory in the Union. It contains, indeed, the aggregated and condensed richness of vast areas of vegetable growth that have been accumulating for ages on the sides of the mountains skirting the valleys. An analysis of this soil shows it to be pre-eminently rich in all the mineral and vegetable elements necessary to the growth of all the cereals, vegetables, fruits, etc., etc., usually grown within the limits of the Territory. It is of good depth, is invariably found to superpose a gravelly soil, and is so inclined that perfect drainage can readily and effectively be had. Thermal springs are so abundant that it is no uncommon thing for the farmer to be supplied with warm and cold water direct from the mountain side. The mountains being high and not very precipitous, the valleys are generally well protected from the cold winds, and in the hollows or gulches wood grows plentifully, and yields a supply of fuel and fencing for the home and farm necessities, and an abundant and grateful shade for stock."

The northern portion of the Territory, included between the Clearwater and the British Possessions, is chiefly mountainous, interspersed with prairie lands and a number of lakes, some of them of exquisite beauty. Along the shores of these lakes and in the river bottoms are good arable lands.

The region between the Boisé River and the Clearwater consists of table lands naturally rich in grasses, heavily timbered mountains and fertile valleys. The best known of these are the Clearwater, Salmon, Payette, Weiser, and Boisé. These valleys are all well watered, possessing extraordinary fertility of soil. With the aid of irrigation these lands produce abundant crops of cereals, as well as the fruits and vegetables of the Middle States. There is sufficient timber to contribute to the salubrity and humidity of the climate.

Between Boisé Valley and the southern boundary line there are fertile valleys traversing sagebrush plains and table lands. The proportion of timber in this region is small, being confined chiefly to the lines of streams and mountain sides. Three fourths of this vast surface is capable of reclamation by irrigation, and will produce abundant crops. In the south-west section of this district are several fertile valleys tributary to the Owyhee. In the south-east section among others are the upper end of Cache Valley, which produces all kinds of cereals and vegetables, and Malade Valley, fifty miles long by from three to four miles wide. The last-named is a fine, fertile valley, containing several farming settlements. It contains 175 square miles of irrigable land. The valley is flat, and though the streams have but slight fall, still, as the benches are everywhere low, the water can be taken out all over the valley. Bear Lake Valley contains about 275 square miles of tillable land. It extends in a broad belt on both sides of the river southward from Soda Springs for fifteen miles, when the river is forced into a narrow cañon, but begins again at Georgetown and extends up the lake. In the valleys of the Blackfoot and its branches there is much valuable land. Professor Gannett estimates that probably 175 square miles of the Blackfoot Basin can be made productive.

In southern Idaho irrigation is generally necessary. So far from being a drawback, however, the farmer has now come to regard this fact as an advantage. Crops thus cultivated are not subject to the vicissitudes of rainfall; the possibilities of drought are avoided; the farmer's labors are seldom interrupted, and his crops rarely injured by storms. This immunity from drought and storm renders agricultural operations much more certain than in the eastern States. Again, the water comes down from the mountains and plateaus freighted with fertilizing materials derived from the decaying vegetation and soils of the upper regions, which are spread by the flowing water over cultivated lands. It is probable that the benefits derived from this source alone will be full compensation for the cost of the process. Experience will correct the errors occasionally resulting from permitting too great or too rapid a flow of water, and the irrigator soon learns to flood his lands gently, evenly, and economically. "It may be anticipated," says Professor Powell, "that all the lands redeemed by irrigation in the arid region will be highly cultivated and abundantly productive, and agriculture will be but slightly subject to the vicissitudes of scant and excessive rainfall. A stranger entering this arid region is apt to conclude that the soils are sterile, because of their chemical composition; but experience demonstrates the fact that all the soils are suitable for agricultural purposes when properly supplied with water."

Boisé Valley, especially in the neighborhood of Boisé City, affords an excellent example of the truth of the foregoing. Within twenty years a barren sage-brush plain has been transformed into a paradise. Trees and shrubbery adorn the streets and gardens. Orchards bending beneath the burden of their fruit, fields of waving grain, gardens producing every variety of crops, are on all sides. The larger and smaller fruits, perfect in form and flavor, and the mammoth vegetables whose characteristic flavors are not affected by their size, surpass the much-extolled products of California. During the past season Boisé Valley has supplied not only her home market and Wood River; but also the neighboring territory, with her fruits. Official figures show that out of a total of 433,435 pounds of fresh fruit received at Butte, Montana, this season, up to November 1st, 253,430 pounds were from Boisé Valley, the remainder being from California, Missouri River, Utah, and Portland. J. A. Munroe, Esq., acting general freight agent of the Union Pacific, in referring to this circumstance, writes: "I am satisfied in my own mind, that the business of the Boisé Valley in the fruit line this year is but the commencement of a better and more prosperous business each year to come."

From November 1st, up to which date the above figures are given, an additional 150,000 pounds of apples have been shipped to Butte from this valley, making in all over 400,000 pounds of fruit contributed by Boisé Valley to the single mining camp of Butte.

Immediately south of Boisé City, Mr. Thomas Davis has an orchard of some 10,000 apple trees which have produced this season an immense quantity of the choicest fruit ever grown in any country in the world. The orchard is about twenty years old, and in excellent condition, except that the superabundance of the yield this year broke down the limbs of some of the younger trees. Since the apples began to ripen, men with carts have been constantly engaged in gathering the fruit carefully and assorting it for the market.

Preparatory to shipment the apples are packed in fifty-pound boxes. They readily find a market in all parts of Idaho and adjoining States and Territories. No less than 250,000 pounds of this fruit have already been sent by rail to various parts of the North-west, and Mr. Davis still has as many stored away in a three-story building, specially prepared for the purpose, on his premises, and shipments continue to be made almost daily. Apples boxed and shipped net about $1.25 per hundred pounds, so we may safely calculate that the fruit already disposed of and that yet in store will bring Mr. Davis a clear $6,250. Besides this, he has 150 barrels of vinegar, 20,000 pounds of choice dried apples, and a considerable quantity of pears and cider. Altogether this year the net profit derived from this sample orchard will reach a handsome $10,000. This is only a sample of what Idaho is doing in the way of producing fruit which is everywhere pronounced of superior quality and delicious flavor.

Lest the reader may think this an exceptional instance, he is referred to the article on Ada County, for a more complete description of the agricultural resources of this section.

The area formed by the junction of the Boisé, Payette, Weiser, and Owyhee valleys is a vast agricultural region. In the immense basin formed by the confluence of Idaho's great rivers is a compact body of farming lands millions of acres in extent—the largest agricultural area between the great prairies and the plains of the Columbia. In soil, climate, and facilities for irrigation it is unsurpassed. It is mainly the rich, warm loam that produces sage-brush to perfection in its natural state, and all the cereals, fruits, and vegetables of this latitude when cultivated. There are acres upon acres of apples, plums, pears, peaches, and small fruits, and alongside of them, almost as far as the eye can reach, are stretches of wild farming lands awaiting claimants and cultivation. It is not unusual for immigrants to locate on wild lands in these valleys, put up comfortable houses, good barns, good fences, etc., and pay for all such improvements with the first year's crop of potatoes, or other vegetables taken from only a small portion of their farms. The fact that Idaho farmers were, as a rule, very poor when they embarked in business a few years ago, and that they are now generally well off, and have fine buildings and the best improvements, with large herds of stock, are proof that this is a lucrative pursuit.

The cereals do almost as well in Idaho as the fruits. Oats yield fifty-five bushels per acre; wheat, thirty bushels; rye, twenty-five bushels; potatoes, 250 bushels. The truth is, Idaho is one of the best grain-producing regions in the United States, and in proof of this statement I submit the following official table of the yield per acre:

	Wheat.	Rye.	Oats.	Barley.	Potatoes.	Corn.
Idaho	30	25	55	40	250	35
Nevada	12		31		95	30
California	17	15	30	23	114	34
Oregon	21	14	31	23	95	33
Eastern States	13	15	31	23	69	26

In one case fifty-four pounds of wheat were produced from a single square rod, being at the rate of 140 bushels to the acre. The wheat produced in this instance has been called "Idaho white wheat," and is thought to be superior. It matures from fall or spring sowing; is white, beardless, and heavy, and produces a large proportion of flour.

The mountain slopes of Idaho are watered by abundant streams, and checkered with alternate tracts of forest and rich prairie. Even in the least favored regions are localities adapted to specific branches of agricultural enterprise. These will ultimately be occupied by a thrifty farming population.

In north Idaho crops are raised without irrigation. The precipitation of moisture on the mountains is said to be greater than on the lowlands, but the hills and mesas adjacent to the great masses of mountains receive some of the supply condensed by the mountains themselves, and the lands have been found to be favored by this condition to an extent sufficient to warrant agricultural operations independent of irrigation. There are about 1,000,000 acres of prairie land in north Idaho, between the Cœur d'Alene Indian reservation and the Salmon River.

North Palouse, Genesee, Paradise, and Potlatch valleys, in Nez Percé County, are rapidly filling up with an intelligent and thrifty farming population. In the neighborhood of Lewiston fruits and vegetables of all kinds are raised in perfection. Peach trees have been known to bloom there in February. Lewiston and Moscow are the two chief distributing points for this vast agricultural area. The following yields of grain in the neighborhood of Moscow have been furnished us, and can be vouched for as correct. On the farm of Mr. M. W. Smith, on Ceder Creek, 200 bushels of wheat (machine measure) were threshed from two and one-half acres of measured ground. R. B. Hogan threshed 3,000 bushels of oats from thirty-four acres of ground on the farm of O. S. Cochran, near Kamiack Butte. B. Maxer, who also lives near Kamiack Butte, threshed 812 bushels of oats from nine acres of ground. Potatoes raised in the Palouse soil, known as the "Palouse Beauty," weigh frequently over four pounds. A single potato vine measured ten feet in length. The laterals, together with the main stalk, measured just 304 feet six inches. The production of flax is also becoming an important industry in north Idaho. The first crop was sown in 1878, and yielded from twenty to twenty-five bushels to the acre. Near Genesee, at M. Hensen's ranch, thirty-two bushels are raised to the acre. Last year it was worth $1.62 per bushel.

South of the Clearwater is also an area of agricultural land quite as rich and extensive as that to the northward. It is claimed to be preferable, as its altitude is lower, its climate more genial; it is well watered by running streams and ever-living springs; the grasses and native vegetation grow spontaneously and with tropical luxuriance on its prolific soil; it is within easy distance of the markets of the world, and accessible at all seasons. "With all these advantages," writes a gentleman familiar with that section, "it is a country given over to the loneliness of desolation. With an area and a soil capable of supporting a dense population, it is as unproductive as the desert. Where should be homes of American freemen, the virgin soil cries in vain for the plow. Where towns and cities should be built, no living thing greets the eye. All this vast region of three-quarters of a million of acres which should support a dense population, is lying as uninhabited and uproductive as upon the day of creation."

STOCK-RAISING.

It is in no spirit of disparagement to other sections of the north-west that we assert that Idaho to-day offers the best inducements for the stock-grower. The area of grazing lands is practically unlimited, being from twenty to twenty-five millions of acres. Her plains are covered with indigenous grasses of nutritious quality, affording unsurpassed facilities for stock-raising. The cañons in the lower valleys often afford the shelter necessary for wintering stock, while the pastures, covered with snow but for a portion of the year, present a cheap and effective subsistence. The grass drying on the stalk is naturally cured into hay of a superior quality. Stockmen reserve their lower meadows for winter pastures, while during the milder portions of the year the stock range on the higher lands. The great extent of the table lands and the adaptability of the bottom lands to cultivation have suggested the economic value of this method. The natural and long-continued dryness of the atmosphere, summer and winter; the inexhaustible and wonderfully nutritious grasses which cure as they grow, making them as sustenance for animals almost equal to the feeding of hay and grain; the infrequency of snow or other storms during the year; the warm breezes from the Pacific; the ability of stock to live without shelter and take care of themselves prove Idaho to be one of the best stock-growing regions in the world.

In Owyhee and Ada counties, and all along the Snake for 400 miles, as well as in northern Idaho, are vast and only partially occupied cattle ranges, where the fortunate few who are already established are on a sure road to fortune. Dairying is also a lucrative pursuit. Dairymen in Boisé and Lemhi valleys contract their butter the year round at the uniform price of fifty cents per pound.

The cost of keeping cattle on the range varies from fifty cents to one dollar per head, according to the size of the herd. In some of the higher valleys, winter feeding is followed to a slight extent, which, of course, increases the expense. The loss of cattle does probably not much exceed three or four per cent. "Great and lucrative as mining has proved and is proving," says Governor Bunn, "stock-raising is destined to play a still greater part in our history. The advantages of stock-raising in Idaho are manifold and manifest. I need not point out to you the twenty-five millions of acres of grazing lands covered with white sage and other herbs and nutritious grasses that make such superior food for stock, within our borders; or that where there are desert lands the finger of God has directed streams to flow, to make them reclaimable."

A territorial cattle-growers' association has been recently organized for the purpose of protecting the interests of stock-growers in the territory. Its secretary, Mr. W. C. B. Allen, of Shoshone, presents the following estimate of the number of cattle in Idaho at present:

Owyhee County		50,000	Washington County		15,000
Cassia	"	50,000	Boisé	"	10,000
Alturas	"	50,000	Custer	"	25,000
Oneida	"	50,000	Lemhi	"	15,000
Bear Lake	"	25,000	Other counties		50,000
Ada	"	20,000			
Total					360,000

The probability is that this estimate is below rather than above the actual amount. In Bear Lake County, for instance, there are probably double the number here credited. (See report from that county.) Even assuming the number in the Territory to be 400,000, there is still room enough on the vast ranges along Snake River, Lost River, Pahsimmari, Salmon River, and Owyhee mountains, and Camas Prairies for many times that number.

The following tables of farming and live-stock interests in Idaho are taken from the census of 1880. Though these figures should probably be more than doubled to represent the present condition, yet the reader will readily perceive what an insignificant portion of the agricultural and grazing lands are taken up, and how vast is the area of these lands simply awaiting settlement and occupancy.

FARM AREAS AND FARM VALUES, 1880.

Counties.	Farms.	Improved land.	Value of farms, including land, fences, and buildings.	Value of farming implements and machinery.	Value of live-stock.	Cost of building and repairing fences, 1879.	Estimated value of all farm productions sold, consumed, or on hand for 1879.
Ada	256	62,842	800,475	84,545	522,264	43,400	517,809
Alturas	90	929	28,050	3,225	11,870	1,685	34,550
Bear Lake	109	11,604	138,050	23,380	81,731	5,620	52,805
Boisé	64	4,444	116,050	12,710	71,079	5,080	97,604
Cassia	143	7,336	110,900	15,963	106,319	10,675	44,122
Idaho	155	22,830	254,225	30,370	170,838	19,904	140,816
Kootenai	20	1,100	14,200	2,877	7,117	2,179	8,030
Lemhi	89	17,730	135,850	18,460	164,460	13,875	110,931
Nez Percé	258	18,992	540,460	70,240	260,067	27,430	210,600
Oneida	422	30,148	359,890	63,785	349,588	27,205	117,315
Owyhee	66	4,807	117,000	12,865	237,405	2,982	64,795
Shoshone	5	699	12,100	830	6,250	2,210	5,600
Washington	149	13,846	198,650	24,680	257,812	14,392	110,318
The Territory	1,885	197,407	2,832,890	363,930	2,246,800	176,237	1,515,374

LIVE-STOCK AND ITS PRODUCTIONS, 1880.

Counties.	Live-stock.				
	Horses.	Mules and asses.	Working oxen.	Milch cows.	Other cattle.
	Number.	Number.	Number.	Number.	Number.
Ada	4,994	148	112	2,204	20,367
Alturas	181	33	10	166	593
Bear Lake	926	30	57	1,117	1,454
Boisé	559	36	7	331	1,689
Cassia	1,844	87	241	553	2,697
Idaho	3,088	20	26	1,162	5,606
Kootenai	75	0	8	77	42
Lemhi	1,057	53	48	866	6,696
Nez Percé	3,852	28	55	1,539	4,537
Oneida	3,163	81	123	2,156	11,843
Owyhee	1,976	49	10	1,750	12,332
Shoshone	69			58	318
Washington	2,596	40	40	859	3,098
The Territory	24,300	610	737	12,838	71,292

LIVE-STOCK AND ITS PRODUCTIONS, 1880—Continued.

COUNTIES.	LIVE-STOCK—Cont'd.		Wool.	DAIRY PRODUCTS.		
	Sheep.	Swine.		Milk.	Butter.	Cheese.
	Number.	*Number.*	*Pounds.*	*Gallons.*	*Pounds.*	*Pounds.*
Ada...........	4,525	3,171	14,900	112	69,482	1,090
Alturas........	....	65	....	....	1,150	500
Bear Lake.....	3,255	275	13,639	50	28,685	4,805
Boisé.........	102	846	500	800	10,160	....
Cassia.........	1,473	323	9,565	60	13,200	350
Idaho..........	3,988	2,252	16,158	....	8,289	....
Kootenai......	60	37	300	....	1,520	....
Lemhi.........	....	262	....	1,500	30 000	150
Nez Percé.....	7,814	2,387	41,070	10,175	27,823	....
Oneida........	2,420	717	8,896	450	82,818	12,600
Owyhee........	3,600	308	21,600	2,480	20,900	200
Shoshone......	....	107	....	....	400	....
Washington....	89	3,438	521	....	16,217	....
The Territory..	27,326	14,178	127,149	15,027	310,044	20,293

As it is the object of this chapter simply to give an outline of the agricultural and pastoral resources of the Territory, the reader is referred for more specific information particularly to the articles on Ada and Nez Percé counties, though Oneida, Bear Lake, Cassia, and Washington are rapidly assuming prominent positions among the agricultural counties. In Owyhee, mining is gradually being succeeded by stock-raising. Lemhi, Custer, Alturas, and Idaho, though known chiefly as mining counties, have each fine agricultural and pastoral areas. The two Camas prairies in Alturas and Idaho counties respectively, bid fair soon to become the granaries of Idaho; Kootenai, the northernmost county of the Territory, possesses some fine prairie lands capable of sustaining a large agricultural population.

THE RECLAMATION OF DESERT LANDS.

Governor Bunn, in his report to the Secretary of the Interior, said on this subject:

"During the past year there has been a marked movement in this direction, and within another year thousands upon thousands of acres of splendid arable land will be added to the already great area of the Territory. In a very few years an acreage greater than the whole State of Rhode Island will be reclaimed in the Snake River Valley alone, and changed from an arid, parched, and unsightly desert into rich and blooming agricultural lands, safe from drought or floods of rain. This happy condition is entirely attributable to the desert land act, which should not be, and I beg to express a hope will not be, changed. True it is, the act might be amended in some particulars that would redound to the general good, but if it were tinkered at, it would open the way toward a repeal or a radical change, which would be little less than a public calamity.

"Near Blackfoot, a canal is nearly finished that will reclaim between forty and fifty thousand acres. In Cassia County—along the south side of Snake River—Raft River, Goose Creek, and many smaller streams, are owned entirely by the Mormons, and used by them for irrigation purposes. At Shoshone, in Alturas County, twenty-five miles north of Snake River, Little Wood River has been turned on the desert, and a thriving town, with its outlying farms, has grown and is growing, where but two years ago was a sagebrush covered, desert plain. In the Bruneau Valley, some sixty thousand acres are already under cultivation, and a canal has been started to cover from twenty-five to thirty thousand acres more. In the Wood River Valley a canal has been constructed, and irrigates over twenty thousand acres, while below these now fruitful acres lie fifty thousand acres which will shortly be covered with water and cultivated. The Idaho Mining and Irrigating Company, of New York, is constructing a canal with a capacity of four thousand cubic feet of water per second, which takes the water of the Boisé about 75 miles above its confluence with Snake River. This canal will irrigate and reclaim about 600,000 acres of land lying north of Snake River, and south of Boisé City. On the Payette River two canals are nearly completed, that will cover about fifty thousand acres, while a third is contemplated, that will reclaim thirty thousand acres more. On the Weiser there are about seventy-five thousand acres being brought under irrigating ditches, there being three or four different canals now building. In addition to the above, a plan is maturing to take the waters of Snake River and reclaim nearly two millions of acres of valley land. This, if carried into effect, will give Idaho land enough to supply the entire Pacific slope with cereals, fruits, and vegetables, and make her the richest of the Territories."

CHAPTER VI.—COUNTIES OF IDAHO.

There are at present fourteen organized counties within the Territory, as follows: Ada, Alturas, Bear Lake, Boisé, Cassia, Custer, Idaho, Kootenai, Lemhi, Nez Percé, Oneida, Owyhee, Shoshone, and Washington. Of these, Alturas, Boisé, Custer, Idaho, Lemhi, Owyhee, and Shoshone may be described as mining counties. Ada, Bear Lake, Cassia, Nez Percé, Oneida, and Washington are chiefly agricultural. Kootenai has both mining and agricultural resources, but at present is chiefly remarkable for its magnificent forests of timber. This classification is, at the best, only general, as the mining counties of Alturas, Lemhi, and Owyhee are rapidly receiving attention for farming and stock-raising, while those above mentioned as agricultural, notably Washington County, are beginning to produce considerable mineral.

ADA COUNTY.

Though one of the smallest in size, Ada is the most thickly settled county of Idaho. Her valleys are the most highly cultivated, and her farms, orchards, and vineyards present a sight that recalls the landscapes of California. The valleys of Boisé and Payette Rivers are lined with prosperous ranches, and much of the permanent wealth of the Territory is concentrated in this neighborhood. Its county-seat is Boisé City, the capital of the Territory.

Boise City.—The capital city of Idaho is situated on the north side of Boisé River, about fifty miles above its confluence with the Snake. Should one of the old French voyageurs, who have left so deep an impression on the nomenclature of the West, visit the spot to-day, he would naturally conclude, from the numerous orchards, shady streets, and pleasant groves, that Boisé (wooded) City was named before the river, from which the town in fact derives its name.

Far more wonderful than the splendors of the ancient Cities of the Plains, whose glories have for ages formed the theme of verse and song, is the story of the growth of the true American Western towns. On what was once a sage-brush plain, apparently almost a desert, such as constitutes so vast an area of Western territory, clear-sighted American grit and enterprise have within twenty years built a town which is the pride of its citizens and the admiration of strangers.

Here, far from the main lines of travel (until 1883, 250 miles from the nearest railroad communication), accessible from the great world outside only by long and tedious journeys by stage or teams for days and nights, over forbidding, desolate, and uninhabited stretches of sage-brush desert and alkali plains, in what was so long considered as a far-off corner of the country, the pioneers and settlers of Idaho have built their little city, founded their homes, and established their places of trade and business.

What is now known as old Fort Boisé was established near the mouth of Boisé River many years ago. A writer who visited it in 1845 states that even at that time the Hudson's Bay Company had been maintaining a trading post there for many years. It was never a military post, however. The present Fort Boisé (more properly designated now as Boisé Barracks) was not established until 1863, fifty miles above the site of the old fort. To the founding of this military post the town may be said to owe its origin.

A town-site company was immediately organized, and six of what are now the most valuable business blocks in the town were staked out. Lots were rapidly disposed of. The excitement attendant upon the discoveries in Boisé Basin brought thousands of miners into the country, the benefits of which were reaped in large measure by Boisé City. It is upon her agricultural resources, however, that Boisé chiefly relies at present.

Commercial and Statistical.—Boisé City is at present reached from Kuna station on the Oregon Short Line, from which it is distant about fifteen miles, and with which it is connected by two daily stages each way. A branch line is projected from a point down the valley, and is expected to be completed early in the spring.

The growth of Boisé City has been firm from the start. While slow as compared with more favored localities like Denver, and subjected to no fictitious "booms" or temporary excitements, she has been steadily advancing, each year witnessing substantial improvement over the last. In 1880 her population according to the census was 1,899. Judging from the vote polled at the last general election, her population at present is about 3,000. Her assessed valuation this year is about $1,000,000, and the city debt on the first of January will probably not exceed $12,000.

The business part of the town is substantially built of brick and stone, a city ordinance prohibiting the erection of frame or wooden buildings within certain limits. The streets are wide, clean, and shady, crossing each other at right angles, the blocks intersected lengthwise by convenient alleyways. The town was incorporated January 11, 1866, and as the citizens have always taken special pains to elect responsible business men for its officials, the government has in general been wisely administered. There is a regularly organized fire department, with a Silsby steamer, three hose-carts, and 1,500 feet of hose. There are two companies, Boisé Engine, No. 1, and Ada Hook and Ladder, No. 1. The city has recently erected a neat two-story brick engine-house at a cost of 3,000. Mountain water is introduced into town through Eastman Brothers' water-works.

There are three excellent hotels—the Overland, Central, and Western. There are about a dozen general merchandise stores, besides a number of dealers in special merchandise, such as stationery, drugs, jewelry, furniture, etc. The aggregate amount of business done by the merchants monthly is about $200,000 cash sales. All professions and mechanical trades are well represented. There are sixteen saloons.

Besides the branches of industry common to a town of this sort, there are several flour, grist, planing, and lumber mills, two breweries, a distillery, and brick and marble works.

The First National Bank has an authorized capital of $500,000; present capital $100,000.

A telephone exchange has been established between the leading business houses, hotels, and public buildings. A Board of Trade has been recently organized, which has rendered valuable service to the business interests of the city. There are three newspapers—*Statesman* (tri-weekly), *Democrat* (semi-weekly), and *Republican* (weekly).

Six stage-lines center here. The same advantages which are offered as a concentrating point for stage-lines will doubtless, in the near future, make it an important railway center. There are many handsome two and three story frame and brick dwellings that would reflect credit upon a much older and larger town.

It is a significant fact that there has not been more than one important mercantile failure here since the organization of the town, over twenty years ago.

Government and County Buildings.—The United States Penitentiary is located about two miles from town. It is of three stories, solid masonry. There are sixty inmates at present. The convicts are dressed in regular prison uniform, and are compelled to work. The institution is a source of considerable trade to the town.

The United States Assay Office is the finest government building in the Territory. It was built by the United States, at a cost of $81,000. It is of stone, about 60 feet square, and 45 feet high. It is of great convenience to bullion producers, as the assayer in charge is kept supplied from the Treasury Department with a bullion fund with which to purchase deposits.

Ada County court-house is built on Capitol Square. The grounds occupy an entire block, and are surrounded by a fine iron fence. The building is of brick, three stories, and handsomely fitted up with court-room and rooms for county officers and district judge's chambers. The entire cost was $68,000.

Other objects of interest in the city are the United States Signal Office, established in 1877, and the Territorial Law Library. The latter is under the supervision of the territorial secretary. There are now several thousand volumes of law books, the supply being constantly added to.

The military post overlooking the town was established, as before stated, in 1863. There are two companies stationed there, one cavalry and one infantry.

Societies and Churches.—Boisé City is more than commonly well supplied with religious, benevolent, and charitable organizations.

The Masonic societies are Boisé Lodge, No. 2, and Shoshone Lodge, No. 7, A. F. & A. M.; Boisé Chapter, No. 3, R. A. M., and Idaho Commandery, No. 1, K. T. Odd Fellows: Ada Lodge, No. 3, I. O. O. F., and Idaho Encampment, No. 1. Order of Workmen: Idaho, No. 5, A. O. U. W.

There are also organizations of Champions of the Red Cross, and Boisé Lodge, I. O. G. T., besides the Boisé City Turn-Verein. Each of these societies is on a solid financial basis, owning valuable real estate and buildings in the heart of the town. Besides these there are a free library association and a literary and dramatic club. There are five churches, the Methodists and Presbyterians each having a fine substantial brick building. The Episcopalians, Roman Catholics, and Baptists each have a frame building.

Public School.—The glory of the city, however, is its graded public school. The Independent School District of Boisé City was established by law February 4, 1881. The school-house is a handsome four-story brick building, with mansard roof. It is 100 feet in depth by 82 feet in width. The rooms are capable of accommodating from fifty to seventy pupils each. It has all the modern improvements possible, including means of ventilation, heating, ingress and egress, and electric clocks, securing uniformity of time in each room. It was built at a cost of $50,000, and the citizens feel a just pride in an institution which boasts of having no superior on the coast. Many families have moved into the town in order to give their children an opportunity to attend the school. So successful has the school been under the present management that there has been no demand for private schools, though there are over seven hundred school children in the district. Professor Daniels, the principal, is ably supported by a corps of six assistants selected with great care. The school is visited almost daily by strangers, who always leave with but one impression, that of admiration for the systematic and orderly arrangement of the whole institution.

Resources.—While the trade and business incidental to a territorial capital and flourishing county seat are not to be ignored, Boisé has resources of far more importance. It occupies an eligible position as a distributing point. The Owyhee country, Bruneau Valley, Boisé Basin, the Weiser country, and Wood River are all more or less tributary to it. A healthy rivalry will be stimulated by the new towns springing up along the Oregon Short

Line, and we may look for a future for Boisé far more brilliant than anything in the past. The mines in the vast scope of country tributary to the town will furnish a ready market for the produce and fruit of Boisé which have become famous throughout the West.

After the completion of the Boisé branch of the Oregon Short Line, with its round-house and shop at this place, it is expected that a narrow-gauge railroad will be constructed to connect Boisé with Atlanta, the mining camp, ninety miles distant, which has made such a brilliant record during the past season. In fact, Boisé City offers the only natural outlet to the famous Boisé Basin section as well as the Atlanta country.

The climate of Boisé is salubrious. The atmosphere dry and clear. Snow rarely falls to a great depth. Situated at an altitude of 2,800 feet, the winters are mild, while the heats of summer are tempered with the cool mountain breezes, though wind storms are unknown. From a sanitary point of view, the place is the admiration of every one except the doctors and undertakers. The sportsman and angler will find plenty of employment in the neighboring creeks and sloughs.

For a mountain region the roads are good, offering facilities for pleasant drives in all directions. By ascending Table Rock, back of the town, the spectator on the hottest day in summer will be welcomed by refreshing mountain breezes, while the view of the valley for miles around spreads out before him in all the beauty of mingled wilderness and cultivation. A favorite drive is to the Hot Springs, a few miles east of town. The Springs are highly medicinal, containing iron, sulphur, soda, lime, and magnesia. There are vapor, shower, plunge, and mud baths. The temperature of the Springs varies from 125 to 220 degrees Fahrenheit. They are already a favorite resort, and need only to be known to become as celebrated as the Hot Springs of Arkansas.

In social attractions Boisé is far ahead of much larger towns in the East. The lawlessness supposed to characterize so many frontier towns is unknown here. The culture, refinement, and hospitality of the people of Boisé are proverbial.

With easy railroad communication so soon to be established, a new stimulus will be given to enterprise. There is land enough in the neighborhood for all who may choose to come. The history of the past twenty years in this valley shows what pluck and determination can accomplish in the face of apparently almost insuperable obstacles. With these obstacles now removed, easily accessible to the immigrant seeking a home, or capitalist seeking investment, with a strong determination on the part of the settlers to stand by the home altars which they have reared, and a boundless faith in its own resources, the Queen City of the Valley retains unshaken confidence in the security of its future.

Boisé Valley.—When General John C. Fremont first visited Boisé Valley, on the 7th of October, 1843, he wrote:

"When we had traveled about eight miles we were nearly opposite to the highest portions of the mountains on the left side of Snake River Valley; and continuing on a few miles beyond, we came suddenly in sight of the broad green line of the valley of the Riviere Boisé, black near the gorge where it debouches into the plains, with high precipices of basalt, between walls of which it passes on, emerging from the mountains. Descending the hills after traveling a few miles along the plain, the road brought us down upon the bottoms of the river, which is a beautiful, rapid stream with clear mountain water, and as the name indicates, well wooded with some varieties of timber, among which are handsome cottonwoods. Such a stream had become quite a novelty in this country, and we were delighted this afternoon to make a pleasant camp under fine old trees again."

The deep impression thus made on the mind of the Pathfinder, forty years ago, is renewed in the glad surprise experienced by every stranger who for the first time passes up Boisé Valley, save that what was forty and even twenty years ago a wilderness is now adorned with pleasant farms, extensive orchards, and waving fields of grain.

Boisé Valley is about sixty miles long, containing about 200,000 acres of good arable land. Forty-five bushels of wheat to the acre is an average crop.

The valley is capable of sustaining a large, thrifty, and prosperous farming population, who, with their established homes, will continue, as in the past, to make a permanent market for Boisé City.

Under the direction of a company of New York capitalists, known as the Idaho Mining and Irrigation Company, a new irrigating canal, thirty miles long, fifty feet wide at the top, and thirty-five feet at the bottom, carrying four feet of water, is being taken out of Boisé River on the south side. When completed it will reclaim 500,000 acres of what is now desert land.

Through the courtesy of A. D. Foote, Esq., engineer in charge of the Idaho Mining and Irrigation Company, we have been enabled to make some copious extracts from his official report concerning the lands in Ada County to be reclaimed by this undertaking.

They may be roughly described as lying in the form of a triangle, the apex of which is necessary for the irrigation of the lands. This triangle is nearly equilateral, measuring about forty miles on each side, and containing approximately four hundred thousand acres, three hundred and fifty thousand of which are available for irrigation and occupation.

These lands lie in immense benches, or broad plateaus, which for long distances slope gently toward the meeting of the rivers; at intervals, the general slope is broken by a sharp mesa or bluff, and dropping fifty feet, they stretch out again as before. In proposing to reclaim by irrigation a tract of land of the size just mentioned, the first requisite naturally is water. The Boisé River, heading in the Sawtooth Mountains of central Idaho, has a catchment basin above the entrance of the company's canal of about sixteen hundred thousand acres, which gives five acres of catching surface to each acre it is proposed to irrigate. The amount of moisture in the form of snow which falls in the upper Boisé region is purely a matter of conjecture, as no statistics on the subject are to be had. It is known that there is very little rainfall, and a great deal of snow. Whatever traveling is done there in winter is done on snow-shoes. The river never rises suddenly; but beginning about the middle of March, gradually rises, reaching its highest about the middle of June, and then, gradually falling, reaches its lowest point again during the long frozen period of the winter. The great banks of snow in the mountains work as self-acting reservoirs, as well as if actual reservoirs were constructed there by man—better, perhaps, as the dam never gives way. They hold the year's collection of moisture until the time when most needed on the plains; then, sending it down in a steady stream, increasing as the crops grow, and dwindling as they ripen.

By careful measurements of the cross-section of the river-bed, where the canal dam is being built, and a reasonably accurate measurement of the velocity of the current, I find the quantity of water flowing in the river at its very lowest stage to be about fifteen hundred cubic feet per second. At its highest flood-line, as shown by the drift-wood on its banks, and estimating its velocity at eight feet per second, it carries about twenty-five thousand cubic feet per second.

As the above-mentioned quantity is fully twice that required in the winter, and six times that required in the summer, for the purposes of the company, there is no doubt about the amount of water flowing in the river being at all times sufficient. It may be well to state that from many inquiries made of old residents here, it appears that the river was never so low as at the time of my measurement, since Americans began coming into the country.

In Colorado, the average duty of water, as near as I can learn, is about one hundred acres per cubic foot per second. It would certainly seem as if Idaho would need less water than southern California, or even Colorado; but in order to be perfectly safe, I have calculated on one cubic foot per second for one hundred acres of land. At this rate, the canal will irrigate four hundred thousand acres; or at one hundred and fifty acres per cubic foot per second, six hundred thousand acres.

The area of irrigable land lying under the canal, between the Snake and Boisé rivers, is approximately three hundred and fifty thousand acres. On the south side of Snake River there is a tract of irrigable land roughly estimated at thirty-five thousand acres, which can be easily covered by the company's water, by carrying it across the river in a pipe, or flume. Along the east side of Snake River, below or north of the mouth of the Boisé, are some two hundred thousand acres of excellent land, which could be easily and cheaply reached from the company's canal by a pipe or flume crossing the Boisé just above the mouth of Ten Mile Creek. It may appear needless to take water out of the river on one side, and carry it down twenty miles and then cross the river with it; but it is much cheaper and better than to take it out of the Boisé on the opposite side, or lower down, as the country is not adapted on that side of the river to canal building, nor is the river bottom adapted to dams. The foregoing gives 585,000 acres controlled by the canal.

It is the experience in Colorado, Utah, and California that desert lands, after being irrigated a few years, require much less water than at first. This being the case, four thousand cubic feet per second will certainly be enough to irrigate not only the lands of the peninsula, but those across the rivers as well. It will probably take several years for the settlers to thoroughly irrigate their lands; and in the mean time, there is excellent use for a large portion of the water on the placer lands of Snake River.

In a preceding general description of the lands of the company, they are described as in broad benches, or plateaus, which is correct in a general way; and to one looking over them from the surrounding hills, they have a perfectly flat appearance. When looked at in detail with a leveling instrument, however, there is found to be a general descent toward the Boisé River, and also toward the junction of the Boisé and Snake Rivers. This descent averages about twenty-five feet to the mile. It is also found that there is an immense number of slightly rolling plains, each with its system of divides and drainage channels on a small scale.

The Snake River has a fall of only about two feet to the mile, and its course is generally in a deep cañon, with a high wall of lava-capped bluffs on the north side of it. For this reason most of the drainage of the tract of land under consideration is towards the Boisé. This subject of the drainage of irrigated lands is nearly if not quite as important as the irrigation itself. Some, in fact nearly all, of the failures that are recorded of irrigating enterprises were caused by not taking into consideration the question of draining the lands after irrigating them. These lands are generally covered with a dense growth of sage-brush, some of it very large, interspersed with what is locally called "white sage." In places, large areas have been accidentally burned off and are slowly being covered again. I mention this burning merely to show that the land is very easily cleared.

In regard to the quality, richness, or productiveness of these lands, there is a certain amount of possible evidence to be obtained from the farmers located on the north border of the tract along the Boisé River. There is but a narrow strip or fringe of land on which the crops are now grown. Some might think for this reason that this fringe was the only land of the tract which is arable. On the contrary, every farmer along this narrow strip, and every one knowing anything about soils, will testify that the higher lands farther from the Boisé River are far better, both in climate and soil, than the lowlands now cultivated. The expense of getting water from the Boisé River to the higher lands has prevented and always will prevent any being taken out on a small scale.

Numbers of farmers along the river have already applied to me for opportunities to get land higher up, most of them desiring to get on to Deer Flat, which is the highest tract of all. The reason for the higher tract being the richer is simply that it is composed in large part of decomposed lava, which makes the richest soil known, while the lower lands have a large proportion of clay and sand from the Boisé River.

The following analyses, made by Professor Johnson of Yale College, show the composition of the soil in two places. (Sample No. 1 was taken from near the wagon road, about five miles north of Henderson's Ferry. Sample No. 2 was taken about midway between the two rivers and about twelve miles east of their junction.)

A. D. FOOTE, Esq.   NEW HAVEN, CONN., February 25, 1884.

DEAR SIR: I give you herewith the results of analyses of the two samples of soil lately received from you. The analyses show that both soils contain a good store of all the elements of fertility, with the single exception of nitrogen. The considerable quantity of matters soluble in hydrochloric acid, and the fineness of the soils, afford strong presumption that they will, under due supply of water, yield abundandant nourishment to crops. Since ordinary crops, under favorable conditions, forage by their roots, through a depth of several feet, no less than ten million pounds of soil per acre contribute to their nourishment; and in such a mass of soil the small amounts of sulphuric acid and nitrogen stated in the analyses represent considerable quantities, each hundredth of a per cent corresponding to one thousand pounds per acre.   Yours very truly,

S. W. JOHNSON.

ANALYSES OF SOILS BY PROFESSOR S. W. JOHNSON.

	No. 1.	No. 2.
Silica (soluble in hydrochloric acid)	.016	.024
Oxide of iron and alumina	1.624	2.025
Lime	1.200	.383
Magnesia	.768	.503
Soda	.026	.043
Potash	.119	.239
Sulphuric acid (S O^3)	.026	.023
Phosphoric acid (Pr O^5)	.111	.004
Carbonic acid (C O^2)	.866	trace
Chlorine	trace	trace
Silica (soluble in carb. soda, sal.)	1.938	2.461
Titanic oxide (Ti O^2)	.869	.303
Matters dissolved or set free by cold concentrated hydrochloric acid	7.583	6.118
Sands, silicates, etc., insoluble in acid	92.417	93.882
	100.000	100.000
Organic matters contain of nitrogen	.035	.040

Supposing, however, that the higher lands are no richer than the lower, I give the following results as showing what can be done on the low, poor lands, it being remembered that no manure is used, except that contained in the muddy water of the Boisé. Mr. I. N. Costau, a member of the legislature for many years, and one of the most prominent farmers in the Boisé Valley, made the following statements to me while I wrote them down:

"Last year, 1882, on ten acres of poorest land, with imperfect irrigation, raised forty tons of red-clover hay. Sold 75,000 pounds (1,250 bushels) of onions from two acres. Potatoes only gave 200 bushels to the acre. Have raised 1,000 bushels on two acres. Have raised 113 bushels of barley on an acre. Wheat from forty to sixty bushels; oats one hundred to one hundred and fifty bushels; carrots and turnips equally good with potatoes. Connecticut flint-corn will grow well, especially on the higher benches; have raised sixty bushels to the acre in the bottoms. Prunes, the Germans say, grow better than in their own country. Apples, pears, peaches, plums, apricots, cherries, etc., as good, if not better, than in the most favored spots in California. The elm, soft maple, black-walnut, locust, etc., make our best shade trees."

Mr. B. B. Stewart, whose farm is situated nearly opposite Boisé City, is said to have the poorest land in the valley. He admits it is rather poor when first broken up, but the muddy water of the Boisé seems to have a powerful effect on it. He gives the following as examples of what he can do with his land:

"I have been farming for five years on this same tract of land. My principal crop has been grass, which improves by irrigation. I grow alfalfa and clover; my average crop is four tons to the acre, in two cuttings, and it is now better than when first seeded. Raised about fifteen acres of potatoes this year which averaged 150 bushels merchantable potatoes to the acre, which is about an average crop. Have raised corn every year I have worked the land, until this year. Have grown flint-corn, never less than twenty-five bushels to the acre, and on an average from thirty to thirty-five bushels to the acre. This past year raised an Early Dent corn, which has yielded better than the flint-corn. I have raised wheat, but only in small quantities, and not often, which averaged twenty-two bushels to the acre. Do not consider my land as well adapted to wheat as other crops. I can cut and put hay in the stack for the cost of one ton of hay to the acre, which leaves a net of three tons of hay to the acre. I have a small apple and pear orchard of about an acre, which has been set three years; would have had quite a crop this year if the fruit buds had not been killed by the unusual cold weather of last winter; have about a half acre of small fruits, currants, raspberries, strawberries, etc., etc. I sold last summer, from eighteen square rods of land, $125 worth of strawberries, besides using all we wanted in the family. I find I can grow larger crops of small fruit, as well as other crops here, than in Massachusetts, Missouri, or Oregon—in all of which States I have cultivated fruits, etc. To sum up, I can raise larger crops and with more certainty, on this sage-brush desert, with irrigation, than in either of the above States, depending upon the usual rainfall, besides always having clear weather to secure crops after they have grown."

Mr. Payne, a neighbor of Mr. Stewart, went on his land in the spring of 1873. Having irrigated a year or two longer than Mr. Stewart, he has better crops. This year he raised 360 tons of alfalfa on sixty acres of land (six tons per acre), 160 tons of clover on forty acres (four tons per acre). He does not raise much wheat, because he thinks feed crops pay better. Oats sown with clover gave him thirty bushels per acre this year. Has usually raised very good flint-corn, but did not plant any this year.

Four years ago he set out two hundred apple-trees, and this year realized an average of two bushels per tree. The potatoes yielded 200 bushels per acre.

Dr. Wright, of Boisé City, who has a farm near Middleton, told me that one field of ten acres has produced from five to six hundred bushels of wheat every season for the past fourteen years, and it still appears well, if not better than ever.

I mentioned that the climate on the higher lands is preferable to the river bottoms. In all temperate climates low, wet places, surrounded by hills and away from the sea, are the first to be touched by a white frost in the autumn, and the last in the spring. The cause is easily shown, but need not be stated here, so long as the fact is admitted; consequently, the first blossoms and tender plants are more likely to be killed when confined by the mesa along the Boisé River than when only a hundred feet or two higher on the broad, open plains. The average temperature for the year is probably lower on the plains than along the river, but it is also much more even, and it is quick to change from cold night to bright, warm day, which ruins fruit blossoms. The fruit orchards along the Boisé Valley have suffered very slightly from this, it is true, losing peaches only twice, I think, since its settlement; but the probabilities are that one of these times, at least, they would not have been destroyed on the plains above.

The climate is about the same as that of Virginia, as a rule, but with fewer storms, less wind, and is much drier. Last winter it was much colder than ever known in Virginia. Exceptional winters, however, occur everywhere, I believe, and need not be considered in a general estimate of the climate. There are none of those terrible tornadoes known here which devastate the mid-west. I believe they are impossible in a valley shut in by mountains.

The following letter, written by Judge John B. Miller, late Register United States Land Office, Boisé City, in reply to a series of questions by an inquirer in Iowa, truthfully covers many important points, and as it is written by an old resident to a friend in the East, probably will convey the kind of information desired better than I could:

"Referring to your letter of the 2d inst., making inquiry in relation to the climate, amount of arable land, the prospects of new settlers, etc., I will state that, as you are perhaps aware, I have resided the greater portion of my life in

Iowa, but have been residing here for three years past, and am pretty well acquainted with all portions of the Territory, but more especially with the Boisé City land district. The climate here is fine in summer; while it is quite warm in the sun, yet in the shade it is always cool, and at night, in the warmest weather, you will need a blanket over you while sleeping. The summers have certainly reminded me of my summer in California in 1850. There we could work all day, in the hottest sun, without feeling oppressed by heat. I do not recall any day that I have felt uncomfortable here. The fact is, you can endure more here than you could in a more level country, the air being more exhilarating. There is a buoyancy in the step of the people peculiar to those residing in a mountainous region. While the summers are cool and pleasant, the winters are delightful; perhaps not one half the people of the Territory have overcoats, and of that half not one in ten uses them except when riding. As a result of the mildness of the winters, the dwelling-houses, as a rule, have thin walls, and people live comfortably in houses which would be untenantable in an Iowa winter. In speaking of the mild winters, I refer only to the valleys; in the mountains the weather is cold, and snow falls to a great depth.

"I would estimate the tillable land at about one acre in twenty, the balance consisting of mountains and their foot-hills, which cannot be reached by irrigating ditches. None of the valleys are wide, and a large portion of them have to be irrigated in order to raise crops. However, irrigating is not nearly so expensive or troublesome as I had supposed before I came here, and with the main ditches once made, the farmer has but little trouble, and can control the flow of water as he pleases; and with an absolute immunity from rain in summer, he can count with a reasonable certainty on a pleasant time for harvest and the number of bushels he will raise.

"The crops generally raised are wheat, oats, and barley, and all the vegetables common in Iowa and Illinois. All kinds of fruit trees and shrubbery grow finely here; the finest variety of rose-bushes, which can only be raised in Iowa with extreme care, live through the winter without any protection. The varieties of fruit grown here are greater than in any portion of the United States, except California; frequently in the same garden you will see trees loaded down with apples, pears, peaches, nectarines, apricots, plums, and prunes. The fruit yield of last year was simply enormous, while the crop of this year is good.

"I fully realize the difficulty of explaining the climate so that it will be understood by an Iowa man. In mid-winter we may have one day a snow from five to eight inches deep, and will wonder how on earth the cattle, sheep, and horses are to live out on the range without feed, when in perhaps twenty-four or forty-eight hours we feel the chinook (coast wind) commencing to blow soft like an evening breeze in summer, but steady, and in a short time the snow will disappear, and the ground become completely dry. As you are perhaps aware, all kinds of stock are allowed to run out on the range in winter, without feed, and, as a rule, come out fat in the spring. You can, perhaps, get a more correct idea of the mild character of the winters here when I tell you that birds which are usually migratory remain here summer and winter. The wild geese breed and remain here at all seasons.

"A man coming here from Iowa would at first dislike the country, and if profane, would curse the Fates—or, more likely, the fellow who tempted him to come.

"If in summer the roads will be deep with dust, the valleys will appear more narrow than they really are, and when not irrigated the grass will appear like dry hay; while for miles, sometimes, he will see nothing but sage-brush and jack-rabbits; but take out irrigating ditches and cover the sage plains with water, and the sage will disappear; and the land which before appeared worthless will produce, on an average, twice as much wheat to the acre as can be raised on the best Iowa lands, while the farmer and stock-raiser have the endless mountain range free of taxes to raise their stock on. From the very nature of the country, there will always be comparatively few towns in Idaho. The real business will be farming, stock-raising, and mining. While fortunes will be made for ages to come at the last-named business, stock-raising and farming will be the more certain investments. Stock-raising must always be good; for, as I said before, it costs nothing to raise stock, and farming will always pay well, as the mines will not consume all that can be raised in the valleys, and the produce will command higher rates than can be obtained in the States.

"I could pick out here and there, all over the Territory, valleys that whole neighborhoods from the States could move into and find homes which, in a short time, they would not exchange for their old ones.

"It is hard to tell which is more profitable here, raising cattle or horses, as I find a wide difference of opinion on the subject. It certainly takes less capital to start in the cattle business; but with capital to start on, I am inclined to believe raising horses and mules is the most remunerative. There are not many sheep here, but the business is a good one."

The following is copied from R. E. Strahorn's pamphlet on "Idaho and its Resources," which is mainly correct:

"Idaho valleys cannot be excelled by any region east of California for the production of fruit. Apples, peaches, pears, nectarines, apricots, plums, prunes, grapes, and all the small fruits are produced in the greatest abundance, and of a quality unsurpassed. The sage-brush lands, naturally the very emblem of sterility and desolation, are in a few years turned into the finest fruit farms, with less trouble than attend a similar transformation on the wild prairies of Iowa or Nebraska. A prominent fruit-grower estimates that twenty thousand large fruit trees have been set out annually for the past five years in the valleys surrounding Boisé. Several of the orchards in this locality produce from twenty-five thousand to forty thousand bushels of fruit each annually, there having been but one failure of the crop for ten years. General L. F. Cartee, ex-Surveyor-General of Idaho, has forty varieties of grapes in his vineyard, none of which have ever failed to bear a full crop, save the Catawba. John Krall, in the suburbs of Boisé, has one hundred and twenty-five acres in fruits (twenty thousand trees), embracing all the varieties known in this latitude. His production last season was five hundred thousand pounds. He finds no fruit insects yet, and pears are never troubled with blight or other disease. His market is mainly in the mining camps, and his fruit commands from five to twelve cents per pound. Thomas Davis, also near Boisé, has a seventy-five-acre orchard (ten thousand trees). His orchard has failed to produce but *once in the last ten years*, and his last season's crop of forty thousand bushels of large fruits, and five hundred bushels of berries, must have returned him a snug little fortune alone. His orchard is seventeen years old, and not a tree in it looks like decaying. Mr. Davis has extensive fruit-drying apparatus, and a cider and vinegar factory, in which he works up vast quantities of fruit annually. Indeed, fruit-drying and the manufacture of cider is a prominent and very profitable industry. One firm dries from thirty thousand to forty thousand pounds of fruit annually, and the interest bids fair to grow until at least the demand of Idaho and adjacent territory is supplied.

"The fourth year's growth of apples in Boisé Valley has yielded two hundred pounds; of cherries, seventy-five pounds; of peaches, one hundred and fifty-two pounds; of pears, one hundred and thirty pounds; of plums, one hundred and fifty pounds; while small fruits, such as strawberries, currants, gooseberries, blackberries, and raspberries, are very prolific. The growth of wood made by fruit trees, and the quantity of fruit often found loading the branches, is almost incredible. John Lamb, in Boisé City, has black locust trees on which I was shown limbs which had grown from twelve to fifteen feet in one season; and plum, peach, and apple trees, two years from the graft, full of fruit. In the yard of Governor Neil, at Boisé, I counted one hundred and forty nearly ripe greengage plums on a branch seventeen inches long, the plums averaging one and one half inches in diameter.

"There is a grand future in store for the Idaho fruit-grower. Montana to the north, Wyoming on the east, Nevada to the south, produce practically no fruit. With her railroads soon reaching the remotest corners of these Territories, and with a vast consumption at home, Idaho is assured the best fruit markets in the land. Fruit can be produced in all her lower valleys, and short-sighted is the settler who does not take advantage of the above facts."

I have once or twice in this paper used the expression, "muddy water of the Boisé River." This "muddy" part of the water is of immense importance to the enterprise contemplated. If the water were not muddy it would be a serious, if not fatal, drawback to the undertaking as far as irrigation is concerned. I mentioned Mr. Stewart as saying that his land was poor, but the muddy water enabled him to get along. He says: "If a ditch, in which the water has been running for several weeks, be allowed to run dry, a fine greenish gray coating will be found to cover the bottom and sides from a quarter to half an inch thick. The sun shining on this will cause it to smell badly in a few hours. I find on my land that wheat does not do very well for the first few years after it is broken up, but after irrigating it a couple of years it will grow wheat well. One portion of my land gets its water from a pond or reservoir where the water has settled and become clear. It does not make good crops like the 'muddy water.' I would rather give two dollars an acre for muddy water than one for clear."

General Cartee of Boisé, late Surveyor-General of Idaho, says: "Open a trench, or furrow, through a newly plowed field, and let that muddy water through it; at first it will soak through its banks, and by percolation wet the earth each side for a distance of perhaps two feet; by that time there will be a lining of fine silt to the trench, and no water will go through it. You cannot irrigate by percolation with this water, and you need fear no seepage from your ditches or canals. There will be a little in the beginning, but it will not last. We have to irrigate here by letting the water over the surface in a sheet, or better, little drills, such as are formed by a harrow, and the result is that we get a layer of fine silt over all the land, which is the best fertilizer we can have." "Our lands grow richer by cropping, instead of poorer." Mr. Costan and Mr. Payne tell me the same thing, but it is needless to multiply the testimony.

In the matter of location, these lands at first glance appear somewhat isolated, and without a market or outlet for their produce. The extensive mining regions of the Owyhee County on the south and west, of central Idaho on the north, and of eastern Idaho and southern Montana on the east, will for many years make a lively market for fruit and vegetables. These mining districts are just beginning to give promise of great and continued productiveness.

There is no market the pioneer farmer likes so well as a mining market for his produce. Prices are invariably high and sales are quick. The Oregon Short Line Railway, just completed, bisects these lands near the middle, and has located three towns thereon. Two of these are merely side-tracks, or water-stations; the third, Caldwell, is a rapidly growing railroad town, and is the point of connection with a branch road building to Boisé City. Of course its stability depends almost entirely on the irrigation of the lands around it. The advantages of the railroad communication thus already established with the mining regions of Wood River and Butte, with the Pacific Coast, via the Oregon Railroad and Navigation Company's lines, and also with the rest of the country, are too evident to need description.

I anticipate, however, that the greatest advantages in the peculiar location of these lands will be found in their proximity to the great summer pastures of central and western Idaho. At present the few scattering herds can find sufficient nutriment in the exposed knolls and in the sage-brush of the low valleys during the winter.

Camas Prairie, Little Camas Prairie, and the hills and mountains around and to the eastward and northward, can fatten a million cattle every year where now they fatten a thousand, if there were any place to keep them through the winter. Stockmen know this, and already numbers of them have inquired of me about locating on these very lands for the purpose of raising alfalfa to feed in the winter. With alfalfa they can keep the stock fat and ship fat cattle East in the spring.

One who has not seen them can form no idea of the extent and richness of these mountain pastures of central Idaho. I have wandered over a large extent of them, and know whereof I write. The soil is rich and moist, and does not wear out as do the Wyoming plains. Water is plentiful. The hills and prairies are rolling, often steep but not rocky. Quaking-asp thickets are scattered through them, making plenty of shelter from sun or storm; and the fattening properties of the grass is something bordering on the marvelous. I repeat, therefore, that the peculiar location of these (when watered) rich, hay-growing plains, near these immense grass-growing hills, makes a combination that cannot be excelled for stock-raising purposes. It enables the stock-grower in Idaho to ship fat cattle East in the spring with a decided advantage on the more expensive corn-fed cattle of Nebraska and Kansas; and finally, the beef fatened in the Idaho hills and kept on alfalfa, will be found to have more and better flavor, be more juicy and tender, than corn-fed beef.

Caldwell, named from the Kansas ex-Senator, is situated on the south side of Boisé River, at the crossing of the Oregon Short Line, at an altitude of 2,500 feet. It is hardly a year old, but already boasts of a number of substantial dwellings and business houses. It has a telephone exchange, connecting the town with Boisé City, 30 miles away, two hotels, several merchandise and hardware stores, and all the other accompaniments of a much older town. It has the advantage of having a settled and prosperous community surrounding it, so that when it sprung into existence upon the arrival of the railroad, it found a market ready made. A weekly newspaper, the *Tribune*, advertises its resources to the outside world. Before a building on the town site had been completed, the money was raised to erect a good, comfortable school-house. The Baptists have already built a neat, commodious edifice. The Boisé Valley Branch of the Short Line running to Boisé City is to have its junction here. The canal constructed by the Land Improvement Company takes its water from Boisé River, about ten miles east, is led over a high plateau to the south-east, and reaches the reservoir near the summit of the "Terrace," on the eastern edge of town, by a line fifteen miles long. It covers about 15,000 acres of some of the finest farming lands in the west.

Situated in the center of an agricultural, grazing, mining, and forest region, there seems no reason why Caldwell should not, in a few years, be one of the leading towns in Idaho.

Payette Valley is a fine agricultural region, situated about 50 miles north-west from Boisé City. It is several miles in width, and contains rich belts of alluvial bottom-lands. It is surrounded by foot-hills covered with nutritious bunch-grass, furnishing feed to thousands of cattle, horses, and sheep. The section is attracting much attention as a stock country. Wheat, oats, barley, hay, corn, potatoes, and other vegetables, besides fruits, are successfully raised.

Emmettsville is a rapidly growing agricultural settlement in the heart of Payette Valley. A fine bridge across the Payette is near this town, and it already commands considerable trade for miles around.

There are two large irrigating ditches, carrying about 25,000 inches of water. It is estimated that the two ditches together will cover sixty sections of agricultural land. Another irrigating scheme is projected, second in importance only to that in Boisé Valley. It is proposed to construct a canal on each side of the river, beginning near the Boisé County line, and flowing thence westerly. When completed, these ditches will reclaim from 200,000 to 300,000 acres, and furnish farms for hundreds and even thousands of colonists.

Ada County being chiefly agricultural, but little attention has been devoted to its mineral resources. The cretaceous rock of the foot-hills of the Boisé Mountains, which traverse the whole length of the county, are said to be coal-bearing, and the lignite discovered in several places for a distance of thirty miles is of a superior quality. In the same formation beds of a very fine fire-clay are found.

ALTURAS COUNTY.

Alturas has an area of over 19,000 square miles, or larger than Vermont and New Hampshire combined. It is about 200 miles in length, with a width varying from 70 to 130 miles. It is the banner county of the Territory, not only in size, but also in wealth and population. In it lies the great Wood River region, the phenomenal richness of whose deposits, as well as those of the Sawtooth, have made the name of Alturas known all over the world. Situated in central Idaho, watered by the river from which the section takes its name and by a score of tributaries, at an elevation of from 5,200 to 9,000 feet, are the great mineral fields of Idaho. With a mineral belt extending for 110 miles, with easy communication by means of the Wood River branch of the Oregon Short Line, with a record already brilliant though hardly four years old, this may be truly regarded as an attractive country.

A correspondent of the Chicago *Tribune* writes : " Veterans in mining business stood amazed as the belt, if I may so term it, broadened and lengthened, and it seemed that it absolutely had no limit. From the mountains bordering Wood River Valley at Bellevue, across the divide into Croy Gulch, across this into Bullion, beyond this to Deer Creek, over this divide into Warm Springs Creek, and beyond this to the Smokies, the almost solid column of locations extends ; and scattered throughout this entire fifty-mile stretch there are proved to be good paying mines, while the prospects with an actual value of from $1,000 to $10,000 are myriads. Beyond the Smokies, on this chain, comes we know not what ; the country is too young to have told; but is rich with promise for the next season."

Among the several thousand locations it would be not only impracticable, but tedious, to give a detailed catalogue descriptive of every claim. We shall therefore content ourselves with a general description of the country, referring simply to some of the more important mines. We are indebted to Mr. T. E. Picotte of Hailey, Major Wm. Hyndman of Ketchum, and Major Wm. H. Pettit of Atlanta, for much of the information in the following pages concerning the resources of the country.

Within its boundaries may be enjoyed at all seasons quite a diversity of climate. All fruits and cereals pertaining to the temperate zone can be cultivated there, with the same result of really wonderful returns. On fresh-broken ground, or common "sod," a yield of fifty bushels of wheat or barley is generally expected and secured, while from the same planting the yield of "volunteer" grain the second year is even greater.

At Armstrong's Willow Creek ranch, this year, five acres of volunteer wheat yielded 522 bushels, or at the rate of over ONE HUNDRED AND FOUR BUSHELS PER ACRE !

This is, of course, an extreme case—in fact, it stands unequaled even on Camas Prairie, that garden-spot of Idaho — but several instances could be cited where the yield of volunteer wheat has reached 75 bushels per acre.

The soil is so well adapted to the raising of potatoes and vegetables that a yield of less than one ton of potatoes per acre is a great disappointment, while with ruta-bagas, carrots, etc., less than two tons is not considered an average crop. And this, it must be borne in mind, is in fresh-plowed ground that three years ago had never even felt the tramp of civilized man.

As a Stock-raising Country.—There is probably no better country in the world for stock-raising. The would-be cattle king can here indeed realize his dream of seeing his flocks feeding on a thousand hills, with no other trouble than two annual round-ups to change from the summer to the winter range, and *vice versa*, and for branding purposes.

The drives from one season's range to another are short, not exceeding seventy miles, and stock keep fat and ready for market the year round. Surprising as this may appear, it is nevertheless a fact that when fat beef cattle are needed for market, no matter what the season, the butchers can go to any herder in the county, with entire confidence of finding what they seek. In summer the stock feed on the fine growing grass of the foot-hills of the Sawtooth range ; in the winter months the abundant bunch-grass of the great Snake River lava fields enables them to thrive and fatten.

This industry is making such rapid strides that several cattle-raisers have already begun the importation of thorough-bred stock, and E. R. Leonard, assessor and tax collector of Alturas County, who brought out two car-loads of Jersey and Holstein bulls and heifers last spring, will visit Wisconsin and Illinois this winter, to purchase three or four car-loads more. His experiments made the past season have convinced him that a Jersey cow will yield much more and richer milk fed on native grasses, than the best native milker, even when stall-fed on the most approved diet. This gentleman has just established a creamery, with which he expects to compete very successfully with the choicest products of the trans-Mississippi creameries. One of the best permanent ranges in the world, according to its size, is undoubtedly to be found in Alturas County to-day; as the lava fields can never be settled, while the mountain ranges will probably remain in the same condition, except where a mineral-bearing outcrop may induce a miner to locate a claim.

As a Mineral-bearing Section.—Probably no other region on the face of the globe is equally favored with Alturas County in this respect. Whithersoever the prospector may direct his steps from the lava fields, he cannot fail to strike ore. And the only other questions that may puzzle him, next to that of "Shall I strike ore?" which he can always surely answer in the affirmative, are: "How much will there be of it?" "What character shall it be?" As to its grade or accessibility he need not worry; the first will be high, the second easy, as the country is becoming almost as equally noted for the exceeding richness of its ores as for the beauty and smoothness of its natural roads.

The mines have made Alturas County what it is to-day. But for the mines, its numerous small valleys, and gulches, and extensive lava fields would have in time afforded feed to thousands upon thousands of heads of stock; but the remoteness of the region from market would have prohibited all agricultural enterprise except such as would be needed for individual wants. With the discovery and exploration of the mines, however, a local market has been afforded the agricultural producer, who finds rapid cash sales for all his "truck" at $40 to $50 for hay, four to five cents per pound for vegetables, the same for oats and barley, and so on. The mines of Alturas County were discovered in the early 'sixties by gold-hunters on their way to some far-off El Dorado. The first discovery was made in the extreme northwestern end of the county, in an aggregation of granite bowlders, since known as Rocky Bar. Soon after placers were worked at Atlanta, and permanent settlements made. From these two points many expeditions were sent out to the eastern portion of the county, which was then indicated on the maps under the general name of "unexplored region," and many good prospects found; but the fear of the Bannock Indians—a warlike tribe which at that time roamed about Lost, Little Wood, and Big Wood Rivers, and over Camas Prairie—prevented any settlement other than on one of the Smoky creeks, where Newton Revis, a hardy old gold-seeker, located a placer at least ten years ago.

These expeditions brought back such glowing reports that the miners of Rocky Bar and Atlanta, consumed with a burning desire to occupy this "unexplored region," could hardly restrain themselves from invading it, even though to do so seemed to be certain death; and the Indian outbreak which resulted in the Bannack tribe being driven from Camas Prairie and the entire Wood River and Sawtooth region was a most welcome event. The prospectors soon followed the retreating Indians, the sound of the pick and shovel was heard in the land, discovery followed discovery, until a large population flocked in, and towns, hoisting works, concentrating and reducing mills, and smelting and sampling works sprung up in almost every gulch.

Three Years' Progress.—Since that time Alturas county's progress has been really wonderful. Scarcely three years have passed, and yet the trackless desert has been spanned by 252 miles of standard-gauge railway, fully equipped, with an equal extent of telegraph lines; the tax-paying population has increased from almost 500 souls to 2,900; the taxable property from $750,000 to $3,250,000; the annual county revenue from $25,000 to $130,000; the annual yield of the mines from $250,000 to $5,000,000; and everything else in the same proportion. The increase in property values can perhaps be better appreciated if the following mine sales be quoted—the reader bearing in mind that a few years back the very existence of these mines was unknown:

The Minnie Moore sold last spring to an English syndicate, which includes among its members one of the directors of the Bank of England, for $500,000. The purchase price is paid.

The Idahoan is sold to a London and New York company, of which the Count de Barranca, a noted German financier, is one. Price $450,000.

The Mayflower, at Bullion, was sold to J. V. Farwell, the Chicago merchant prince, for $375,000. In less than eighteen months it reimbursed the purchaser for his outlay.

The Narrow-gauge Bannock group, purchased by the same for $85,000 cash, sold only the preceding season for $5,000.

The Muldoon mine, discovered in the spring of 1882, was sold the same fall to a Philadelphia company for $125,000.

Numberless other instances might be quoted, but these suffice.

The Reduction Works.—As above stated, the ore is of wonderfully high grade, but of exceedingly diversified character. On the outskirts of the Big Wood River Valley—in Resurrection district—is found a gold-ledge thirty feet wide, of ore that averages $25 per ton, an enormous yield for a free-gold vein of that size. This vein crosses the valley, and reappears again south-west of Hailey, where it is known as the Big Camas.

About four miles north of Resurrection district some silver-bearing galena begins to be found. Its value per ton varies of course, but scarcely falls below $90. From that point past Bellevue, Hailey, Bullion, Ketchum, Muldoon, Bowlder, on to Galena, from north to south, and Soldier Creek and Smoky districts to Little Lost River, from west to east, this character of ore is found. North of Galena, east of Little Lost River, and west of the Smokies, the character of the ore again changes to gold and silver bearing.

Such a variety of ore of course necessitates an equal variety of modes of reduction. The free-gold ore is therefore reduced in gold mills, the silver-gold ore in silver mills. The last-mentioned kind of ore being refractory, roasting furnaces are attached to the mills constructed to reduce it.

The reducing capacity of the mills and smelters now in the county is about as follows:

	Tons.
The Bellevue smelting works	5
The Hailey smelting works	10
The Ketchum smelting works	120
The Galena smelting works	30
The Little Wood River smelting works	60
The Vienna Company's mill	50
The Columbia and Beaver Company's mill, at Sawtooth	50
The Atlanta Company's mill, at Atlanta	50
The Buffalo Company's mill, at Atlanta	40
The Big Lode Company's mill, at Atlanta	30
The Last Chance Company's mill, at Atlanta	20
Making a total daily milling and smelting capacity of	465

In addition to the above, there are several concentrating works, that is, works which concentrate the metal in from three to ten tons of ore into one, by separating it from the waste. Of these the most noted are:

	Tons.
The Minnie Moore Company's, with a daily capacity of	80
The Queen of the Hills Company's	50
The Hailey Concentrating Company's	40
The Wood River Company's	60
The Mayflower Company's	30
The Narrow-Gange Company's	40
The North Star Company's	40
The Buzzo Company's	40
The Ontario Company's	40
The Silver King Company's	30
The Little Wood River Company's	30
Making a total daily capacity of	510

These works do not all run steadily, however, our mining men not having lost their habit of spending the winter months in the East, the works remaining closed in the mean while.

The Towns.—The importance to which the mining and cognate industries have attained in this county led to the location of several towns, whose enterprising citizens vie with each other in advancing the interests of their respective localities.

The first large town which the traveler by rail sees in the county is

Shoshone, which is located at the junction of the Wood River Branch Railway. Here the Oregon Short Line Company have constructed the most extensive and complete railway shops west of Omaha. The town is also the terminal point of the toll-road to the great Shoshone Falls, which have been very properly named "The Niagara of the West," and which will attract and delight large numbers of tourists from this time on. There is a good weekly paper published here—the *Journal*—and the place is the center of a thriving stock-raising district. Present population about 700.

Bellevue.—This is the next important town reached. It is located on the east branch of Wood River, about fifty miles north of Shoshone, via the Wood River Branch. The Minnie Moore, Queen of the Hills, Queen Victoria, Monday, Oswego, and other rich mines are within one to two miles, and 200 men are steadily employed in and about the mines, at wages varying from $3.50 to $6 per day.

Across the river, opposite Bellevue, is the new town of Broadford, the miners' headquarters. Population of Bellevue and Broadford, about 2,000. A weekly newspaper—the *Chronicle*—is published here.

Hailey.—Five miles north of Bellevue is Hailey. This is the county seat of Alturas, and the commercial, financial, political, and social center of the Wood River and Sawtooth mining region. Admirably situated at the intersection of Croy Gulch and the Wood River Valley, and in the very centre of the county, her enterprising business men draw trade from all parts of the surrounding country in a radius of 150 miles. Three daily and three weekly newspapers are published here, viz.: The Wood River *Times*, the *Inter-Idaho*, and the *News-Miner*. The *Times* also publishes a weekly edition, as do the *News-Miner* and *Inter-Idaho*. The former is in its fourth year; the *Inter-Idaho* is but five months old. Population of Hailey about 2,500 souls.

Bullion lies about seven miles west of Hailey. It is exclusively a mining camp, situated in a narrow gulch. In its neighborhood are some of the richest mines in the Territory. Conspicuous among these is the Bullion Mine, operated and owned by the Wood River Gold and Silver Mining Company, of which Colonel E. A. Wall is manager. The ore is largely composed of gray copper, assaying 180 ounces in silver. There are over two miles in tunnels and drifts. The mill in connection with the mine paid for itself the first week. "That is," says Colonel Wall, "we had ore we could not use, ore not worth anything to us, and in one week I sold enough from that ore to pay for the mill."

The Mayflower, referred to above, the Jay Gould, O. K., Eureka, and the Idahoan (the last named having been recently sold for $450,000), are all fine paying properties.

Deer Creek enters Wood River a short distance above Hailey. The Montana, Silver Moon, Mountain View, Wolftone, and Davitt are all promising claims. The Narrow-gauge Group is owned by Chicago parties; they have produced considerable ore, 125 tons of which sold for $30,000. In

Quigley Gulch is the Ophir group of mines. There are four claims, all showing high-grade galena. They are owned by a Chicago company, are advantageously located for working, and there is an abundant supply of wood and water.

THE GREAT CENTRAL WOOD RIVER REGION.

Warm Springs Mining District and Ketchum.—Mineral was first found on Warm Springs Creek in 1877, by Major Cavanah and Dr. Marshall, on a tour through that region from Atlanta; but no locations were made then, nor in fact until after the Indian war in the following year.

During the seasons of 1879 and 1880 several parties of prospectors found their way over from the Salmon River country, and discovered the mineral regions of Wood River in general, and large numbers of locations were made, several mining districts being organized.

The upper Wood River region is known as Galena, the lower as Bellevue, and the central as Leadville, the name of Leadville being changed by the post-office department when application was made for a post-office to that of Ketchum, which is now the center of this central Wood River region, the most promising and prosperous district in Idaho. Most of the large tributaries of Wood River join in the Warm Springs Creek district, Warm Springs Creek itself being the largest, known also as the west fork of Wood River, the town of Ketchum being directly opposite its confluence with Wood River.

The north fork, with Lake Creek and Eagle Creek, join the main river above Ketchum, and the east fork, Greenhorn Creek, and Deer Creek below Ketchum. All of these tributaries, especially the main forks, have sources fully 25 miles from their confluence with main Wood River, and from their mouths to their sources are lined with vast growths of timber, fir and black pine predominating, mineral being found in abundance on all.

The first mineral locations were made on Warm Springs Creek, about 12 miles from its mouth, on what is known as Boyle Mountain, and the producing mines of the Philadelphia Mining and Smelting Company, the Warm Springs Consolidated Mining Company, the Black Horse Mining Company—all foreign incorporations, based on property in the vicinity—have made the Wood River region prominent; such as the Ervine and Ten Broeck of the P. M. & S. Co., the Ontario of the W. S. Consolidated Mining Co., and the Black Horse Mine. Large quantities of high-grade lead ores have been taken from these and various other mines in this vicinity.

The extensive concentrating works of the Warm Springs Con. Co., under the able management of Col. J. H. Moyle, turn out many tons of most perfect concentrates from lower-grade ores daily.

The numerous warm springs on this creek are a source of much wonderment, the principal of which, one mile from its mouth, has become a prominent resort, known as the "Guyer Hot Springs," owned by I. I. Lewis and Capt. Henry Guyer, both prominent mining men.

A large hotel and various other buildings and bath-houses, both tub and plunge, have been erected, and a town-site surveyed and platted, called "Saratoga."

On the bench or table-land at the mouth of Warm Springs Creek are situated the reduction works of the Philadelphia Mining and Smelting Company, the largest enterprise in Idaho, consisting of four large smelting furnaces, five roasting furnaces, twenty charcoal kilns, with all the latest modern appliances for moving ores and material, lighted by electricity, and facilitating the manufacture of bullion.

These works have been in successful operation for nearly three years, and in that time have sent out several thousand tons of fine lead and silver bullion, the season of 1880 showing a manufacture and output of over 3,000 tons alone, and all from ores produced in the immediate vicinity of Ketchum.

The location of these works, at the confluence of Warm Springs Creek and Wood River, is all that could be desired, the site in itself being perfect for convenience, power, proximity to timber, wood for fuel, and the various fluxing materials, lime and iron being found in abundance in the immediate vicinity.

The situation, with all its facilities, is the envy and admiration of smelting and ore-reducing men from every place.

Smelting the high-grade lead ores of this region has been considerable of a problem hitherto, abounding, as they do, in sulphur, with some zinc, arsenia, and other base metals, which somewhat retard and obstruct the free manufacture of bullion. Coke in large quantities has been found necessary, which had to be brought from Pennsylvania, and proved very expensive before the completion of the railway to the works. It was proved, after a trial of several seasons, necessary to erect roasting furnaces and roast all high-grade lead ores before smelting, and prevent the accumulation of matter, which was both difficult and expensive to handle and again reduce.

But with the completion of the railroad to the works during the season of 1884, and the erection of the five roasting furnaces, thus insuring cheap coke, and transportation hence on bullion, and facilitating the smelting process, a grand success of the smelting proposition in Idaho is assured, and the Philadelphia Mining and Smelting Company, after a series of embarrassments and discouraging experiences, now enters upon the fruits of persistent endeavor and persevering hope that it richly deserves.

And their works will continue to grow and expand over their magnificent location as the ore production of the surrounding region increases, which it most surely will, it being merely in its infancy as yet.

Among the partially developed and largest ore-producing mines of the district may be named the following :

The Elkhorn mine, three miles east of Ketchum, owned by I. I. Lewis and others, which on a scale of limited operations for the past two years, never employing more than fifteen men at any time, has turned out a quarter of a million dollars' worth of ore, fully two thirds of which is net profit.

In the same vicinity is the Parker mine, owned by W. H. Watt and others, which likewise operated on a small scale for only a year past, has turned out almost one hundred thousand dollars' worth of very rich ores. Bordering on what is known as the Elkhorn are also found the Baltimore and Victoria companies' mines, of which the Baltimore in the past eight months has produced in mere development work fully $40,000 worth of ore.

Other mines and prospects in the vicinity of these, the Back-pay, Noonday, Buckhorn, Quaker City, Independence, Mattie, Keystone, Triumph, and many others, have all shipped ore in quantities large and small, but all high grade, and all give promise of proving good and permanent mines.

On the east fork of Wood River the North Star group occupies the foremost place, the North Star itself being an exceedingly large and promising ledge, from which an average daily output of forty tons is made. The ore is high grade in character but more base than usual in this region, and the owners, the Philadelphia Mining and Smelting Company, have erected a fine concentrator near the mines, and by a process of concentration dispose of most of the base and refractory metals and refuse matter, sending fine, clear concentrates to the smelters.

The American Eagle and Ketchum mines of this group, with but little development, indicate future ore-producing mines equal to any in the region.

The east fork locality is especially rich in iron, immense bodies of the finest fluxing iron being found, which carry a considerable percentage of silver.

The numerous prospects and mining locations along East Fork and its sources are bewildering, and in the limits of this work it is impossible to do justice to them.

Opposite East Fork in Greenhorn Gulch are found the producing Imperial and Occidental mines, both of which are worked on a very limited scale by the independent owners, but make a good showing yearly. Many other promising locations and prospects are in the same vicinity. But it would be utterly impossible in the scope of this work and of the space allotted to this district, even to mention all of the ore-producing mines, large and small ; suffice to say that within the past three years over three thousand lode-mining locations have been made and recorded, and are mostly held and worked, very few of them proving barren or worthless.

The future of the district promises almost anything in the range of the wildest imagination, there being absolutely no limit. Every facility is now offered for the influx of population and the investment of capital, now setting in strongly.

The Union Pacific Railway Company, in the progress of construction of their great north-west through line to the Pacific coast, had their attention drawn to the Wood River country by the great immigration thither, and large freighting business done and promised, and as soon as the Oregon Short Line Railway had reached a desirable point for a branch divergence to the Wood River region, it was made, and in August last completed to Ketchum the present and probably permanent terminus. Passenger and freight trains now arrive and depart daily from and for all points east and west by a thoroughly equipped and perfectly constructed standard-gauge railroad, with all modern conveniences and comforts.

Ketchum is a natural railroad terminal point, situate in the center of a broad, beautiful, well-watered valley, with routes, roads, and trails diverging in all directions to numerous mining camps and mountain towns and villages; in the main inaccessible to railroads, especially standard-gauge lines.

The town lies on a high level gravel bench at the confluence of Trail Creek with Wood River, and opposite the mouth of Warm Springs Creek. The Wood River Valley for fifteen miles below from its mouth to fifteen miles above is a grand, unbroken, almost level valley, with an average width of one half a mile, and an average elevation of 5,500 feet above sea-level, susceptible of agricultural production of almost all the staple grains, vegetables, and fruits of the Middle and Northern States, with but little irrigation, for which there is abundance of water, and which the lay of the land renders easy and inexpensive. The lands have all been surveyed and platted by the government, and are open to location and settlement under the various acts of Congress, and much has been settled upon and improved. All of the potatoes, onions, and vegetables consumed in the country are produced, and hay of most excellent quality is a natural production of rank growth. In the mature spring-time the whole valley is a very Eden for stock, and the region abounds in game of all kinds.

Into this beautiful valley came the first settlers, mainly mining prospectors, only four years ago, and where then only existed smiling inviting nature, now loom up the works of man on every hand: railroad, telegraph, telephone, electricity in harness, water power utilized, and the homes of several thousand pioneers and prosperous settlers, engaged in agricultural, manufacturing, and mining pursuits.

The town of Ketchum is now a thriving community of 2,000 inhabitants, the registered male voting population being 517 in the town alone. Buildings, first of log and stone, later of lumber from the numerous saw-mills in the town and vicinity, and progressing in fine substantial brick business blocks and houses. Three good churches, a large public school, with male and female teachers, benevolent and social organizations, three banks, one a national, a daily and weekly newspaper (the *Ketchum Keystone*), and almost one hundred mercantile, manufacturing, and trading enterprises. Life and activity on every hand, and naught but indication and promise of the prosperity of all the people. The town site was located under what is known as the old ten-dollar-lot law, or act of Congress, which allows each inhabitant two lots at the minimum price of ten dollars each, where the size does not exceed 4,200 square feet. Lots were surveyed larger in the Ketchum, and the price fixed by government at fifteen dollars each. The town plat contains 1,600 lots, which have all been taken and located by actual settlers, and improved in the main by erection of business houses and homes, many of them fine and substantial, comparing favorably with cities and towns decades older, East and West.

Rhodes Addition to Ketchum.—The original town site having been all taken up, and occupied by actual settlers, it was found necessary by the railroad company, on the completion of their railroad, to establish its terminal point, sidings, reversing tracks, depot buildings, engine-houses, and machine-shops, at a point convenient and adjacent to Ketchum, which was determined to be immediately north of the now four-year-old town, and in the line of its growth and expansion, on lands belonging to the Alturas Land Improvement and Manufacturing Company, an organization incorporated by the owners of the lands in the valley north of Ketchum, who having acquired lawful titles, and surveyed and platted a beautiful addition to the older town, named Rhodes Addition to Ketchum, after the president of the company, James M. Rhodes of Philadelphia, who is also president of the Philadelphia Mining and Smelting Company.

This addition consists of a tract of 1,000 acres of land, and is handsomely laid out along the steppes or benches of rising ground, receding from Wood River, the railway company's tracks, works, and buildings occupying the foreground, with all the attachments, surroundings of forwarding houses, ore-sampling mills, lumber, wood, and coal depots, etc. Six beautiful wide straight avenues, over two miles in length, named respectively Idaho, Arizona, Wyoming, Washington, Oregon, and Montana, extend along the valley north from Ketchum, intersected by cross streets numbered to twenty-six, so far as platted; the surveyed portion containing 2,000 most desirable business and residence lots, and all so arranged as to result in a charming city in the near future. It is claimed that past progress and present indications insure it being the metropolis of Wood River and central Idaho.

The managing agent for the sale of lots, Major Wm. Hyndman, is authority for the statement that they are in active demand, sales in large numbers being made, a reasonable price being fixed to encourage settlement and induce immigration.

There is no more favorable or promising point in the States and Territories of the west for founding a home. Surveys have been made for water-works, which will be constructed early next season, an abundant supply of clear mountain-spring water having been secured from Lake Creek, two miles north, to furnish water for irrigating and manufacturing purposes and domestic use; a line of pipes being also contemplated to the hot springs to carry hot water for household use, bathing, etc. Building material of every kind abounds in the immediate vicinity, excellent stone, and first-class clay for brick manufacture; while Ketchum is the lumber depot of Wood River and central Idaho, being at the very door of the vast timber region. No less than six large saw-mills, with planing, shingle, and other attachments, being in operation at full capacity constantly.

In view of all the facts, the astounding mineral future foreshadowed, the hitherto phenomenal growth and progress, and the wonderful facilities for the pursuit of almost every vocation and line of business; there is no more promising point in America to-day to cast your lot in than the immediate vicinity of Ketchum. It can be reached by the Union Pacific Railway system direct, on standard-gauge trains.

The man of family, or the single person, casting about for a change of residence and a start in life, can do no better than strike with all his effects and responsibilities for Ketchum, Idaho.

The **Smoky Districts** are about twenty-five miles west of Ketchum. The ledges are large veins of low-grade galena ore, carrying from twenty to fifty ounces silver, and thirty to fifty per cent lead. The Smoky Bullion Consolidated Mining Company, a New York corporation, are the owners of a group consisting of the Providence, Smoky Bullion, Ophir, Blake, and Wallace. They have erected one of the largest and most complete concentrating mills in the Territory. The machinery is the most massive in use and embodies all the latest improvements.

The Smoky Bullion and Ophir mines yield fine bodies of high-grade ore, containing lead, silver, and gold. The Forest, Chance, Buckeye, Fisher, and Little Smoky are owned by the Huntington Company of Pennsylvania. The Fourth of July yields both gold and silver. The Isabella, owned by James McFadden, is probably one of the finest in the district. Several tons of its ore yielded several thousand dollars. The ore of the Carrie Leonard samples 187 ounces silver per ton. There is a regular defined vein, ranging from two to four feet in width.

The Silver Star and Salamander were sold about a year ago to the Philadelphia company for $50,000. There are numerous other locations, such as King of the West, Winterest, and Galore, all more or less developed.

The **Galena District** embraces the region about upper Wood River, with the town of Galena as its distributing point. The chief group of mines is the Senate group, owned by the Senate Mining and Smelting Company. The Senate, Red Cloud, Chief, None Such, and Kid mines constitute this group, and are all rich and permanent-looking prospects. A thirty-ton smelter has been built by the company near the property. The President, Delta, and Conway Castle mines are owned by the Conway Castle Mining Company of New York. The Conway Castle mine is a five-foot vein. Assays have been made of the gangue, which show fifty per cent lead and as high as 350 ounces in silver.

The Dresden mine has a cropping of white lime which is traceable for 2,000 feet, and so far wherever this cap is removed the galena appears. The ore averages about 140 ounces silver per ton.

Across the divide from Wood River are the Sawtooth mines, which are frequently included in the Wood River section, though of essentially different character. They are fissure veins in granite, carrying black sulphurets, ruby and antimonial silver being free milling but requiring roasting. A ten-stamp mill dry crusher has been erected near the Columbia mine, owned by Courtwright & Co. of New York. A twenty-stamp mill has been erected at a cost of $250,000 near Vienna, by the Vienna Company, of which Mr. Chris. Johnston is superintendent.

The district is divided into three principal cañons or gulches, known as Lake, Beaver, and Smiley gulches. In the first named is situated the Atlanta mine, showing a strong vein from four to six feet in width, yielding fine rich ore. A quantity of ore was extracted from the Lucky Boy running as high as $5,000 per ton.

In Beaver Gulch, where the town of Sawtooth is situated, one of the earliest discovered was the Pilgrim mine, which was located in 1879 by four immigrants from Nebraska, and sold the same season for $30,000. The vein is from ten to twenty-five feet wide. The ore is sulphurets and ruby silver. The Bidwell and Beaver extension mines have produced several tons of ore assaying from $500 to $2,000 per ton. Fifteen tons of ore from the Silver King yielded $500 per ton. In Smiley Cañon are located the five claims known as the Nellie group. A rich stratum of ore in the Nellie assayed from $70 to $3,000 per ton.

The Mountain King mine has been compared to the great Custer mine of Yankee Fork in general formation and character. The vein projects above the surface for from two to seven feet. In places the vein widens to sixteen feet, five feet of which is ruby sulphuret ore and gold. A shipment of 100 tons yielded $240 per ton. The Solace mine is high-grade ore. Thirty tons were sold, realizing $10,000. The Vienna is a vein two to seven feet wide, containing streaks worth $2,000 per ton. The town of Vienna is the supply point for this section.

The Little Wood River district is about twenty miles east of Hailey. The principal mines are the Muldoon group, owned by the Wood River Mining and Smelting Company. The company also operate smelting and sampling works, which are lighted by a Brush electric light. The company also own a large deposit of bog iron twelve miles distant, which is used as a flux. An ore body was struck in the Muldoon mine which showed a breast of five feet of solid galena assaying 170 ounces of silver. There are a number of other locations on which more or less work has been done.

The Blackburn District is in the north-eastern part of the county. The Tyndall lode is the oldest location. The ore is galena, carbonate, gray copper, with some chloride and ruby silver. Assays yield from 130 to 500 ounces silver. Some of the copper ore from the Ingersoll assays 1,000 ounces of silver per ton, some as high as 1,500 ounces, and much of the steel galena carries over 300 ounces silver per ton.

Rocky Bar.—This district is one of the oldest in the Territory. The Idaho, Vishnu, and the Ada Ellinore have been most productive. The Vishnu and Ellinore have each yielded over $1,000,000 in gold. Fifteen miles north of Rocky Bar, on the middle Boisé, is

Atlanta.—The Atlanta Mining District was discovered in 1864 by parties of the great wave of placer miners sweeping over Idaho from the north, coming from Florence and other places in that direction. The great Atlanta ledge was located that year from discoveries on what is now the Buffalo and the Atlanta mines. These discoveries (which were named from the battle of Atlanta) gave the mining district and the town their name of Atlanta. The Atlanta ledge, which is an immense fissure, not less than fifty feet wide in any place yet seen, with bold croppings for a distance of not less than three miles, runs diagonally across Atlanta hill, which rises 1,500 feet above the town. The town is situated in a very pleasant valley on the middle Boisé River, eighty-five miles above Boisé City, and about eighty miles from Mountain Home station on the Oregon Short Line Railroad. The only wagon road at present runs to the latter place and crosses a high range of mountains. Steps are now being taken to build a wagon road directly down the Boisé River to Boisé City, which can be made on a good grade, and is the only natural outlet for the camp. This road will add greatly to the prosperity of the camp, as it could be used both winter and summer, while the present road to Mountain Home cannot.

The principal mines of the camp are the Atlanta, the Buffalo, the Tahoma, the Last Chance, the Jessie Benton, and the Big Lode. The Atlanta and the Buffalo are adjoining mines on the Atlanta ledge, and have been worked the most extensively, and so far have proved the richest in the district. Both mines have steam hoisting works, and working shafts down 500 feet. There has been taken from the Atlanta mine up to date about $1,200,000 worth of high-grade ore, as follows: about 700 tons averaging $800 per ton, and about 5,000 tons averaging $125 per ton. Large amounts of lower-grade ore have been left standing in the mine, owing to a lack of cheap methods of milling. The Atlanta Company has now about completed a new dry-crushing silver-mill of fifteen tons capacity per day.

The Buffalo mine has produced a large amount of ore similar to the Atlanta, and has a ten-stamp dry-crushing silver-mill which has been in operation for the past six years.

The Tahoma mine is proving itself to be among the best ore-producers in the camp, having started up a new ten-stamp wet-crushing silver-mill last spring, which has been running continuously since, crushing about eighteen tons of ore per day. These three mines are the only ones operating continuously at present; but the Last Chance (owned by the Atlanta Hill Company), the Big Lode, and the Jessie Benton have produced very rich ores, and are likely to prove valuable properties. The Last Chance Company have commenced the erection of steam hoisting works, and have a working shaft down 150 feet.

The formation of the district is granite, and the ore principally ruby and native silver, with sulphurets carrying a large per cent of gold.

The present prospects of the camp are very bright indeed.

Camas Prairie, already mentioned, is not to be confounded with the prairie of the same name in Idaho County. It is about twenty miles west of Bellevue and Hailey. It is about thirty miles long and half as wide, and has been termed the "cream of the land of Camas Valley." Along its southern portion runs Camas Creek, a tributary of Wood River. The whole prairie is magnificently watered, and in season covered with a luxuriant growth of grass, making it a paradise for stock. The soil is a rich black loam about twenty inches in depth. Irrigation is said to be unnecessary, for the reason that there is a heavy clay subsoil which holds water and moisture. The resources of Camas Prairie have been thus described: "The numerous creeks which are flowing through the valley keep the clay soil wet, so that however dry the top soil may look, you will always find plenty of moisture within a few inches of the surface. In demonstration of this fact we have only to say that water in endless quantities can be found almost anywhere on the prairie, at a depth of from two to eight feet below the surface. Many settlers have wells with sufficient water for all stock at that depth. This condition of soil renders the lands of this prairie very productive. Immense crops of oats, wheat, barley, and all small grain, and all kinds of vegetables and fruits, can be grown easily and to great profit. The natural grasses yield wonderful crops of hay; and tame grasses, wherever tried, flourish amazingly. Timothy, alfalfa, and clover have been sown, and have proved to be big croppers and very hardy in growth. We know of fields of timothy which were sown on sod, that yielded two to three tons per acre; tame grasses and all fine small grain find their natural elements here, and consequently yield enormously. Squire Abbott, one of the residents of Camas Prairie, sowed one pound of wheat, which he received from the East, and on harvesting and cleaning up, realized *one hundred pounds* of nice, clean wheat. Barley sown on sod this year produced from fifty to sixty-five bushels to the acre, *without any irrigation*. Potatoes planted in the same way, without irrigation, produced from one hundred and fifty to two hundred and fifty bushels to the acre. All kinds of garden vegetables, such as beets, turnips, pease, beans, onions, cabbages, etc., are successfully and very profitably cultivated; the crop is monster, the quality 'par excellence,' and the market for all that is not needed for home consumption is sure and at paying prices. In fact, the soil of Camas Prairie cannot be excelled in any State or Territory in the Union.

"Timber.—The mountains in the north are covered with a heavy growth of pine timber, thus giving plenty of wood for fuel and lumbering purposes. Two or three saw-mills are here, from which good building and fencing lumber can be obtained for from $20 to $40 per 1,000 feet. This is another inducement for settlers to come and locate here, as fuel is so handy and cheap. In the hills surrounding the prairie are found the choice grazing lands of the country, where stock find good living and keep fat all the year round. Cattle, sheep, and horses require but little prepared feed here, and scarcely any shelter, the bunch-grass of the hills affording splendid feed all through the year. There can be no doubt that this valley will prove a wonderful agricultural belt, and that it is the spot for all new-comers in search of a pleasant home or ranch to put their stake. No more fertile or productive lands can be found in Idaho, where such a diversity of crops can be raised with so little labor and expense.

"To all in search of a place to make a new home, and who contemplate locating lands, we say, Come to this section of Idaho and take an observation of Camas Prairie and its wonderful resources. Here a poor man can, with little means, but with plenty of spirit and 'go-aheadativeness,' soon surround himself with all the comforts of life."

Several settlements have sprung up on Camas Prairie within the past two years.

The first house in Soldier City was built about the 24th of June, 1884. This town is situated about in the center of the prairie, is distant about 30 miles from the Wood River mines, 18 miles south of the Little Smoky Mining District, and 45 miles north of Shoshone. There is a fine market, and a good outlet for anything that can be raised. Lumber sells for $20 per 1,000 feet; shingles, $3.50 per 1,000; fence-posts, 8 cents apiece; wood, $4 per cord.

A Good Place to Grow up in.—Alturas County offers opportunities to the capitalist, to the agriculturist, to the miner, to the business man—briefly, to all classes of people. The region is young, hardly touched, filling up rapidly with the very hardiest and most enterprising people, and the opportunities for all are such as cannot be equaled anywhere. To the *rustling, energetic* young man in search of a location where he may "grow up with the country," we most emphatically and confidently say: "Come to Alturas County, Idaho." It matters not what you can do, what profession or vocation you may follow, you will do well if you are determined to succeed.

BEAR LAKE COUNTY.

Bear Lake County was organized January 5, 1875. Estimated number of acres of land under cultivation, 9,000. The cereals that return the largest profits are wheat and oats, although barley is grown at a fair profit in some localities. Rye is also grown in limited quantities, but is not very profitable, owing to the slow demand. The average number of bushels of cereals and vegetables to the acre are as follows: wheat, 25; oats, 40; rye, 40; barley, 30; potatoes, 75.

The average weight of measured bushels of the various products is as follows: wheat, 60 pounds; oats, 37 pounds; barley, 50. Rye is not grown in any locality as an industry. The number of pounds of flour usually made from a bushel of wheat is 36.

This valley is not adapted to the growth of fruit trees, except the hardy kinds of apples and plums. Many of our settlers are sanguine of success in the growth of fruit; but at present very little has been done by way of experiment. The hard winters are not so fatal to our fruit trees as is the action of the sun and snow in the spring, which tends to scorch the bark and injure the tree when the sap is running up. Some fair apples are raised nevertheless. Berries do well, and yield abundantly; strawberries grow very prolifically and yield a large profit to the growers; raspberries are a prolific growth also, and yield large profits; gooseberries grow thriftily, and are well adapted to this climate; currants do well, and the English varieties yield abundantly; the kind known as "native currants" are a remarkable variety, and grow to an enormous size, and are very hardy and prolific. Some have been measured and found to be two and a half inches in circumference. In some localities vines thrive and do well, especially where they are protected by the cañon breezes and adjacent mountains from early frosts.

The estimated number of acres of arable land not under cultivation is 10,000.

The industrious home-seeker can find a good selection of land to establish a home, and every comfort usually found in the valleys of the West.

The estimated quantity of wild hay land is 20,000 acres. The estimated quantity of cultivated hay land is 500 acres. The number of tons of wild hay usually harvested to the acre is one and one half tons. The number of tons of tame hay usually harvested to the acre is, red-top, 2 tons; timothy, 2 to 3 tons; alfalfa, 3 to 5 tons. The kinds of grasses that thrive and mature best are, lucern (alfalfa), timothy, and red-top; lucerne is a very profitable crop; it is cut in some localities as often as three times in the season.

The grazing land cannot be even estimated in acres. The ranges for hundreds of square miles are covered with a luxuriant growth of bunch-grass. Cattle and horses thrive and fatten, and horses are kept in good condition summer and winter on the range. The number of cattle, horses, and sheep that our ranges would sustain annually are estimated as follows: cattle, 50,000; horses, 1,000; sheep, 50,000.

The profits stock-growers realize are enormous; it is one of the chief industries, and surpasses nearly all the pursuits of the husbandman. The present high price of cattle tends to make this industry still more lucrative. Cattle usually return 25 per cent per annum on the money invested. Horses are very profitable, as it costs but little to raise them. Sheep are a good investment, and yield enormous profits in wool and mutton to the grower. The climate is mild and salubrious in the summer; the spring and fall seasons are short; the winter is generally severe, although some winters are very moderate and even mild. The severe weather usually sets in about the first of December, and winter usually breaks up about the latter end of March or beginning of April; some winters last till May, but this is exceptional.

We have no forest timber in the valleys; our mountain sides and ravines are covered with a thick growth of pine, balsam, aspen, mahogany, and cedar. The pines are red, white, yellow, and pinion. The cedars are chiefly white. The mahogany is properly mountain-box. The pines furnish us an excellent article of lumber; the balsams are manufactured into a fine article of shingles; the aspen (quaking asp) and mahogany make excellent fuel, and also the cedars—the latter are also used in manufacturing furniture.

The mineral resources of the county are not as yet developed. We have no mines that pay to work, although galena, copper, iron, and silver-bearing lodes have been discovered. The ores are low grade, and owing to high transportation cannot be profitably extracted. A short distance from Montpelier is located a good salt spring, from which is manufactured a good quality of table-salt. Lime is manufactured in quantities for home consumption. Building stone is found of a fine quality, and especially on the east side of Bear Lake, where a fine quality of red sandstone exists, and is a handsome as well as a durable building stone.

There are two flour-mills in the county. There are fourteen school-houses in the county. There are fifteen churches; fourteen Mormon and one Presbyterian.

Paris is the county seat. The population of the county is as follows:

Paris	1,000	Preston	50
Montpelier	400	Cottonwood	125
Bloomington	450	Nouna	50
Bennington	211	St. Charles	456
Georgetown	120	Fish Haven	130
Ovid	125	Ranches, etc	300
Liberty	125		
Total population of county			3,512

There are in the county the following stores and manufacturing establishments: Twelve general stores, two book stores, two drug stores, one saloon and billiard hall, one boot and shoe factory, one tailoring establishment, one tinner, three harness shops, three steam saw-mills, ten wagon and blacksmith shops, five water-power saw-mills, three shingle mills, three lath mills, three planing mills, one wood-turning establishment, three millinery establishments, one brick yard, one tannery, six dairies, six cheese factories, one watchmaker and jeweler.

Bear Lake County is bounded on the north and west by Oneida County; on the east by Uintah County, Wyoming, and on the south by Rich County, Utah. Its area is 2,000 square miles. At the south end of the county is a beautiful body of fresh water, called Bear Lake. The lake proper is about twenty miles in length by eight miles in width. It is divided in the center by the Utah and Idaho line from east to west. It abounds in fish of various kinds. Several kinds of trout, viz., salmon trout, silver trout, speckled trout, and mountain brook trout, also mullet and white fish, as well as chub, are found in abundance. The lake is fed by several mountain streams, and these also abound in fish. It has an outlet emptying into Bear River in the north. This acts as an inlet in the spring and an outlet in the fall. The shores of the lake are sandy and gravelly, and afford a clean and easy approach. The water is shallow for a distance of about a hundred yards, when it gradually deepens, to an extent not as yet determined. The water is very clear, affording a view of the bottom at a depth of ten to fifteen feet. It is a splendid bathing resort, and the inhabitants living on its shores delight in this exercise, as well as others who visit the lake in the summer from distant localities. No doubt can exist in the mind of any one who has visited this beautiful lake, but in the near future this will be a favorite summer resort for the tourist and pleasure-seeker, and good hotels and accommodations will be provided and the lake decked with sails. The hunting as well as fishing facilities cannot be surpassed. Deer, bear, and elk abound within a short distance of the lake, while in the immediate vicinity can be found pheasants, prairie chickens, sage hens, rabbits, hares, and several varieties of small game. Geese, ducks, pelicans, shypokes, gulls, swans, and nearly all kinds of aquatic birds incidental to the North American region, are to be found here in abundance. The west and south side of the lake is fringed with timber of the cottonwood species; the north and east side is sparsely bordered by willows and a few scattering trees. The lake forms a complete basin, as the hills approach it on three sides. Good wagon roads encircle it, and a pleasant drive can be had along its shores. It freezes over about January, and continues a vast body of ice till April. Wagon or rather sleigh roads cross it in various directions, and it forms an easy means of transportation for winter freights. The Oregon Short Line Railway traverses the county on the east side, and Montpelier promises to be a town of no mean proportions. Paris is connected with Montpelier by telephone. This line is owned and operated by Woolley Bros., of Paris, who have large mercantile interests in Paris and Montpelier. A project is on foot to connect all the settlements by telephone. Paris has also an office of the Deseret Telegraph Company, a line running from there to Franklin, Oneida County, across the mountains west of Paris.

Paris is the center of the county, or nearly so. It is divided into two wards, and has a good share of the business of the county. A good and substantial brick court-house has been lately built here, and a term of the District Court is held here every six months.

The altitude of Bear Lake County is 5,900 feet above sea-level, and is one of if not *the* highest cultivated valleys in America. Irrigation is the only means of producing fertility. The rains during the year fall chiefly in spring and fall. For the purpose of irrigating the land, large and expensive canals and ditches are constructed, which convey the waters of the mountain streams to the benches and lands under cultivation. A very little dry farming is carried on, but it is a very scanty and precarious means of obtaining a livelihood.

The system of co-operation is carried on in the principal towns, and co-operative stores and manufactures are a source of employment and remuneration. The system of establishing and carrying on the mercantile business and the various manufacturing industries, such as cheese-making, dairy farming, boot, shoe, and harness making, etc., etc., has been demonstrated a success, and the little space afforded here is insufficient to describe its merits. The Paris co-operative institution may well be called the parent institution of the county, as it has branched out in nearly every industry, and forms a means of employment to a great many artisans and laborers.

BOISÉ COUNTY

Is one of the original counties of the Territory. It is situated north-west of Ada, which formerly formed a portion of Boisé. It has an area of 3,300 square miles, and has been known in mining history chiefly for its placers.

The history of the discovery of Boisé Basin, and of its productions, will be found in the chapter on mining. The basin is about thirty miles long, with an average width of fifteen miles. It is surrounded by rolling hills, heavily timbered. The country rock is granite. Her placers yielded for eighteen years an average of more than a million dollars per annum, and some are still worked with profit.

As the placer grounds, however, grew gradually less paying, attention was given to quartz, and as it is claimed that the county lies wholly within the eastern and western limits of the mineral belt of the Territory, there seems no reason why her quartz mines should not produce as great a yield as any mineral section in the Territory.

Quartz Mining.—For a distance of forty miles or more, a rich mineral belt, beginning with Gold Hill, extends through the county. The Banner District lies about thirty miles north-east of Idaho City, the county seat. Most of the developments have been made since 1878.

The Elmira Company owns a group of mines, called the Banner, Crown Point, Wolverene, Idaho, Star of the West, and the Washoe. In the Banner the pay chute is over five hundred feet in length. There are two veins. The tunnel struck a vein fifteen inches wide at a distance of eight hundred and seventy-one feet; after being driven eight feet farther, it struck a second vein, which varies from six to fifteen inches in width. The first vein dips to the south, the second to the north. The ore is chloride, occasionally black sulphurets, antimonial, ruby, and native silver. The Crown Point is opened to a depth of over four hundred feet.

The following statement of assays was furnished by the assayer of the company:

							Ozs.
Crown Point, Wolverene,	} ore runs to 6,000 ounces, averaging						70
Banner,	"	"	400	"	"		40
Idaho,	"	"	400	"	"		50
Star of the West,	"	"	200	"	"		70
Washoe,	"	"	200	"	"		50

There is a fine twenty-stamp mill in connection with the works, besides a roasting furnace, and an assay office.

The Deer Lodge is a comparatively new discovery. Three assays are reported, as follows: No. 1, $210.25; No. 2, $374.50; No. 3, $1,351.98. The average of the rock, taken from wall to wall, was $312.21. Other locations in the neighborhood are Monarch, average assay, $219.12; Homestake, $230.19; Daisy, $67.54. The Comet is an extension of the Daisy, and the Northwest an extension of the Homestake.

Several locations have been made near the head waters of the Payette, close to the county line. Principal among these are King of the Forest, Summit, Julia, Mammoth, Romeo, and Benaune.

The Quartzburgh District, north of Idaho City, has been producing gold since 1867.

Three claims on the Gold Hill lode are owned by the Gold Hill Mining and Milling Company, for a distance of 2,900 feet south-west and 1,400 feet north-east of the discovery shaft. Perhaps the best description is the following from the pen of a well-known writer: "The vein carries two to three feet of easily worked decomposed sulphureted quartz, yielding from $10 to $100 per ton. Thousands of tons have been worked in the company's twenty-five-stamp mill, giving an average yield of over $30 per ton, while large runs have been made yielding from $50 to $100 per ton. The main shaft is down about 500 feet; from this six levels have been extended along the vein at intervals of about seventy-five feet. These various underground openings aggregate a length of over two miles, and have almost universally followed paying quartz. The material now being raised from the deep workings pays almost double what that did from the surface. Seventy men are employed.

"There is a vast extent of productive ground exposed in the Gold Hill mine above the 600-foot level, and the company's product is as steady as the returns of interest on our government bonds. Indeed, this success has been almost phenomenal. The mill now at work has run twelve years with only a brief stoppage for repairs. It has produced $2,650,000. It reduces the Gold Hill quartz at an expense of less than $1.25 per ton. When, occasionally, its proprietors wish to do custom-work (crush quartz for other mines), it earns $56 per day for each battery of five stamps; and yet it is that same old Cobden mill which in 1865, in the hands of New York capitalists, made a flat failure, and did much to bring Idaho into bad repute as a mining country. Its present owners, who are thorough miners and millmen, bought it in 1869, and it has paid for itself, and the mine, and all other improvements, a dozen times over. About 5,000 tons of refactory ore, worth $30 per ton, lies on the dump; this grand reserve will be held, and added to, until the incoming railroads are near enough to render the transportation of roasters, salt, etc., and the working of that grade of ore practicable. The Gold Hill enterprise is a splendid monument to the skill and nerve of the practical miners in charge, and, as an illustration of what the right men can do with the right machinery in Idaho, is the pride of every citizen."

The Gambrinus District is eight miles from Idaho City. The Forest King mine is a twenty-foot ledge, cut up with paying veins. It is gold-bearing quartz, averaging from $25 to $30 per ton. A new five-stamp mill has just been erected during the past season, making very successful runs. The Golconda is a similar formation. It also has a five-stamp mill, and the owners, Monroe & Company, intend to erect hoisting works in the spring.

The Silver Chief is also owned by Monroe & Company. The latest cleanup, taken from a depth of three hundred feet below the surface, yielded $109 per ton; one bar assayed $1,294. The fineness of the silver is .951, which is extra fine.

The Trade Dollar is a new discovery, having been located late in the fall of 1884. Its ore assays $41 gold and $55 silver.

The Mammoth mine is on Summit Flat, owned by Willson & Whitney; gold-bearing quartz, same character as Golconda. There is an eight stamp mill. A small force of men took out $60,000 during the past summer. It is an old discovery, and has always paid well. Vein averages about two feet.

The formation of all these mines is contact vein between porphyry and granite.

Placers.—The chief placer grounds at present worked in Boisé County are owned by Mr. Ben Wilson of Pioneer, who was one of the first men to introduce hydraulic mining in the basin. He now controls forty ditches, aggregating over one hundred miles in length, and covering nearly twenty miles of mining ground. He runs nine giants (one man with a giant is said to be equal to 100 men with picks and shovels for ground sluicing), two derricks, and a saw-mill, where, during the mining season, two men saw from 3,000 to 5,000 feet of lumber per day, which is all consumed in flumes, sluice-boxes, out-buildings, etc. Mr. K. P. Plowman's gravel claim is on East Hill, near Idaho City. The bank, which is nearly 100 feet high, is worked by a "Little Giant" hydraulic. This claim in 1883 averaged a yield of $2,000 per week. Messrs. Buzzini & Co.'s gravel claim is on the hillside south of Moore's Creek. The gravel bed is eighty feet deep. Their claim is about half a mile in length with a width varying from 400 to 600 feet. The ground pays handsomely, and it is said there is enough of it at the rate it has paid so far to yield nearly a million dollars.

W. B. Noble has a fine claim at the head of Grimes Creek at Grimes Pass. There are two ditches taking water from Grimes Creek, one two miles in length, the other three. There is a saw-mill in connection with the claim, which manufactures all the lumber needed. Day and night shifts are working constantly, and it has paid well for a number of years.

On Ophir Creek near Placerville is Henry Reed's hill claim. The gravel is from ten to sixty feet deep. There are two machines at work, one for washing and one for cleaning up. The water is carried from Ophir Creek through a ditch six miles long.

B. F. Channel's claim at the head of Willow Creek on the summit between Idaho City and Centreville, has paid well for several years, yielding about $10,000 a season. The water is brought through a ditch twenty-five miles long.

East of Placerville is the Granite Creek Ditch Company's claim, which yields from $15,000 to $20,000 per season. The gravel bank is from twenty-five to forty feet deep, and is worked with little giants. The Ranch Company work a large claim on Granite Creek Bar.

A company of fifty Chinamen are working a claim in the bed of Granite Creek. It has been worked for fifteen years, and yielded $25,000 a season.

In Deadwood Basin two placer mining companies are at work. The quartz ledges are but partially developed.

There is still a large amount of gold and silver in the bed of Moore's Creek awaiting the arrival of capital and enterprise. The project of a bed-rock flume has been discussed for years, but has never been put in practical operation. There is said to be an extent of six miles in Moore's Creek and one mile in Elk from its junction with Moore, that may be treated as ground that can be profitably worked through a bed-rock flume on a large scale. These seven miles will average more than 600 feet in width and twelve feet in depth of tailings, top dirt that was stripped off of bottom gravel in early days, and occasionally new ground. The lowest possible estimate of the amount of gold contained in this seven miles of creek will exceed eleven million dollars, besides what is contained in the thousands of acres of low bars and flats which skirt the creek, and cannot now be worked for want of fall or dump. In addition to this amount of gold, it is estimated safely that 100 tons of quicksilver lie so intermixed with the tailings that a company working the creek would have the advantage of at least a hundred thousand dollars' worth of this article so indispensable in the working of mines.

Timber.—Next to its mineral, Boisé County is especially rich in its magnificent timber. It is estimated by the best-informed residents of Boisé Basin, we are told, that there are at least a million acres of fine, heavy pine timber lands accessible in the water-shed of Boisé River. Besides the vast amount of merchantable lumber, there is apparently no limit to the amount of post timber. The opportunity offered to the immigrant to get his lumber and fencing cheaply is an important item. On the Payette River, in fact in nearly all sections of the country, are forests of pine and fir, clear and of the finest kind for lumbering.

Agriculture.—Notwithstanding the average high altitude of the county, farming and stock-raising are becoming important industries. Garden and Long valleys both present rare opportunities for ranching and stock-raising. Grain and cereals of all kinds are produced. The first named is about fifteen miles north of Placerville, near the Middle Fork of the Payette. Long Valley is seventy-five miles long and about fifteen wide. It is traversed longitudinally by the North Fork of the Payette. There are few settlements. The soil is rich, and offers excellent inducements to those desiring to go into the business of dairying and stock-raising.

Upper and Lower Squaw creeks and Horseshoe Bend form one continuous valley country, where grain can be raised in abundance, and where there are ranges capable of sustaining many herds of stock.

Towns.—Idaho City, the county seat, dates its existence back twenty years. Its population has been fluctuating, sometimes counted by the thousands, at others by the hundreds. Three times reduced to ashes, it has been as many times rebuilt. It now contains several stores of all kinds, a bank, a semi-weekly newspaper (the *Idaho World*), a good school, churches, Masonic and Odd Fellows lodges, and the usual accompaniments of a mining town.

Quartzburgh, Placerville, Centreville, Pioneer, and Banner are flourishing mining camps.

CASSIA COUNTY.

Cassia County is one of the southernmost counties of the Territory, lying between Owyhee and Oneida counties, and bounded on the north by Snake

River, which separates it from Alturas. The county was organized in 1879, and the county seat established at Albion, by a vote of the people, on the second Monday of June of that year, at which time, also, a set of permanent county officers was elected to take the place of the temporary officers appointed and provided for by the act organizing the county from a portion of Owyhee County, approved February 20, 1879.

The new county assumed a portion of Owyhee's debt, amounting to ten thousand dollars, seven thousand of which has been paid up to the present time, by the sinking fund provided for that purpose. In addition to this, the county has incurred a debt of about twelve thousand dollars, existing in the shape of county warrants, bearing interest at ten per cent per annum. The finances of the county have been extremely well managed, and the credit of the county is on a firm basis, county scrip being worth eighty-five to ninety cents on the dollar.

At the time of its organization, the county contained a population of about one thousand. There was a small settlement in Marsh Basin, a few families on Cassia Creek and Raft River, four or five houses on lower Goose Creek, and as many at Oakley, on upper Goose Creek, a small settlement on Rock Creek, and one on Dry Creek, and quite a number of miners along Snake River, at Salmon Falls, Shoshone Falls, and Bonanza Bar. In five years the population has increased to over three thousand; the assessed valuation has increased from $199,409 in 1879 to $597,171 in 1884; and every interest of the county has flourished.

The area of the county is 5,100 square miles. Of this at least one half is good stock-range, which is capable of supporting well twice the amount of stock that it now supports. Of the remaining one half, the larger portion is high mountains, where horses range to a considerable extent. A small portion, about 50,000 acres, is under fence; and about 10,000 acres of this is under cultivation, the remainder being hay and pasture lands.

The county is essentially a stock-growing county, and as such ranks among the first in the Territory. There are some fine agricultural districts, however, and for the production of grain and some kinds of vegetables no part of the country can surpass it.

The topography of the county is varied, rising gradually from Snake River south to the Utah line, where it becomes very rough and mountainous. Numerous spurs shoot out from this region toward Snake River, dividing the county into numerous valleys of greater or less extent, widening toward the north, and opening out into the broad valley of Snake River. Raft River Valley, occupying the eastern portion of the county, and extending north and south entirely through it, is for the most part a grazing country. It has an average width of from ten to twelve miles, and although a considerable portion of it is worthless for agricultural purposes—and apparently for any purpose—the stunted growth of white and yellow sage, which gives it so much the appearance of an absolute desert, makes it one of the finest winter ranges in the Territory. There is a narrow strip of land along the river, however, varying from one to three miles in width, consisting of good agricultural and natural hay land. There is plenty of water, and some good land yet unoccupied. There are four or five hay-ranches under fence, consisting of from 500 to 5,000 acres each, and the foot-hills on either side of the valley afford extensive summer ranges for stock. Sublette Creek, coming in from the east, waters a fine little valley about three fourths of a mile in width, and five or six miles in length, where fine crops of grain are produced.

That part of Raft River Valley known as Lower Cassia Creek, which takes its name from a stream that comes into Raft River from the west, is fast being settled for farming purposes. Grain has been produced abundantly there during the past season. At the head of Cassia Creek, about ten miles southwest of where it empties into Raft River, is the largest settlement in the valley. Looking down upon this settlement from the south stands Independence Mountain, the highest point in this region, being 10,000 feet above the sea. About five miles down the valley, on Connor Creek, is pointed out the spot where General Connor had his famous battle with the Bannocks and Shoshones in 1864. On the opposite side of Independence Mountain, on the head waters of Raft River, in the vicinity of what is known as the Cove, and about three miles north of the City of Rocks, are the remains of rifle-pits and earth-works, of some rods in extent, to mark the place where a whole train of emigrants were massacred by Pocatello and his warlike followers in 1862. Here is a broad valley or basin, just above the Raft River Cañon, and near the Utah line, which contains about thirty settlers, who raise good crops of grain and grass, and whose cattle, horses, and sheep grow fat on the surrounding ranges, and bring wealth and plenty to the settlers.

About ten miles north-west from Independence Mountain, and about fifteen miles from Snake River, is Cloud Mountain, about 9,000 feet above the sea, looking down to the north upon Marsh Basin and Albion, the county seat. Diverging from this mountain are two low ridges or spurs, extending one to the north-east and one to the north-west, inclosing Marsh Basin, and almost coming together again six miles to the north, leaving only a narrow gorge, through which the basin is drained into Marsh Lake, and thence through Cañon Creek into Snake River. Marsh Basin is a circular valley, about six miles in diameter. There are about 2,000 acres under cultivation in the valley, which give excellent returns in grain, hay, and vegetables; while the surrounding ranges support a few head of horses and cattle belonging to the settlers.

Passing over a low ridge to the west, we come to Goose Creek Valley, which extends north and south from Snake River to the Utah line. This is the most extensive valley in the county, and one of the finest in the Territory. There are now over 3,000 acres under cultivation, and with the water that is in Goose Creek it is thought that 10,000 acres can be cultivated. The valley is about five miles in width at its southern extremity, and widens quite rapidly toward the north, until it opens out into Snake River Valley. Extending from Snake River up Goose Creek is a body of over 200,000 acres of the finest land, that only requires water to make it one of the best agricultural districts in the Territory. Several attempts have been made to organize a company to take out the waters of Snake River for the purpose of irrigating this tract, but as yet no practical results have followed.

Extending away to the west, for forty miles down Snake River, is a low, undulating country, through which extend the narrow valleys of Dry Creek, on which are three or four hay-ranches; and Rock Creek, which is occupied by a few settlers who raise good crops of hay and grain. For fifty or sixty miles farther to the west the country is rough and broken, until you reach Salmon River, in the extreme western part of the county, which affords some good hay land, and is the headquarters of some extensive stock-growers. The larger portion of the western half of the county is rough and broken, and contains no agricultural land to speak of, but affords extensive and valuable stock-ranges.

Climate.—Our climate in the winter is cold and changeable. The amount of snow-fall in the valleys is not very extensive, but immense quantities are accumulated in the mountains, which afford vast stores of moisture for the growing crops when the hot days of summer come. We have a great deal of rain in the valleys during the winter season, or from about the 1st of November to the middle of April. During the remainder of the year rain seldom falls, except occasionally a shower or two about the 1st of July. Consequently no crops ordinarily can be raised without irrigation, although during the past season there have been exceptions to the rule. Our climate is remarkably healthful.

Schools.—Our school system has been much neglected, perhaps necessarily so, from the newness of the country and the scattered condition of our population; but under the county superintendency system the condition of our schools has been much improved. The school tax has been much increased, and a growing interest is being manifested by the people. A move has been made to establish a good school at Albion, and it is hoped we shall soon have a school that will be a credit to the county. The county is divided into twenty school districts, and each settlement has a school within a reasonable distance.

Mills.—There is at present but one flouring-mill in the county, but another is in course of construction, and will be in operation before spring.

There are three or four saw-mills located at different points throughout the county, which furnish a fair quality of lumber.

Timber.—Black and red pine and balsam fir are the principal kinds of timber from which lumber is made. Good sawing timber, however, is getting scarce, although there is plenty of an inferior quality to furnish the county with rough lumber for a long time to come. The supply for fuel is inexhaustible. Cedar grows abundantly on the low mountains, and there are large bodies of pine of small growth farther up on the mountains and in the cañons. There is some mountain mahogany, and nut or pinion pine, both of which make a very superior quality of fuel.

Grain.—There were about 10,000 acres of grain raised in the county this season (1884). Wheat averaged 35 bushels, oats 55, and barley 40 bushels to the acre. This was over an average year, however, and the general average would be about 30 bushels of wheat, 45 of oats, and 30 of barley. As high as 120 bushels of oats and 72 bushels of wheat to the acre have been raised this season.

Wheat weighs 60 to 65 pounds to the bushel, and oats and barley are proportionally heavy. The production of flour is about 40 pounds to the bushel of wheat.

Timothy.—As a hay-producing country this has few equals. Timothy especially produces almost beyond reason. I have seen heads of timothy eleven and twelve inches in length, and whole fields of it with heads six to eight inches long. It produces, when well watered, three to four and one half tons of hay to the acre.

Alfalfa.—As a hay-producing plant, alfalfa, or lucerne, or French clover, as it is often called, is even more productive than timothy. Two crops are taken from the same ground during the season, averaging from two and a half to three tons each to the acre. When once well established, it will produce a fair crop with very little or no irrigation.

Vegetables.—Most vegetables do well here, but for vines the seasons are generally too short, although in some localities fine melons and squashes are raised. In Goose Creek Valley tomatoes are raised without difficulty, and some corn is grown. Potatoes, cabbage, and all kinds of root crops do well; potatoes especially, both in quality and quantity, are excellent. Three to five hundred bushels to the acre have been produced on virgin soil without manure. A number have been exhibited this season from various parts of the county weighing from six to ten pounds apiece.

Fruit.—All kinds of small fruit produce abundantly. Currants of a wild variety when cultivated grow literally as large as gooseberries, and gooseberries as large in proportion. The growth of these kinds of fruit is something remarkable. Strawberries and raspberries flourish and produce an excellent quality of fruit. Apples, pears, etc., have not been tried sufficiently to judge of their production. Some trees have been planted during the last two years, and there are also one or two orchards that are bearing slightly. The fruit is fair and free from worms. The trees that have been planted make a vigorous growth, and look healthy and thrifty. It is believed that cherries and plums will thrive, but our winters are most too severe for peaches.

Stock.—There are in the county about 50,000 head of range cattle, 5,000 head of horses, 50,000 head of sheep, and 800 head of Angora goats. The latter were lately brought in from Nevada by J. S. Harris, who is an original importer from Asia.

Some pains are being taken to improve our native stock. Frank Gwin has imported a number of Spanish and French merino bucks for his herd, and other parties have gone to some expense to improve the quality of their wool. James Pierce has brought in a number of Hereford bulls and cows from Illinois. Keogh Bros. use short-horn bulls in their herds, and have some very good grade cows. Col. R. L. Wood has introduced a fine Maltese jack, and J. E. Harroun, E. A. Jordan, and S. J. Nutt have some fine stallions of the Hambletonian and Norman breeds.

Mines.—There is a mineral belt extending through the southern part of the county, which bids fair to develop some good mines. There are a number of prospects, some of which are considered valuable, although none of them have been thoroughly developed, and there are no paying quartz mines in the county. The Vipont mine, situated twenty miles north-west of the City of Rocks, was sold a year ago for $10,000. On the east slope of

Independence Mountain are the Corinne and the Hawkins, from which are shown some very good specimens, assaying $150. They have not been thoroughly prospected, but the Corinne mine was recently bonded for $20,000. Near the eastern border of the county, in the Black Pine Mountains, is a mine from which has been taken some very rich ore of ruby silver; and a quartz mill costing $25,000 has been erected there. As yet, no considerable body of the ore has been struck, although several shafts have been sunk, and a 700-foot tunnel run.

Marble.—Marble also, of good quality, has been found to exist in this region, about twelve miles north-west of the City of Rocks. Another ledge, of superior quality, has been discovered in the north-eastern part of the county, near Fall Creek.

Mica.—At the City of Rocks, in what is known as "The Circle," is a mica prospect, which is thought to be valuable. Sheets a foot in extent are obtained, which show a quality of mica which may prove to be of commercial value. It is tough and transparent, but with a slight tinge of brown, however.

Placer Mines.—The Snake River placer mines have for a number of years been the subject of a great deal of attention. All the richest deposits, however, have been worked out, and the problem now is how to save the fine gold, together with the valuable ingredients of the "black sand," which are found almost universally in the gravel banks along Snake River.

A large amount of money has been expended in experimenting, but no process for saving all the gold, that is practicable and cheap, has yet been discovered. The Midas Company has erected on its property, twenty-five miles from Albion, machinery that cost $60,000, by means of which it is claimed all of the gold and the black sand are saved, but the expense of running it is too great to warrant a continuance. Other parties have experimented with similar results. What is known as the "blanket process" is now considered the best. By running the gravel over common burlap sacking, through variously contrived sluices and boxes, most of the gold is saved, and at little expense. A number of bars are being worked in the county by this process, with good results. The amount saved per day to the man varies from three to fifteen dollars. The following description of coal prospects in the county was kindly furnished by Mr. C. D. King:

These mines are situated in Cassia County, Idaho, 16 miles south of Oakley, on the west side of Goose Creek. The principal bed has an elevation of 5,000 feet above the sea, and 250 feet above Goose Creek Valley.

The carboniferous formation extends over an area of perhaps 20 miles square; the principal outcropping besides those of the main beds on Goose Creek are to be found on Trapper Creek and on Grouse Creek, where a limited amount of fine coking coal has been found.

The coal of the beds on Goose Creek is pronounced by experienced geologists to be a brown lignite, and similar to the famous German brown coal. It is of an excellent quality for heating, steam, and gas purposes. The beds, ten in number, vary in thickness from 3½ feet to 18 feet, and lie in two distinct series, with 75 or 100 feet of sandstone between. All the parting between the various veins is of sandstone, and rather hard, requiring no timbering in working. One of the beds, and one upon which the greatest amount of work has been done, is 18 feet in thickness, with one small parting, showing a face of solid coal 14 feet in thickness. Access to the region is easy from two main lines of railway, viz., the Central Pacific Railroad, and the Oregon Short Line Railroad. From the former the route is up Grouse Creek, and across a low pass in the Goose Creek Mountains, and from the latter across the Snake River plains and up Goose Creek Valley.

The history of the mines dates back to June, 1879, when a party of cowboys hunting stock came upon pieces of float-coal, and upon further search they found a bed of coal that burned readily at the surface. Shortly afterwards, they, with other parties, located the ground and commenced prospecting and mining operations. Improvements so far made consist in tunnels, or drifts, run in the principal beds, and short, open cuts, and facing up of the others. I am informed that the company holding these mines intend shortly to commence mining and prospecting on a much larger scale than heretofore; and as the working of the beds will be of the least difficult kind, viz., tunneling (the slope of the beds being such that no hoisting or pumping apparatus will be required), they hope to be able to show up a fine body of coal at a comparatively small outlay.

The rapid progress of Cassia County in wealth and population proves that it presents many inducements to the settler. Fortunes have been accumulated in the stock business in a few years, and until recently, since the advent of the Oregon Short Line Railroad, grain has brought good returns. There is no railroad in the county, but the prospect is good for a railroad in the course of two or three years. With the development of our mines, and the increase of our agricultural and stock interests, Cassia County is coming to the front; and it is hoped in the near future she will be one of the first counties of a new and prosperous State.

CUSTER COUNTY.

General History and Description.—Among all the inducements held forth to settlers and capitalists by Idaho, their promises are nowhere more fair and their realization more perfect than in Custer County. Its beautiful scenery, its enterprising people, its varied resources, and its brilliant prospects not inaptly commemorate the name of General Custer, whose dashing, romantic, yet productive career has become a part of our national history. The mushroom growth of the West is world-renowned, and Custer County is a conspicuous illustration. Twenty-five years ago, when placer mining was in its prime and quartz mining in its infancy, the territory now embraced in its confines was known only to Indians and an occasional party of prospectors traveling to or from Montana. To them a wilderness, to the makers of maps it was "unexplored." During a few years subsequent to 1862, placers were actively worked in Stanley Basin, on what is now its western border; and in 1869 a few venturesome men found rich ground on Loon Creek, nearly north of Stanley Basin. For three years a town built thereon flourished with a rough population of four hundred to fifteen hundred men, and then its life departed as suddenly as it came. In 1870 other placers were discovered and yielded handsome returns, but until quartz claimed attention, five years later, the region now forming Custer County was practically unknown. From 1875 to 1879, the fame of its rich mines spread abroad—attracting capitalists and increasing its population—until the following year, by legislative enactment, Custer County was created; and for four years it has thrived in all respects, with a life distinctly its own. Embracing in irregular outline about 5,000 square miles, it is as large as the State of Connecticut, and larger than Delaware and Rhode Island together; situated in central Idaho, it is within easy reach of two railroads, the Utah and Northern branch of the Union Pacific on the south-east; and the Oregon Short Line, Wood River branch, on the south-west; and possessing the elements essential to local support of a railroad, it is but a question of time—a year or two—when our "modern civilizer" will traverse its entire length. The resources of Custer County are found in its mines and its agricultural and grazing lands. The following statement of facts easily verified will furnish the best testimony to the inducements offered:

Mining.—In some States and Territories mining and agriculture, though progressing hand in hand, are yet nearly independent of each other. The farmer's market is widened by the miner, to be sure; but not relying on home consumption exclusively, he can exist and prosper, although the pick and shovel of the miner are silent. Particularly is this true in California, with its railroads, its steamships, its Eastern and foreign marts; but the farmer of Custer County is dependent upon home demands, which are great or small according to the activity of its mining industry. The prosperity of agriculture, then, bears at present a pointed relation to the prosperity of mining in this county. They must rise or fall together. Hence, mining demands the attention of not alone the capitalist, but the farmer, the merchant and the professional man as well. Keeping its importance in view, the following history of mining—present, past, and prospective—together with statistics relating thereto, is given as fully as space will allow:

Placers.—Beginning with the discoveries in Stanley Basin in 1862, it is found they were actively worked for ten years, producing, according to reliable estimates, $500,000 in that time; since then a few men have worked there a few months yearly, producing about $100,000 more. To show the richness of this ground, it may be stated that in early days one man with a "rocker" took out as much as $900 in one day. Loon Creek, before mentioned, produced $600,000 in three years. Placers on Yankee Fork were first successfully worked in 1870, and a few men, in brief yearly seasons since, have produced at least $150,000.

Quartz.—The existence of so much gold in the beds of the creeks led to the reasonable theory that nature was somewhere hiding away huge ledges of mineral wealth, from which the waters had washed away but the outcropping quartz. As usual, the placers in those regions stimulated the energy of prospectors for quartz. In both Stanley Basin and Loon Creek gold quartz claims, rich on the surface, have in recent years been discovered, but still await development. From one claim on Loon Creek ten tons of free gold ore were last year crushed at Custer Mill, yielding $120 per ton. On Yankee Fork, in 1875, the Charles Dickens was discovered; in 1876 and 1877 the Custer, Unknown, Montana, and other famous mines were found. About this time, the Rainshorn and other claims were located in Bay Horse district, followed up by discoveries at Clayton, East Fork, and Squaw Creek; and last year important mines were found on Lost River. At present there are about 2,000 mining locations in Custer County, divided in six prominent districts, viz., Lost River, on the stage road from Blackfoot to Challis, about fifty miles south of the latter; Yankee Fork, thirty-five miles west of Challis; Bay Horse, twelve miles up Salmon River, south-west of Challis; Kinnikinik, sixteen miles south of Bay Horse, on Salmon River; Squaw Creek, four miles farther south; and East Fork, thirty-five miles up the stream of the same name.

Yankee Fork District.—The group of mines on Custer Mountain, collectively known to the mining world as the Custer Mine, has been by far the largest bullion producer in Custer County. Considerable litigation hung over two mines of this group—the Custer and Unknown—soon after their discovery, and beyond shipping about 320 tons of ore for reduction elsewhere, valued at $160,000, there was no work of importance done until 1879, when their development was begun by the present owners. In addition to the two named, there have been added by purchase, the Grey Eagle fraction between them, the Summit, above the Unknown, on the apex of the mountain, and the Grand Prize, below the Custer. These mines contained within their boundaries, from the top of the Summit, through the Unknown and Custer, to the lowest workings in the Grand Prize, a huge vein with regular walls, varying in thickness from six inches to thirty feet, and carrying chutes of fine ore throughout, which in some respects have been a marvel to mining men. Dame Nature, usually so chary of her favors in the mineral kingdom, was in an amiable mood when she uncovered to the eye of man her treasures on Custer Mountain. At the points of discovery on the Custer and Unknown, there were exposed to view great quarries of ore, from which, through force of her agencies, the hanging wall had become loosened, sliding down the steep mountain. Experts were able to recommend fancy figures in purchasing this property, merely by estimating the value of ore thus in sight. In 1880, during the skillful management of Colonel William B. Hyde and T. R. Butler, a substantial 20-stamp dry-crushing mill was erected, with the usual roasting and amalgamating appliances—the machinery therefor being made by Fraser & Chalmers, Chicago. This mill, with the addition of ten stamps erected under the management of Superintendent William McCaskell, in 1882, has pounded away continuously up to this time, with several thousand tons of ore in sight yet to be crushed. About 33,000 tons of dry ore have been reduced from the group mentioned, and about 900 tons more that were brought from other mines in the district. The result has been 1,260 bars of doré bullion, whose assay value approximates $3,000,000. The ore, which carries from fifteen to forty per cent of gold, has been so free of rebellious metals as to produce bullion averaging nearly 990 in fineness. With a milling capacity of over 900 tons per month, it is saved to ninety-five per cent of its value, and converted into bullion at a cost less than $25 per ton. A Hallidie's wire rope tramway—3,600 feet long, and carrying seventy buckets—delivers the ore from the mines to the mill. J. B. Haggin and George W. Grayson, of San Francisco, the principal owners, have benefited this district greatly by receiving custom ores at reasonable rates. The records of this property—at present under the management of Chris. Morler, superintendent, M. L. Crafts, assayer, and C. L. Rood, cashier—furnish in detail an exhibit of a remarkable mining and milling operation.

On Custer Mountain, and to the east and south, are a great many other claims—among them the Badger, Continental, Blue Wing, Lucky Boy, and Whistler—which have produced good pay ore, and have in sight now large quantities of a low-grade character. The Continental has at least $40,000 in sight. The Badger has recently sold several hundred tons of good ore to the Custer mine, and is now leased to it for a long period.

On Mt. Estes, five miles north of Bonanza, are situated a number of good claims; those which have attracted the most attention being the Montana and Whale mines. The former, celebrated for its rich gold ore, is well developed by shafts, tunnels, and cross-cuts, and has not only paid handsomely from the date of its discovery, but now has fine prospects ahead. It has shipped about 720 tons of ore, including 585 tons to the Custer mill, of the gross value of $261,000. In addition, there are large bodies of low-grade ore in place, and the ore dumps are well filled. It is owned by James Hooper, superintendent, J. W. Faulkner, D. Cameron, Amos Franklin, and D. B. Varney. The Whale mine, with ore containing almost entirely silver, has not been developed until the past few months. With three or four men at work its production has been over $15,000. The Charles' Wain, Hidden Treasure, and other good prospects are found on this hill.

Charles Dickens.—As widely known as this celebrated author is in the literary world, so is the mine bearing his name known to mining men. Situated half a mile above Bonanza, on Norton Hill, and traceable east and west therefrom for two miles, with a true fissure vein; with ore so rich in gold that its discoverers pounded out in hand-mortars during the first month about $17,000; and with a system of development more thorough than any other mine in this district, it is a property which, with proper facilities, will rank high as a producer of bullion. In 1875 the first ore shipments netted 15,000; in 1876 twenty-three tons shipped to Salt Lake City assayed $17,000; in 1878 an arrastra costing $19,400 was erected. Crushing two tons per day, it had produced $32,000 in seventy days, at the close of the working season. During the summer of each succeeding year the arrastra has been in operation, and in addition has made ore shipments to Custer mill and other reduction works. From reliable data, the total production in bullion and ore shipments has been $500,000. Two tunnels, of a total length of 1,400 feet, follow the vein in from the surface, giving the mine at present a depth of 400 feet. Careful sampling has revealed thousands of tons of ore in place, worth at a low estimate over $300,000 in silver and gold. Ore bins and dumps are full to overflowing. All this dormant wealth merely awaits the magic touch of a mill to awaken it to its rightful sphere of influence. Originally owned by W. A. Norton, John S. Rohrer, and Fred. Phillips, it is now managed by J.W. Hamilton for J. E. Dooly of Salt Lake City, who is the executor of the estate of W. A. Norton, deceased. Other claims contiguous to the Charles Dickens require more development to determine their worth.

The above claims, chosen from among 200 locations, indicate the vast wealth lying yet unexplored. Remoteness from railroads has been a great drawback in this district; but it is not too much to expect that its future, under more advantageous circumstances, will be more brilliant than its past.

Bay Horse District.—The next to the largest bullion producer in the county is the Ramshorn group of mines—the Montreal, Ramshorn proper, Utah Boy, and Post Boy—embracing an area 4,500 feet in length on the vein, by 600 feet in width. The vein is traceable on the surface continuously through the length of the four claims, beginning with the Montreal at the top of the hill, and running to Bay Horse Creek. It is in a formation of slate and porphyry, with a general direction of north-east and south-west, and dips to the west at an angle of 25° to 30°. Hardly any but assessment work has been done on the Montreal. Ramshorn proper is developed by a system of tunnels running into the mountain on the vein, with various connecting winzes and raises. The Utah Boy has three tunnels on the vein, each from 100 to 400 feet long; and the Post Boy, at the foot of the hill, has three tunnels of yet greater length. About 10,000 tons of ore have been extracted from the Ramshorn proper, at an average of 120 ounces in silver per ton, carrying 8 per cent lead, 30 per cent iron, and sufficient silica for self-fluxing. The other claims have yielded 2,400 tons of ore, at 75 ounces silver to the ton, with 10 per cent lead. But little work has been done on any claim but the Ramshorn proper, except in recent months. With nearly every working showing fine ore in the face, it is a gratifying fact that at no time since its discovery have the prospects of this group been better. In the autumn of 1880 an Omaha smelting company put up on Bay Horse Creek a 25-ton smelter, which yearly made successful runs on the various ores of this district up to 1883, when the present owners of the Ramshorn bought the old plant, and added thereto another stack, with a blast furnace of a capacity in ore, besides the fluxes, of 40 tons daily. The company buys ore from nearly all the mines in this and other districts. A tramway similar to the one at Custer mine, and 3,200 feet long, begins at the Ramshorn proper, and delivers ore at the ore-house on Bay Horse Creek two miles above the smelter, between these points wagon transportation being used. Charcoal is used as fuel, and a large flume has been constructed down the cañon above to convey wood to the coal-kilns just above the smelter. Besides the large force of men employed in cutting wood, fluming it, and burning coal, there are 125 men on the regular force at the mines and smelter. Average cost of smelting, $15 per ton; mining and tramway, $10 to $12 per ton. Owned by J. B. Haggin, J. T. Gilmer, and O. J. Salisbury. It is at present managed by the last-named gentleman.

Three other good mines situated on Ramshorn Hill are the Bull of the Woods, Silver Wing, and Skylark. The first is situated about 1,500 feet west of the Ramshorn, and is developed by four tunnels 850 feet in length, with a few cross-cuts, winzes, and raises. The vein, which carries seams of high-grade ore, is not the Ramshorn vein, but is about parallel thereto. The ore thus far extracted has averaged 303 ounces per ton in silver, with 30 per cent copper, and no lead, and is valued at $91,000. Present prospects are as good as ever. The Silver Wing, situated west of the Ramshorn, and owned George L. Shoup, Owen Long, James Macnab, Al. Barselou, George Clark, and W. T. Stethem, is developed by 3,000 feet of tunnels, etc., and has shipped in three years about $100,000. First-class ore averages 1,000 ounces, and second-class 125 ounces, in silver to the ton. Work is continuous, with no decrease in ore supply. The Skylark, adjoining the Ramshorn on the west and the Silver Wing on the south, has developed a cross-vein of the Ramshorn vein, by four tunnels, with a total length of 1,000 feet, besides the usual connecting works. It was located in 1877, and has produced 212,582 ounces in silver, at an average per ton of 123 ounces. It is owned by an Omaha company, with A. J. Crook as manager. These three mines are in a formation not materially different from the Ramshorn, and the ores are also similar, excepting that they carry a smaller per cent of lead.

Two other mines, situated a quarter of a mile above Ætna, that have a good record, and will better it, are the Excelsior and the Beardsley. The Excelsior, owned and superintended by J. D. Wood, is well developed, having three tunnels of an aggregate length of 800 feet, giving a depth of 277 feet. It has produced up to October 31st 2,385 tons of ore, yielding nearly 200,000 ounces in silver, with 30 per cent lead, and 4 per cent to 6 per cent copper. The ore body now in sight will average from seven to eleven feet in thickness, nowhere being less than seven. It has been followed the past summer for 200 feet, and has been developed upwards for 40 feet. Competent judges have pronounced it to be the finest body of ore uncovered in Custer County, with the single exception of the Custer mine. Shipments from it made the past season to the Clayton smelter, amounting to nearly 1,200 tons of ore, average 90 ounces in silver to the ton. It is in a formation of lime, and has regular walls. The Beardsley, owned by J. P. Spaulding and Robert Beardsley, is contiguous to the Excelsior, contains the same character of ore in the same formation, and all appearances indicate that the Excelsior ore body is continued within its lines. It is developed by 300 feet of tunnels, and 300 feet of raises and winzes, etc., and has produced 800 tons of ore, yielding 40,000 ounces in silver. Having been recently bonded to the Ramshorn M. & S. Co. for $45,000, active prospecting is being carried on to fully develop the mine.

7

The Bay Horse M. & S. Co., which constructed the original smelter plant in Bay Horse, in 1880—operating the same until May, 1883—reduced 6,745 tons of ore, mainly from Bay Horse district, yielding 862,126 ounces in silver, or an average of 128 ounces per ton. This showing and its subsequent record, together with the history of individual mines, must carry conviction to the minds of mining men as to the worth and stability of the mineral resources of Bay Horse district.

Kinnikinik.—In 1880 the Salmon River M. & S. Co. began the erection of a 25-ton smelter, and operated it, under the management of C. B. Rustin, during sixty-six days in the summer of 1881 and twenty days in 1882. The works are substantially built on an advantageous site at Clayton. With a daily capacity of 23 tons of ore, it produced in 1881 220 tons of base bullion, containing 100,000 ounces silver, and in 1882 the production is estimated at one fourth this amount. At the beginning of 1884 the smelter and several mines were sold to A. J. Crook & Co., with Mr. Crook as manager, who at once put the works in shape for a summer's run. From June to October the smelter had reduced 1,810 tons of ore, containing 186,841 ounces silver. Another run in November closes operations for this season; but the present intention is to conduct the business on a larger scale in 1885—a plan well warranted by the richness of the mines in these districts.

Among the prominent mines owned by the new company are the Ella, Overland, Faithful Boy, and Monitor—all on the same vein—carrying a few ounces in silver, but worked principally because they contain nearly forty per cent iron. They are situated near the smelter. On Poverty Flat, four miles distant, this company owns the Silver Bell, Youknow, and Redemption, all of them well developed. The last named has produced about 850 tons of ore, containing about $90,000 in silver. The Silver Bell in 1881 produced $30,000, and has not since been worked.

Squaw Creek.—Four miles above Clayton is situated the Red Bird, owned by the same company. Not only can the ledge croppings be traced 600 feet in length, and 10 to 40 feet in width, but a shaft sunk 100 feet, and 50 feet of levels therefrom, are all in ore varying in value from low to high grade. The average of ore shipments made this past summer is 35 ounces silver per ton, with 35 per cent lead. The Kirk Bros. own the Cinnabar mine. An incline 150 feet long is in good ore, and the production has been fully 200 tons, averaging 80 ounces silver and 40 per cent lead.

East Fork District.—The Germania and Arctic were located in 1879, and are owned by J. D. Wood. He has shipped from them 600 tons of ore, averaging 150 ounces silver, $10 gold, and 55 per cent lead. They are in brown porphyry formation, with a true fissure vein, and promise well. About one half a mile to the east is the Crœsus, with a ledge 7 to 25 feet wide cropping out the length of the claim, 1,500 feet. A shaft has been sunk 70 feet, showing ore in the bottom assaying 100 ounces silver and $20 gold per ton. It is an immense lead, with thousands of tons of ore in sight that will average at a safe estimate 50 ounces silver and $10 gold per ton. Its owners, J. D. Wood, J. W. Birdseye, and William Short, think that cheaper working facilities will enable the Crœsus to earn the right to its name.

A group of mines one half mile farther east embrace three good claims—Bible Back, Idaho, and Tyrolese. The Idaho has shipped 200 tons of ore, assaying 150 ounces silver and $10 gold, with 55 per cent lead; the Bible Back, 100 tons of the same grade; and the Tyrolese, in October, 1884, 30 tons of similar character. The little work done on these claims shows fine ore and a true fissure vein. The Jefferson, Washington, Sutterberg, Sperling, and others have shipped small lots of ore.

The claims made in behalf of this district would seem extravagant, compared with total results, if the disadvantages surrounding it were not stated. Consider an altitude (at the Germania) of 9,500 feet; a fall of snow, beginning in November, which reaches enormous depths by the following May; a working season which lasts about three months in a year. Consider, also, the stoppage of all communication in winter with other districts; the fact that but little capital has so far been at the disposal of the mine-owners; and last, but most important, that transportation charges to either smelter range from $25 to $50 per ton. But such hinderances would be overcome by reduction works located near the mines, with capital sufficient to provide for winter. And for all purposes of mining and smelting there is no lack of water and fine timber.

Lost River Mining District.—Among the principal claims in this district showing galena and silver ores are the Grand Prize, Alice, Mammoth, Black Daisy, and Jay Gould—at present not much developed, but showing good bodies of ore, assaying as high as 200 ounces in silver and 60 per cent of lead. That which has attracted most attention, however, is a group of five locations styled the Big Copper mines, viz.: Buena Vista, Golden Wave, Copper King, Henrietta, and Old Judge. They make a block of mineral ground 3,600 feet long by 1,200 feet wide. The vein is a contact between lime on the east and granite on the west, with a width of 700 to 800 feet. Several strata of ore running throughout vary in width from five to one hundred feet, separated by porphyry dykes. The ore, carrying sulphurets, black and red oxides, carbonates, etc., assays on an average from twelve to twenty ounces in silver, and as large a per cent copper. A 30-ton smelter near the copper mines has been constructed recently and is now in operation. Supt. Center states that the ores, properly mixed, will flux themselves so effectually that forty to fifty tons of material can be run through daily. A contract has been signed for the erection of another smelter next spring. If the recent discovery of these properties be considered, the work already done, the growth of agriculture, and increase in population in Houston and the whole valley, prophesy clearly the greatness of the future in store for this district.

Unfortunately the scope of this review is limited to brief sketches of the most prominent properties. But in addition to other mines now considerably developed, with encouraging results, new "finds" are continually reported. From Pahsimari Valley, from Yankee Fork, from the mountains above Challis—in short, from every section of the county—come reports merely hinting its great mineral wealth yet undiscovered.

Agriculture ably supplements the mining industry in enriching this county. The Salmon River, rising in the Sawtooth Mountains north of Wood River, enters it on its south-western border, and pursuing a zigzag course in a general north-easterly direction, receives the waters of ten large creeks besides the East Fork. These streams, together with Lost River and its tributaries, flow through thousands of acres of arable land still uncultivated. Since the hand of man is forced to supply what nature withholds, irrigation takes the place of rain; and the water that annually goes to waste would make verdant, fruitful valleys out of deserts; would convert the silence of desolation into the sounds from many homes. In Round Valley, containing thirty square miles of arable and grazing land, but a small portion has been put to human use; in Lost River Valley, containing (in Custer County) about one hundred square miles of arable land, four thousand acres of hay and grain will equal the number cultivated this year; in Pahsimari Valley, containing about fifty square miles of arable land, comparatively none is under cultivation. Indeed, the assessor's books record only 11,240 acres of land located and held in 1883, and but 17,000 acres held this year. There are also small portions of land on several creeks that await only human agency to transform their barren acres. A few families have settled in Pahsimari—a valley forty miles in length by eighteen miles in average width—but beyond a few tons of hay and grain, etc., for home use, nothing has been produced. This valley alone will furnish homes and occupation for hundreds of people. The lack of roads leading to markets has retarded its development. Lost River, from its source to the point where it sinks in the lava beds, runs for sixty-five miles through a fine valley rich in natural resources. Since the mining excitement of last year, eight hundred people have flocked thither—of whom perhaps one half are engaged in agriculture. With homes to build, land to inclose and bring under the beneficent effects of irrigation, the new-comers have still found time to cut this year about 5,000 tons of wild hay, and raise 10,000 bushels of grain. The grain crop next year will quadruple this amount. Farming in Round Valley has been liberally rewarded. The acreage under cultivation has steadily increased for five years, until this year its contribution to the county's wealth is 30,000 bushels of grain and 800 tons of hay—besides thousands of pounds of vegetables. The grain crop of 1884 is double that of the previous year. Men who came here penniless a few years ago now own ranches, with houses, equipments, and live-stock, which are worth from $3,000 to $15,000.

Oats is the principal grain raised, being of a very hardy, solid character, and for that reason taking the place of barley. Wheat could be raised as profitably as oats, if there were only flour-mills in the county to grind it. There is no lack of a market, as 400,000 pounds of flour are annually imported to meet the consumption, at prices ranging from $4.50 to $6 per hundred, according to locality and season. Each bushel of oats will weigh forty-two pounds; and the average yield per acre being thirty-three bushels, it will be seen that this is equivalent to forty bushels to the acre of the standard weight of thirty-five pounds. Hay yields about one and a half tons to the acre, in its wild state. Alfalfa, blue grass, red-top, and timothy have been successfully sown. To farmers in Eastern States the lateness of the harvesting season will seem remarkable. The farmer's work, begun the latter part of March, is not really ended until the fall plowing is done, in the middle of November, and he has no fears if by October 1st his hay and grain are safely under cover. The profits accruing to farmers will give no surprise, when it is understood that oats bring $1.20 per bushel; hay $20 per ton; potatoes two cents per pound; cabbage four cents; onions eight cents; and turnips one cent per pound. Other farm produce is sold as follows: eggs at fifty cents per dozen; butter at forty to fifty cents per pound; and chickens at fifty cents apiece. Not only is a ready market found at these prices, but annually thousands of dollars worth of hay, grain, butter, eggs, and poultry are imported from other counties, or Utah, to meet home demands. Hereafter, the tendency of prices will be slightly downward; still the margin left for profits will be extraordinarily large.

Although fruit culture has been neglected, 1,200 trees planted in Round Valley give evidence that apples, plums, cherries, pears, and crab-apples are natural to the soil and climate. Cultivated small fruits, wherever planted, have yielded an abundance. Gooseberries, raspberries, strawberries, serviceberries, and currants of three varieties, growing wild and profuse along rivers and creeks, intimate the wealth nature has in store for those who woo her.

Stock-growing.—This business is not less remunerative in Custer County than in other stock regions where sudden acquisitions have turned paupers into "cattle kings." The highest profits are, of course, realized where the climate and snow-fall are such as to demand but little or no cut feed for the stock in winter. There are thousands of acres of grazing land in Pahsimari, Lost River, and Round valleys—besides small sections in other portions of the county—where the stock is not hay-fed oftener than one winter in three; and then only the weakest and poorest cattle during a few weeks of the severest weather. It has not been the practice of stockmen to provide even to any considerable extent for hard winters. With the grazing lands thus limited to low ranges where the snow-fall is light, still the assessment rolls for 1883 and 1884 show that about 10,000 head of cattle annually range within the county's borders, besides the horses and sheep. This business would remain highly profitable, however, if stockmen would yearly prepare to meet the possible rigors of winter. The principal expense would be in cutting and stacking wild hay. A mild winter would leave a large surplus to carry over to the first severe one, thus mitigating its hardships. Such a plan, earnestly carried out, would more than double the capacity of its grazing lands: first, by allowing an increase of stock in ranges now occupied; second, by opening up thousands of acres of new country in altitudes a little higher, whose summer ranges, already unsurpassed, would thus be rendered safe for winter use as well.

Stockmen heretofore have slighted the truth that the Lost River and Salmon River regions afford the best fields for successful sheep-raising in the West. This branch of industry is certainly growing—evidenced by the fact that whereas only 850 sheep were assessed in 1882, the assessor this year found 3,000 head. The number of horses and mules in 1883 was 1,200, and it reached 1,600 in 1884.

Principal Towns.—Challis, the county seat, safely sheltered in the foothills of Round Valley, invites our contemplation. Being the principal base of supplies for the mining regions, the medium of half the business transacted in the county, and the especial resort of stockmen and farmers, miners and business men, it forms what may be reasonably termed a cosmopolitan town. Particularly is this noticeable in winter, when, because of its educational facilities and its mild and dry climate, families from points less favored come to its pleasant portals. Containing a transient population of 500, it becomes at such times the scene of pleasure as well as of business. It is laid off in eighty-two regular squares, upon a beautiful site, containing nearly 160 acres, upon which are several hundred buildings. A creek running its entire length is fringed with trees and shrubbery, and its general fine appearance maintains the wisdom of its choice as the seat of government. Three miles below Challis, near the Salmon River, are beneficial warm springs, whose curative properties are sought by many guests. The town of Houston, whose existence began last June, now numbers seventy buildings, with a population of over 200, and is located near the prominent mines. A town twelve miles from Challis, in Bay Horse District, presents, in its two names, a striking flight from the depth of the common and vulgar to the height of the æsthetic. Originally known as Bay Horse, Uncle Sam refused to enter it on his post-office rolls, and so it now rejoices under the classic appellation of Ætna. Its population varies during the year from 200 to more than 500 men, mostly engaged in pursuits incident to mining. Small towns exist farther up Salmon River, in the Kinnikinik District, called Crystal and Clayton, principally of use to the mines adjacent. Bonanza and Custer, on Yankee Fork, populated by 200 to 400 people according to season, are exclusively mining camps. They are reached on wheels only through Challis. In picturesqueness of location and in admirable summer climate, they claim superiority over any other towns in Idaho Territory.

General Statistics.—A prudent man, before investing in business in a new county, will carefully scan, not only the evidences of growth, and the resources of particular localities, but will desire to know of the prosperity of the county as a whole. A few figures will express a chapter. From the assessment rolls are obtained the following: In 1881 the valuation of real estate and improvements was $162,000; of personal property, $199,000; total, $361,000. In 1882 the valuation of real estate and improvements was $157,000; of personal property, $232,000; total, $389,000. In 1883 the valuation of real estate and improvements was $183,000; of personal property, $412,000; total, $595,000. In 1884 the valuation of real estate and improvements was $216,000; of personal property, $434,000; total, $650,000.

From the preparations now being made for development of mines, construction of reduction works, and increased tillage of land, the proportionate increase of property shown above will be maintained for several years. From all sources, there has been collected for county and territorial use the following revenue: For 1881, $10,000; for 1882, $14,000; for 1883, $24,000; and for 1884, $27,000—making a grand total of $75,000. With the increase of taxable property, the expenditures have remained about the same; hence taxes decrease yearly, and will so continue.

Schools, Hospital, Mails, Crime, etc.—Creditable to Custer County is its plethoric school fund. With about 200 school children divided between five school districts, there is an annual surplus of money ranging from $2,500 to $5,000. Almost equally good is the maintenance of a county hospital, with first-class surgical attendance, whose kindly protection many an unfortunate has reason to bless. And correlative to the educational advantages afforded is the insignificant criminal element among the population. A small jail and short terms of court fully provide for the welfare of offenders against society and law. The people do not differ in character from that of the average Western community. Their standard of education, their enterprise, and their desire for knowledge are gauged by the immense amount of reading matter daily unloaded at the Challis post-office—now the distributing point for the county. It is the beginning or terminus of six mail routes, weekly, semi-weekly, tri-weekly, and daily. In addition, a six-day service will soon be established from Ketchum, on the Wood River Railroad, to Ætna. A weekly newspaper is published at Challis by R. A. Pierce & Son.

Climate, Timber, etc.—As already intimated, the snow-fall in winter throughout the lower valleys is not of consequence; but it gradually increases with altitude until in the mountains it reaches great depths. At Challis, with an elevation of 5,100 feet, sleigh-rides are well nigh impossible; while in

Bonanza, nestled at an elevation of 6,400 feet, in the very bosom of a mountainous country, the snow attains a depth of three to five feet in its streets. Generally, two short rainy seasons occur in a year. A brief polar wave of cold sweeps down in January or February; but it is a subject of general comment that 30° below zero in this high, dry air, with no wind, is far less penetrating than the cold of Eastern States—damp, windy, chilling. The summer months are pre-eminently delightful: cool nights, days warm, mild, and invigorating, are better appreciated through experience than description. Probably one fourth of the mountainous territory of this county is heavily timbered with spruce, fir, pine, and occasional mahogany. In all the benefits of abundant wood and water, Custer is no exception to the other counties in Idaho.

A General Recapitulation of the foregoing shows that Custer County has added to the wealth of the world $1,350,000 in gold from its placers; and from its quartz mines the large sum of $6,800,000 in gold and silver at assay value. With but two smelters in operation a few months, and one mill at continuous work, this year's production will approximate $1,500,000; while new works finished and others planned will increase this amount by one half in 1885. The old mines in the county show permanency, and new ones are discovered every season. The value of stock on its ranges easily represents the worth of $360,000. The value of its agricultural products for 1884 will equal $175,000; an amount that will be doubled in a few years. Its population has steadily grown until it reaches about 2,000.

With large tracts of farming and grazing land uncultivated; with a list of taxable property annually lengthening with giant strides; with increasing revenue and decreasing taxation; with good schools, and little crime; with stock-ranges of luxurious vegetation; with an admirable climate favorable to health; with a fertile soil, rich in fruitful products; and with a vast mineral wealth in lead and iron, copper and the precious metals—Custer County is blessed with natural gifts and advantages that will prove its brief though vigorous existence to have been but a puny part of its progressive career.

IDAHO COUNTY.

This county occupies a vast region about midway between the northern and southern boundaries of the Territory. Its present area is 10,100 square miles, or nearly as large as the combined areas of New Jersey, Delaware, and Rhode Island.

I acknowledge myself indebted in great measure for some of the statistics regarding this county to the report of a well-known mining gentleman to the director of the mint.

Idaho County was originally the largest county in the Territory. Lemhi and Custer counties were cut off from its eastern end. Boisé County has taken a strip from its southern portion, and one half of Washington County was originally within its limits. On the other hand, it gained in 1875 a strip from the eastern side of Nez Percé County, comprising the agricultural section known as Camas Prairie, and the mining camps of Elk City and Newsome Creek.

The only agricultural portion is Camas Prairie, on its western border; here there are six entire and several fractional townships of arable land, that produce all the usual cereals in profusion. Its elevation is not over 2,500 feet. Along Salmon River there are also a few isolated flats of small extent, which are devoted to gardening and fruit-raising.

The county is watered principally by the Salmon River and its tributaries, the eastern and southern boundary being the water-shed between the branches of the Salmon and the head waters of other streams. The northern portion is drained by some of the forks of the Clearwater.

Salmon River cuts a deep chasm through the county from south-east to north-west. Its valley is from 3,000 to 4,000 feet lower than the average altitude of the mining camps scattered through the adjacent mountains, causing a marked difference in climate. In the winter snow rarely falls before February, and frequently the ground is not whitened during the year, while in the surrounding mining camps the snow covers the mountain sides from 4 to 8 feet in depth.

Idaho County is, however, essentially a mountainous region, the principal portion of the Salmon River Mountains being included within its boundaries. These mountains are in no well-defined range, but are a vast collection of irregularly scattered peaks, overtopping a wilderness of lesser peaks, all of a rugged and forbidding aspect. The average altitude is about 6,000 feet, though many peaks have an elevation of nearly double that height.

The town of Florence is situated 6,600 feet above the sea level, and Warren 6,200 feet.

The Salmon River Mountains are chiefly of granite formation, and appear to have been upheaved at a comparatively recent geological period.

The deep cañon of the Salmon River affords numerous excellent opportunities for studying the character of the subjacent rocks, as surfaces are frequently exposed from 1,000 to 2,000 feet high.

At a point on the river near the mouth of Little Salmon, hornblende slates begin to take the place of granite, and gneiss farther to the eastward. There is an obscure stratification and a general north and south strike.

A few miles farther west, at Carver's ranch, a huge ledge of very pure limestone crosses the river; it is from 100 to 500 feet wide, and extends in a general northerly and southerly direction for about 40 miles, finally dipping under the lava a short distance east of Mount Idaho.

West of this, other varieties of slate, mica, and clay make their appearance, with occasional bunches of quartz, and at the mouth of John Day's Creek the primitive rocks disappear beneath basaltic lava, and are no more seen in the bed of the river from thence to the Pacific Ocean, except in one place in Snake River, about 50 miles below Lewiston, at Granite Point.

The soil of Camas Prairie is derived from the decomposition of lava, identical with that which overspreads most of the Columbia River Valley. Many fossil remains are found in digging wells, but no minerals of value, nor are any likely to be. The mountainous region to the eastward of the lava and the anterior slate formation is probably the source of the mineral wealth of the county.

Gold in paying quantities was first discovered in Idaho near Pearce City, in what is now Shoshone County, in 1860. At that time Idaho was still a portion of Washington Territory. Communication from point to point was slow and difficult, and there was no great rush of miners, nor any great amount of money taken out during that year. By the following spring reliable information of extensive deposits in that section was widely spread, and the search for gold was diligently prosecuted.

Gold was found in the banks and bars of all the forks of Clearwater, and led to the discovery of extensive placer ground at Elk City. Paying ground was also found in many places on Salmon River, and early in July in Florence Basin, in which place thousands of mines were located in a couple of months. On the north side of the Salmon nothing worth mentioning was or has since been found. South of the Salmon gold was found in August, 1862, in Warren's Basin, which is drained by Meadow Creek and its tributaries, and empties into the Salmon River 16 miles north of the town of Washington.

At the present time the ground worth working comprises the upper eight miles of the creek. The shallower portions of the creek and neighboring gulches were worked out in a few years after the discovery of gold. The lower portion of the creek was not abandoned by white men until 1870, at which time the Chinese came in and have since monopolized the gravel-workings, going over the mining ground a second and sometimes a third time.

The lodes of the Warren district vary but little in course from east to west, with a dip to the south from 60° to 75°. They are usually narrow, seldom exceeding three feet in width of ore, and often having less than two feet. The country rock is granite, and vein matter is quartz, carrying, in addition to gold and silver, zinc, blende, galena, and antimony, though but sparingly.

Iron in sulphurets or more or less oxidized is found in all the veins; tellurium, as telluric gold and telluric silver, is found in the Keystone; and tungsten, as tungstate of lime or scheelite, occurs in some quantity in the Charity; previous to its discovery here this mineral had not been observed in auriferous ores.

Cinnabar occurs in nearly all the placer claims; at Miller's Camp, 20 miles west of Warren, it is found in such quantities as to prove troublesome in washing for gold, filling the riffles where gold should lodge; although the vein or lode has been persistently sought for, it has not been found. In one gulch pieces of iron ore containing from 10 to 50 per cent of gold have been found, but its source has not yet been traced. Tin ore has not been observed in the gravel, and copper occurs in vein matter only in minute traces.

At the present time active operations are being carried on only at four mines. The Knott ledge, owned and worked by N. B. Willey, is three miles west of the town of Washington. Running across a ridge at right angles, it is favorably situated for working, and can be opened to a depth of 400 feet by tunnels following the vein. The ore chimney, as at present developed, is from a thin seam to six feet in width, but usually is from two to three feet. One half goes to the ore-house and the rest to the waste pile. The reducing works consist of a five-stamp battery followed by a double arrastra run by water-power, and situated about two miles from the mine. The capacity of the mill is about six tons per diem, and runs but seven months of the year. The present production of the mine is from 30 to 60 tons per month, taken only from the first level; if more fully opened, it would yield 15 or 25 tons a day. The ore pays from $15 to $28 per ton. The cost of extracting is $9, hauling $3, and crushing $2.50 per ton.

The Tramp, one mile from the Knott, owned and worked by Charles Johnson, is a narrow ledge, not well defined at the surface, but increasing to from four to twelve inches in width at the bottom of the 60-foot shaft. An excellent arrastra belonging to the same party is situated three miles from the mine, at which the ore is delivered by pack-train at an expense of $5 per ton. The average yield is from $50 to $65; the production of ore is, however, small.

The Charity, two miles south of Washington, is owned and operated by P. & J. Reibold. It has been prospected by tunnels to a depth of 210 feet, the lowest tunnel being 600 feet in length. The present workings are confined to the upper levels. The reduction works consist of a five-stamp battery at the mouth of the tunnel. There is a large amount of low-grade ore with rich pockets here and there. The average yield is $5 to $12 per ton, though selected lots have reached as high as $1,800 per ton.

The President belongs to Carr & Morton; it is a recent discovery, and a mine of considerable promise. The vein is from six inches to two feet in width, and the ore pays from $17 to $40 per ton. Both the ore and country rock are soft and easily worked, and the ledge lies favorably for development. The ore is worked in custom mills.

The Rescue mine is near Washington, and has been the most extensively developed mine of any in the district. A tunnel taps the vein at a depth of 183 feet, at which point a shaft extends to the surface. The hoisting-works are of sufficient capacity to sink to a depth of 500 or 600 feet below the tunnel level; the shaft is already 120 feet lower, and two levels are opened. A five-stamp mill is erected at the mouth of the tunnel. The ore chimney is from 250 to 300 feet in length, and the ore is all taken out above the tunnel. The first 60 feet below the tunnel is also exhausted, and the next level has the main shaft sunk and the level run about 70 feet, at which point it is in ore. The total yield of the mine has been from $80,000 to $90,000. The mine is leased to a Boston company, who expect to resume operations in the spring.

The yield per ton from the different ledges of the Warren district has varied greatly. Large quantities of rock from the Rescue paid from $30 to $75 per ton. Selected ore from the Charity paid from $40 to $80, and from the Scott as high as $180 per ton. The Keystone ore paid quite uniformly from $30 to $65, and on the other hand, some lots from other ledges scarcely paid for working.

The average yield of ore from this district is not readily estimated. The processes of extraction of the precious metals have been of the simplest character; at first arrastas were used, then stamps with copper plates of limited extent, and at present the arrastra follows the battery, with blanket washings saved for future treatment. Assays of tailings have rarely been made, and it is not easy to estimate the percentage of gold and silver extracted.

A close approximation of the amount of ore taken out and worked during the last fifteen years is as follows: from the—

	Tons.		Tons.
Rescue	1,000	Keystone	200
Knott	600	Eureka	100
Charity	500	Washington	25
Sampson	250	Bonanza	75
Hic Jacet	150	Tramp	100
Knott Treasure	25	President	50
Scott	150	Bullion	100
Alder	50	Other small lots and float-rock	250
General Grant	50		

The ore is generally calcined prior to crushing, and the returns show that more silver is saved by this preparatory treatment. Bullion from calcined ore is usually from .300 to .500 fine, while that from the raw material is .600 to .650 fine. The gold from placer mines varies very much in fineness. That from the small gulches and heads of the streams is from .625 to .675 fine; in the main creek, from .700 to .760 fine, and is the common currency at $14 per ounce. A great extent of ground has been worked along Salmon River, principally by rockers and other primitive appliances; the gold is usually in small particles, known as flour gold, though sometimes in scales; it is current at $16 per ounce, being from .800 to .825 fine.

Near John Day's Creek a few bars of limited extent have yielded coarse gold, and nuggets of from $5 to $15 each, of high grade, over .950 fine, and current at $19.50 per ounce.

The yield from Idaho County can only be approximately stated. Five Chinese companies in Warren's take out more than half the gold of the camp. From diligent inquiry made of the principal members, the following estimate may be stated as nearly correct:

Shun Lee Company	$7,150	Twelve minor companies	$22,800
Wing Wo Company	16,600	Single Chinamen	2,000
Hung Wo Company	9,800	White men	13,500
Leni Wo Company	14,250	Four quartz mills	18,672
Fook Sing Hung	22,700		
Total			$127,472

Along Salmon River there are eight bars worked by Chinese, and five by white men; the product of the year being about $45,000. Nearly the same amount was produced in Florence and Elk City; the smaller camps may be estimated at $43,000, making the total production for Idaho County, $260,000.

The chief agricultural section, as above indicated, is Camas Prairie, estimated to contain 200 square miles of rich arable land. Small fruits, such as strawberries, cherries, etc., grow in abundance. Grain is raised in great quantities, oats yielding fifty bushels to the acre. The prairie is about thirty miles long from north to south, and twenty-five from east to west. Bunchgrass and timothy abound, making it one of the best pastoral sections of the Territory. Horses and cattle thrive well, with little expense to the owners. The camas roots furnish excellent feed for hogs during a great part of the year.

Little Salmon Valley is about 75 miles south of Florence. It contains about 75 sections of good arable land, and produces an abundant crop of grass. It is one of the best watered sections of the Territory. Timber is plenty and of the best quality of pine, fir, and tamarack. The valley is capable of supporting at least 300 families. It is of rich, fertile soil, capable of producing all kinds of cereals and vegetables; while on the surrounding foothills are unlimited pastures for stock. The valley is almost entirely uninhabited, and is but awaiting the arrival of settlers to develop its agricultural wealth.

The chief settlements are Mt. Idaho, at the edge of Camas Prairie, and Grangeville, four miles distant. The former is the county seat, possessing a handsome court-house, several stores, and a commodious hotel. Grangeville is a rapidly growing farming settlement, and is a distributing point for the prairie.

KOOTENAI COUNTY.

This is the northernmost county of the Territory, being bounded on the north by British Possessions, on the east by Montana Territory, on the south by Shoshone and Nez Percé counties, and on the west by Washington Territory. It comprises an area of about 5,530 square miles. As already stated, it is the chief lake county in the Territory. Within its limits are lakes Cœur d'Alene, Pend d'Oreille, Kanisku, Kootenai, Cocollalla, and numberless others. These will be found sufficiently described in the second chapter.

The county occupies the "pan-handle" proper of the Territory, and is in form nearly a rectangle. The Northern Pacific crosses it from east to west, and attains its most northerly point at Lake Pend d'Oreille. Though one of the earliest-created counties, it was not organized till 1881, shortly after the arrival of the Northern Pacific.

Timber.—It has been a great wonder to many that larger and more powerful saw-mills have not been erected on the beautiful streams in north Idaho, for there are mill-sites which for every convenience, both water and fine timber, cannot be excelled in the North-west. This belt has heretofore attracted much attention from careful, far-seeing business men who have come out from the East and thoroughly examined the field, and all unite in the single opinion that the wonderful timber belt of north Idaho is the lumberman's paradise, and that it is equal in extent and quality to that of Minnesota, Wisconsin, and Michigan. In fact, this whole region is one vast forest of the finest fir, cedar, tamarack, and pine. On the banks of Kootenai Lake there is a large body of fine saw-timber. For miles and miles on each side of Pack River there is quite a body of good timber. Pend d'Oreille Lake is surrounded by timber, and Clark's Fork shows patches of timber along its course.

Yet the most extensive bodies of timber in the great North-west are found on the waters of the Cœur d'Alene, St. Joseph, and St. Mary's rivers. On the banks of the first-named immense trees can be seen which will measure from four to sixteen feet in diameter, and many thousands of them.

The St. Joseph and St. Mary's rivers have long been known as the timber section of north Idaho, which is second only, perhaps, to that on Puget Sound. For miles and miles along those streams can be seen giant cedar, tamarack, fir, and pine, and it is to tap this wonderful region that the Northern Pacific last year had a preliminary survey run for a branch road from Rathdrum to Cœur d'Alene Lake, there to connect with steamers from the upper waters of the streams named, the company evidently having an eye on the future importance of the lumbering interests there.

While Spokane Falls has been widely boomed on account of its water power, very little is known abroad of Post Falls, commonly called Little Falls, on the Spokane River, about eight miles below Fort Cœur d'Alene, though as a matter of fact the latter is far ahead of the former, because Post Falls can be readily and cheaply utilized. The mill-site at Post Falls was taken up by Frederick Post in 1871, and at this time he has a large saw and planing mill in active operation. At the back part of this mill one can overlook Post Falls, and it is the grandest sight it has ever been our pleasure to behold. Much has been said of the beauty of Post Falls, yet to be fully appreciated, one must visit the spot. The water surges and dashes down the cañon. The river above the falls spreads out in a quiet, glassy sheet, and little does one suspect, except as the sound of roaring waters reaches his ear, that such a wonderful water-power is close at hand. Immediately above the falls the river is divided by a high, sharp rock bluff, the south branch of the river, on the reservation side, descending in a series of ripples or rapids. The other branch over Post Falls narrows down to about thirty feet in width, and makes an abrupt leap of eighteen feet; then comes a series of falls for the next 300 feet, in which the river drops about forty feet. Something like 100 feet to the north of the falls a canal has been blasted out of the solid rock, and then turns its waters into the river just above the lower falls, but before being discharged must work the machinery of the mill above mentioned. The water-power here is unlimited.

The towering cañon on the opposite side, the great roar of the mighty torrent as it leaps over the falls, somewhat resembling artillery, the seething waters at our feet, and the spray dashing in one's face like a shower-bath, cause many grand scenes of the past to pale into insignificance. Art to a certain extent gives an idea, but nature truly furnishes the real. On the north bank of the river, just above the falls, there is a beautiful level strip of land extending up and down the river for nearly a mile and over one mile back from the river, on which, at no distant day, we believe a beautiful town will be laid out which will rival Spokane Falls. Across the river, high up on the mountain side, springs of ice-cold water gush out which could at but little expense supply a town here with pure, fresh water. From the falls to the lake, a distance of only eight miles, the river is deep and comparatively quiet, the steamer from the lake running to within less that a mile of the Falls.

The Demand for Lumber.—Several mills are running lower down the river on logs secured on the St. Joseph and St. Mary's rivers. These logs are cut, thrown into the rivers named, and run down into Cœur d'Alene Lake, thence to Post Falls and still farther down the stream; yet owing to the rapids and eddies in the river between Post Falls and Spokane Falls, it is very expensive getting the logs to Spokane, and thus it will be readily seen that the cost is very much less to hold the logs above than to drive them below Post Falls. The demand for all kinds of lumber must increase as the country advances in settlement. With the exception of about one hundred and fifty miles along the line of the Northern Pacific (almost the whole distance within the lines of Idaho Territory), there is comparatively little timber fit for lumber, and hence the timber belt of North Idaho must furnish all lumber used along the railroad from the Cascades on the west through Montana and into Dakota on the east; in other words, several thousand miles of country to be supplied from the Cœur d'Alene, St. Joseph and St. Mary's rivers.

Mining.—The advent of the Northern Pacific has rendered easily accessible many hitherto unknown mineral districts in Northern Idaho. In Kootenai County, fifty miles east of Cœur d'Alene, and near the old Mullan wagon road, a vein was recently discovered four feet thick, showing free gold, assaying from $60 to $700 per ton. A number of other rich quartz and placer mines have been discovered recently in the neighborhood. It is supposed to be a continuation of the mineral belt of southern and central Idaho. In the mountains about Pend d'Oreille River, croppings of heavy lead ores, rich in silver, have been found, but owing to their remoteness hitherto, but little has been done in the way of development. Still farther north, from fifty to one hundred miles, is a gold quartz and placer belt. A small amount of work has been done on the placers, and still less on the quartz. The whole region stretching northward is practically unexplored and unprospected.

The Sullivan Creek district was visited by Roger Sullivan in 1863, and the district was named after him. For many years placer mining was carried on to a considerable extent, and much gold-dust and many handsome nuggets were taken out. The placer fields cover an area of about twenty-five miles, and are advantageously situated for rapid development, the water-fall being ample, and it being only two or three feet to bed-rock in the deepest places. The high bars also prospect remarkably well. Very recently rich strikes have been made, and during the past fall the region was considerably prospected. The indications show large quantities of gold near the surface.

The claims so far opened are near the mouth of Sullivan Creek where it empties into Pend d'Oreille River, immediately below the Big Falls. Marvelous tales have been told about caves in which fabulous quantities of gold have been seen near the Big Falls. Making all due allowance for exaggeration, there is no doubt a brilliant future for this district. During the past season miners flocked in from all directions. The owners of several claims have been putting in sluices and running drain ditches for the purpose of opening up their recent finds.

The Pend d'Oreille mines are about thirty-five miles from Rathdrum by way of Spirit Lake Valley. A road is already built to the valley, and from there down to the river is not over fifteen miles. A road will be built the remaining distance very readily, as it is an even grade all the way, there being no mountains or even high hills to cross.

Both above and below the Big Falls, as well as in the tributaries of the Pend d'Oreille, gold is found in paying quantities.

Agriculture.—The beautiful prairie reaching northward from Lake Cœur d'Alene, though settled but recently, has already proved itself capable of raising good crops without irrigation. All kinds of cereals grow readily, and as railroad communication has been established, a ready market can be found for produce raised.

Rathdrum.—Among the most promising young towns of Idaho during the past year was Rathdrum, the county seat of Kootenai County. Built soon after the arrival of the Northern Pacific, its advantages as a distributing point for a large scope of country soon became manifest. Some of the richest soil in the Territory is in its neighborhood. Crops of finest quality can be raised without irrigation. Seventy-five bushels of grain are a fair crop. The climate is mild and salubrious. In its vicinity can be found some of the finest scenery in the land. Cœur d'Alene and Pend d'Oreille, besides a number of smaller lakes, are within easy distance. In September, 1883, the town was visited by fire and nearly completely destroyed. It soon recovered from this loss, however, and rebuilding began in earnest.

At the breaking out of the Cœur d'Alene excitement last winter and spring, Rathdrum was the chief railroad point of departure for those coming from the west. During last February and March, the town was subjected to an exciting boom. The streets were crowded with gold-seekers. Every available space in the hotels, restaurants, saloons, and stores was occupied for sleeping purposes. Houses and stores sprung up like magic. The new buildings were of superior and even costly character. Commodious hotels and elegantly appointed saloons gave the place an appearance almost cosmopolitan, that was strongly in contrast with that of many suddenly developed railroad "cities." The enterprise of the citizens was manifested by the introduction of water through pipes, and brought from neighboring mountain springs. A weekly newspaper, the *Kootenai Courier*, under the editorship of M. W. Musgrove, published to the world the varied resources of the Kootenai country.

In the expectation of a tremendous rush to the Cœur d'Alene mines, merchants and business men laid in heavy supplies of goods. After the Cœur d'Alene stampede, the inevitable reaction set in, and the busy spring season was followed by a summer of unprecedented dullness and quiet. Business languished, many of the fine buildings were deserted, and the enterprising young town found itself stranded on the reefs of a mining excitement. Just at the time when the place was experiencing its dullest and most hopeless period, as if to inflict a crushing final blow, the devastating fire of September 27, 1884, visited it, and within a few short hours transformed to smoke and ashes the substantial evidences of the enterprise of the citizens. The entire business part of the town was swept away. Two or three firms were insured. The rest was a complete total loss. Many of the people were left homeless and shelterless. With a spirit of true grit, however, before the smoldering embers had cooled, the people set to work to rebuild the town.

Spirit Valley is north of Rathdrum about 15 miles, and is indeed a charming spot. It is about 24 miles long, and averages three miles in width. It is covered by the most luxuriant bunch-grass and well watered by mountain brooks. Fourteen claims have already been taken and are now being fenced; besides, several comfortable dwellings have been erected, and it is said there is plenty of room for 500 more. It will not be long before this valley is settled up by a thrifty, enterprising people.

The Place for a Poor Man.—The *Kootenai Courier*, to whose editor we acknowledge ourselves indebted for much of the foregoing relative to this county, has the following sensible remarks for those intending to come to Kootenai in search of homes: "North Idaho is no doubt the best place for a poor man to get a start of any farming country on the globe, if he is willing to put all his ambition and energy into operation, and put up with a few hardships for a year or two. Men have come here with barely enough money to put up their buildings—and some without even enough for that—who are now worth thousands of dollars. We do not mean to infer from this that every one can get rich here in a year or two—and a great many who came here with that idea in their heads have found it out—but we do mean to say that for the right kind of a man there awaits him here a bountiful harvest financially. Some folks in the East get the notion that they can come here and 'show these fellows how to run a farm,' whether they ever saw one or not; and imagine their surprise when they get here to try it and find that there are just as smart men and just as good farmers in Idaho as there are in the States. This is the class that afterwards go back East and try to run down the country, but all they can do does not affect in any way the harvests; and while they are blowing so much about the country, they are only advertising it unknowingly. Then, again, there is a class of people who are of a roving disposition, who are not contented anywhere, and this class, too, will say all they can against the country. Those who belong to either of these classes are a great deal better off where they are; but to the farmers—those who are willing to settle down and grow up with the country, put out shrubbery and engage in general diversified farming—we say again, a golden harvest awaits you."

LEMHI COUNTY.

Early History.—Prior to the summer of 1866, all of that part of Idaho Territory embraced within the present limits of Lemhi and Custer counties was a trackless, unbroken wilderness, over which the foot of the white man had not yet passed. The way to it lay over snow-clad peaks, through rocky gorges, and over deep and rapid streams, fed by the melted snow from the everlasting hills. Many a hard day's march, many hardships and dangers, awaited him who would wrest from the hands of the savage owner this fair, promising region, and open it up to civilization and to settlement. The son of the forest was the sole owner and proprietor. What mattered it to him if in every hill were veins of gold and silver; if in every gulch and in the bed of every limpid stream were golden sands; had he but a sufficiency of game and fish to satisfy the cravings of hunger, and enough skins and furs to shield him in a measure from the rude blast, he was content. But a change came over the scene. With the discovery of gold in California came an influx of adventurers from every land and clime, eager to claim and possess a share in the golden harvest. California, with all its wealth of gold and treasure, was too small to contain them. Like a vessel filled to overflowing, it could not hold them all; some drifted hither and thither, seeking other fields; some, more daring than others, ventured farther into the vast and unbroken wilderness. On every hand new mineral fields were opened, and the lucky discoverers rewarded by rich finds. Can it be wondered at that, with rich mines on every side, this hitherto unexplored country should attract the attention of the prospector, and fill his mind with the thought that where there was so much all around it, there must be something still better within? In the summer of 1866, a party of miners and prospectors discovered rich placer grounds in the Leesburg Basin, about seventeen miles west of the present site of Salmon City. This discovery of rich diggings spread far and wide, and attracted a large number of miners and prospectors, with whose advent came the first permanent settlement of the country. In those early days this was a part of Idaho County, with Florence as the county seat. The county seat was over 800 miles distant by the nearest traveled route, and for a great portion of the year the condition of the roads and trails made communication with Florence impossible, and at best slow and uncertain. The creation of a new county became a matter of public necessity, and in July, 1867, a provisional county government was organized, which was, by act of the territorial legislature, passed in January, 1869, permanently established as the county of Lemhi, with Salmon City as the county seat. Lemhi County is situated in north-eastern Idaho, bounded on the north and east by Montana Territory, the main chain of the Rocky Mountains, and Oneida County, on the south by Alturas and Custer counties, and on the west by Idaho County. Its area is about 4,470 square miles—nearly 3,000,000 acres. Of this vast area, about 300,000 acres are suitable for cultivation, and situated in two great valleys—the Lemhi and Pahsamari—and numerous small vales along the numerous creeks and streams tributary to the main rivers.

Lemhi Valley, the largest, best settled, and most extensively cultivated valley in Lemhi County, is 70 miles in length, and varies in width from 3 to 6 miles, comprising within its limits bottom and bench lands of unsurpassed fertility, adapted by reason of its low altitude and sheltered situation to the successful cultivation of all cereals, vegetables, and fruits. From the first settlement up to the present date, a failure to produce an abundant crop has been unknown. The principal crops raised in Lemhi Valley are wheat, oats, barley, and potatoes.

The wheat crop of Lemhi Valley has never yet proved a failure, yielding from 40 to 50 bushels of a fine, hard No. 1 wheat, weighing 58 to $62\frac{1}{2}$ pounds to the bushel; a steadily increasing home demand creating a good market at $1.20 per bushel: this has been the ruling price for a number of years. Oats have been for years a never-failing crop, yielding from 45 to 55 bushels to the acre, of heavy, full kernels, weighing 45 pounds to the bushel, and commanding a ready sale at from $1\frac{1}{2}$ to 2 cents per pound, with a demand always in excess of the supply.

Barley has been but little cultivated, although as safe and certain a crop as wheat or oats, yielding from 35 to 45 bushels to the acre, and selling at 2 cents per pound. An elevation of from four to six thousand feet above sea-level has been proved to be the natural home of the potato, yielding in that altitude the best crops, of a superior quality. Lemhi Valley has been justly famous for the superior quality of the potatoes grown there, finding a ready market and sale everywhere in the mining camps. The yield of potatoes in this valley has averaged over 250 bushels to the acre, and the market price varies from $1.50 to $4.50 per hundred pounds, according to season. They are of exceptionally large size, white, mealy, and delicious. The writer has seen some of these tubers weighing four pounds eight ounces, and was assured by the producer that he had bushels of the same kind in his field, all sound and solid potatoes. During the 17 years in which Lemhi Valley has been farmed, no failure of this crop has ever been reported.

All kinds of garden vegetables, such as pease, beans, tomatoes, beets, cucumbers, rhubarb, onions, etc., are successfully cultivated, yielding large profits, and the yield everywhere is greater than in other portions of the United States. All the produce in excess of the home demand finds a ready sale at good prices.

Unlike other portions of the United States, where the husbandman puts in his crops in the anticipation that beneficent nature will provide the necessary rain-fall (and in which expectation he is often grievously mistaken, and subjected alternately to heavy loss, if not utter ruin by reason of floods or drought), in this portion of Idaho irrigation is depended upon to insure the ripening of crops. Every eastern farmer who has settled here and made a home has, after a trial of this plan, pronounced it as being a decided advantage over the unaided process of nature. The moisture so necessary to the growing crops can be uniformly applied and regulated, insuring an absolute certainty of crop, enabling the farmer to produce a heavier crop, and to secure a larger growth.

By reason of their gradual slope, and the abundance of water which can be obtained for the purpose, the lands of this valley, and those of the adjoining valleys of the Pahsamari, can all be brought under successful cultivation, thus offering to the industrious home-seeker an opportunity to make a home and rear his family under circumstances and conditions more favorable than in any other section of the great West. Hundreds of families can here find a home. The margins of the streams are sufficiently timbered for all the necessities of the settler; furnishing him with the logs for his house, rails for his fences, and fuel for all his present needs. Should in the course of time this supply of timber be exhausted by consumption, then the pine-clad hills back of the farm will furnish an inexaustible supply of fire-wood, rails, logs, and lumber.

The question of fruit-raising has passed beyond the range of experiment. Although little attention has been given to this branch by the majority of the settlers here, they deeming it somewhat uncertain, a few more enterprising men, foreseeing a source of profit if success should attend their venture, have engaged in this pursuit. The first trees were set out in 1873, comprising the hardier standard varieties of apples, plums, and cherries. Many of these trees were in bearing this season (1884), and have yielded a goodly crop of good, sound apples, free from worms. Orchards have been started everywhere in the valley, and in a few years will contribute their share in adding to the general wealth and prosperity of the county, besides beautifying and enhancing the attractions of the homes of the settlers.

Butter-making has been for many years one of the most successful and profitable industries of Lemhi Valley. The vast ranges in the foot-hills, over a million acres in area, are covered with a rich growth of native grasses, commonly known as bunch-grass, affording the best pasturage in the world, and having that greatest of advantages—freedom to all who may feel inclined to utilize it. The cows feeding upon this grass produce an abundance of rich milk, thus enabling the dairyman to produce butter of unsurpassed quality and flavor. Lemhi Valley butter has a reputation in every mining camp in the Territory, and is preferred by all who have once used it over all other kinds imported from other localities, and commands the best price. The demand has always been in excess of the supply—thousands of cans being sold annually at from forty to fifty cents per pound.

Nearly all the settlers who are now engaged in farming and dairying began in a small way; from small beginnings they have grown up with the country, and have acquired comfortable homes, and are in every sense of the word prosperous, clear of debt, and with money laid by for a rainy day.

Lemhi County has, as before stated, over a million acres of the best public range to be found anywhere on the Pacific slope, the best of pasturage and grazing grounds, well watered by never-failing springs and streams, a dry atmosphere during summer and winter, curing the rich, nutritious grasses as they grow, and which, dry as they are, produce a feed compared with which hay and grain sink into insignificance. With mild winters, exceptionally free from snows and storms, this part of the Territory is especially and peculiarly attractive for the stock-raiser. Here cattle, horses, and sheep can be turned out during summer and winter without shelter and prepared feed, the range affording feed the year round without cost. This range it comparatively unoccupied, and when it is considered that with such natural facilities the cost, including taxes, of raising a full-grown steer, worth from $35 to $50, is not more than $3.50, and the cost of producing a good horse, worth from $85 to $100, is but $6, the profits to be derived from an investment in this industry are easily computed.

Stock-raising has been highly profitable to those engaged in it in Lemhi County. The loss of cattle and horses in all these years has not been more than three per cent per annum. Those who are now rated as wealthy stock-growers in this section made small beginnings, and have grown rich in a comparatively short time. It is capable of accurate demonstration that the profits made in this industry annually are not less than thirty-three and a third per cent on all capital invested. Wool-growing has not been attempted as yet, and the opportunities for engaging in sheep-raising in Lemhi County are as good as anywhere in the Territory, there being ample room on the range for thousands of cattle, horses, and sheep.

Beef steers find a ready sale in all the mining camps at prices varying from $40 to $60. Dairy cows are in demand at from $50 to $75, according to age and breeding. Stock cattle bring from $22 to $28, and yearlings in a like proportion.

The Pahsamari Valley is thirty-five miles in length, and from two to five wide, and as yet unoccupied, save by a few stock-raisers. No farming is being done there. There is room and land for hundreds of the industrious, who can here settle and make homes, and find a ready market for all their produce. The same conditions exist there as in Lemhi Valley, the only difference being a slightly higher elevation, but all the industries so successfully flourishing in Lemhi Valley can be engaged in in Pahsamari Valley with like success.

The following grasses are grown in both valleys: timothy, red-top, bluestem, and clover. The yield is from two and a half to three tons per acre.

Timber.—Around the north fork of the Salmon River, and within thirty-five miles of Salmon City, is perhaps the finest body of pine timber in all Idaho Territory. Trees three and four feet in diameter, and attaining a height of sixty and seventy feet without a limb, are common. All the varieties of the *conifera* are here found. As the forests of the other States and Territories are gradually and surely being swept away by the ruthless hand of the lumberman, and converted into building material, this timber region will prove to be the source of great wealth to the county at no distant day. It is estimated by competent men who have had a large experience in this branch of business, that this timber region of Lemhi County is alone capable of supplying two hundred million feet of as fine lumber as can be found anywhere in the world. Timbers sixty to seventy feet in length, without a knot, can be produced, of unrivaled strength and resisting power. As New England has by reason of its water-power attained and still holds the front rank in the manufacturing sections of the United States, so will this portion of Idaho in some future day become a manufacturing center; with clear, rapid streams on every hand, of sufficient force and fall to turn the wheels of hundreds of mills, the eyes of capitalists cannot and will not fail to observe these advantages. It is estimated that Salmon River alone can furnish the power to run all the spindles and looms of New England. Lemhi River has a fall of about 1,800 feet in 50 miles, and along its banks are hundreds of favorable locations for mill-sites, with ample water-power for all possible needs and demands. The facilities for cheap production are here; it needs but the introduction of capital and enterprise to lay the foundation for a great and prosperous community.

The tourist will find in the limits of this county some of the finest and grandest scenery on the entire Pacific slope. It is admitted that some of the most picturesque mountain scenery is seen on a trip from Salmon City along Salmon River to the mouth of the North Fork, and from thence up that stream to the head waters and the mines of Gibbonsville. The sportsman can here find all the varieties of game common to this mountain region, from the grizzly, the king of the Rockies, down to the agile and sportive jack-rabbit. All the mountain streams abound with that most toothsome of all fish, the mountain trout. The salmon, salmon-trout, and red fish are found in great numbers in Salmon River at their proper seasons in the year, affording unlimited sport for the disciple of Izaak Walton.

The denizen of the crowded and heated cities in search of a cool and shady spot for recreation and leisure can here find all that he could wish for; a rarified, dry, pure atmosphere, with almost constantly bright, genial sunshine, pure water, moderately warm days, and cool nights. While his luckless friend or neighbor is doing some fashionable watering-place or summer resort in the East, penned up like a sardine in a box, in an over-crowded hotel, broiling in the sun by day and sweltering in the sultry heat by night, he is enjoying sunshine without excessive heat, and delightfully cool nights.

Mining Industry.—Lemhi County is situated in what is now acknowledged by all experienced mining men to be the richest mineral field of the Rocky Mountain region. On the north and east the Bitter Root and the main chain of the Rocky Mountains form its northern and eastern boundary for a distance of nearly two hundred miles, on the south and west the famous Salmon River Range, with its many spurs, forms its southern and western boundary. Within these ranges, and entirely within the county lines, fifteen mining districts have been organized within the boundaries, in which both placer and quartz mining are extensively and profitably carried on. The oldest of these districts, and from the discovery of which date the first settlement and subsequent prosperity of the county, is the Leesburg or Nappins mining district. In the summer of 1866, rich placer mines were found, and claims were staked and preparations made for their early development. The fame of these new discoveries spread with its usual rapidity, and a stampede from the surrounding country at once was started, bringing into the region a multitude of miners and others eager to secure some of the riches scattered broadcast by the lavish hand of nature. This district embraces all the country drained by Nappins, Camp, Rapp, Arnetts and Big creeks, with all the bars and gulches tributary thereto. Its production in gold has been about $500,000 annually from 1867 to 1873, being for the period of seven years the princely sum of $3,500,000. Since 1873, when many of the claims were bought up by large companies and consolidated for the purpose of working the ground by putting in bed-rock flumes, the yield has been less. In this way nearly all the claims became absorbed, and are now being worked by these large companies, many of whom have ground enough to last for several generations. The annual yield since 1873 has been about $300,000, making for a period of eleven years $3,300,000, and swelling the total yield to the verge of $7,000,000—truly a magnificent showing. This district will continue to yield for many years to come from $300,000 to $400,000 in gold annually, and thousands of acres are as yet virgin ground, which may at any time swell the annual yield by two or three hundred thousand additional.

Quartz mining has not been carried on very extensively, but a number of fine veins carrying free gold have been discovered, and some development made, with flattering prospects for the future. This portion of our county has as yet received no attention from prospectors for quartz. It is a well-established fact that all placer gold is the result of washings of the gold from quartz veins, the gold in the course of ages having become separated from the vein and been deposited in the gravel. In a district like this, where every shovelful of gravel shows the presence of some "colors" when washed, it is but reasonable to infer that veins of quartz exist in the adjacent hills which only await the patient searcher, and no doubt will richly reward the lucky finder for all the time and money expended in the search. Leesburg mining district is connected with Salmon City by a fairly passable wagon-road.

Adjacent to Leesburg district, and the next oldest in point of discovery, is the Daly Creek mining district, discovered in 1866-7, which comprises all the country drained by Daly Creek and its tributaries. The first discovery was made in Sierra Gulch, in which the Discovery Company worked fifty-four men, paid out $2,100 each week in wages, and every member of which left for the States (the Mecca of all successful miners) in four months with a fortune. This gulch paid $100 a day to the man. This district produced $250,000 the first year, $300,000 the second year, and has ever since 1868, up to the present year, yielded $25,000 in gold-dust, which has been added to the circulating medium of the world, making all told to date nearly $1,000,000. The character and quality of the gold is identical with that of Moose Creek District, being well washed and about .900 fine, worth, according to mint assay, about $18.25 per ounce. Deposit of gravel is about ten feet thick. Claims are developed and worked through a bed-rock flume, about 1,600 feet in length. Unlimited facilities for disposing of the mining *débris* are at hand. The season lasts from five to six months. There is still a large area of ground unclaimed and unworked in this district which would pay very handsome profits for working. No quartz has been prospected for, although the indications are very favorable for finding good veins carrying free gold. This district is surrounded by low hills covered by young pines of sufficient size for all present and future needs.

In Moose Creek mining district is situated the famous Moose Creek hydraulic mine, situated on Moose Creek Flat, several miles in length by a half mile in width, with a deposit of gravel underlying its entire length and breadth, of a thickness of twelve feet at the lower end, which gradually increases to twenty-three feet as the upper end of the claim is reached. The claim was first located by individual miners in 1868, who tried to develop their claims independent of each other, but failed to make a success. The property finally came into the hands of the present owner, who for a number of years worked the ground in the old way, without the use of improved machinery. Becoming convinced that improved machinery would largely enhance the productive capacity of the ground, the profits of several years were expended in a more intelligent and satisfactory development of the ground. A bed-rock flume was commenced and extended along the claim a distance of 2,300 feet to the present workings. This flume is sixteen feet below the bed-rock, five feet wide and seven feet high, and through it all the washings, *débris*, and sands are sent to the Salmon River, six miles below, on a grade of 500 feet to the mile. It is estimated that the water rushes through this flume at the rate of a mile a minute, carrying with it in its irresistible force large rocks too heavy for the strongest man to handle. A large reservoir, of a capacity for storing about ten or twelve million cubic feet of water, has been constructed at great expense. A high flume, 1,275 feet in length, was constructed to secure additional water facilities. Twenty-five tons of iron pipe and two No. 5 giants were purchased, and the entire claim was put in first-class condition for work on the most approved plan, at a total cost of over $100,000, all of which was money taken out of the claim. The gold taken out of the claim was of unusual fineness and value, being none under .900 fine, and worth from $18.75 to $19.25 per ounce. About thirty-five acres have been worked since the first opening of the claim, yielding $400,000. Of this amount $350,000 have been taken out since the new improved machinery has been put in.

In the same district, and about two miles south-east from this claim, is the Shoo-fly quartz-mining claim, discovered in 1873. This mine is from ten to twelve feet in width between walls, and the ore extracted from wall to wall has yielded on an average $40 to the ton. No ore has ever been sorted, but the whole was dumped on the mill floor without sorting. Work has been prosecuted on this vein in a desultory way—working one season and abandoning work for two or three seasons, all except assessment work. The retort obtained from the mill runs shows the extraordinary value of $19 per ounce, which is the highest value ever obtained from quartz gold. A five-stamp mill is part of the improvements on this property, which has yielded $30,000.

A number of other quartz claims have been located in this district, but owing to the lack of capital have not been developed to a great extent. The hills here, as well as in all the other districts before mentioned, are covered by a heavy growth of pine timber of the best quality for mining timbers, etc. This district is about seventeen miles from Salmon City, and connected with it by wagon-road and trail.

North Fork or Dahlonega Mining District is situated about 40 miles north-west of Salmon City, on the north fork of Salmon River and Dahlonega and Anderson creeks, and was first discovered during the early days of the placer excitement in 1867. At that time some rich gold-bearing gravel was found, but not proving profitable to work, was abandoned until 1879, when the first discoveries of quartz were made and numerous claims were located. The mines of this district are true fissure veins from three to nine feet wide, carrying free gold and gold-bearing pyrites. The ore yields from $20 to $180 per ton, and is not refractory, being easily reduced for the free gold in the stamp-mill, and the pyrites after being concentrated readily give up the gold contained in them by roasting and chlorination. An extensive area of placer mining ground has been located on Dahlonega and Anderson creeks in this district, which has paid well and is improving in yield every year, the gold being of a heavy, coarse character; some nuggets have been found worth $20 to $30. Of the many quartz lodes the Huron, Oneida, Rose, Keystone, Sucker, Eureka, Golden Circle, Twin Brothers, Bill Edwards, McCarthy, Monster, Mammoth, Montgomery, St. Joe, and Sucker Extension have been more or less developed, and have paid from the surface down. Many other promising locations have been made which will in time prove to be valuable mines.

A ten-stamp quartz mill chlorination works of a capacity for ten tons per day, and six arrastras, furnish the reduction machinery for the ores, and a saw-mill produces the finest qualities of lumber from the almost inexhaustible pineries of this region. The Golden Circle Mining Company employs about 50 men steadily, and will in the near future double its pay-roll. Dahlonega Creek and the north fork of Salmon River furnish the water-power necessary for all the machinery needed for concentration and reduction of ores. Discoveries of new mines and rich strikes in the old ones are placing this district in the front ranks of gold-mining districts of this county. The past production of placer and quartz gold of this district is about $75,000, and from present indications will be $150,000 this coming year.

Mineral Hill District is situated about 45 miles north-west of Salmon City, and although the latest discovered bids fair to rank with any of the districts in Idaho in point of richness of ores and facilities for large production. This is also a gold camp. The veins are bold, well defined, and strong, varying from four to thirty feet in width from wall to wall.

The Kentuck is a well-defined vein, which has been traced by its outcrop for more than 4,500 feet. The present developments have uncovered in all the workings a body of high-grade gold ore, averaging over seven feet of solid pay dirt, and quartz assaying from $175 to $1,500 per ton. Developments, 350 feet of tunnels, shafts, ore-houses, boarding and bunk houses. The machinery for a complete ten-stamp mill has been shipped for reducing the ores of this mine. On the same vein, commencing at the edge of Salmon River and cropping out a distance of over 500 feet, is the Grunter mine. Considerable work has been done on this claim, and a large quantity of ore has been extracted. The ore is of the same character as the Kentuck, and the vein is as well defined and strong wherever opened as in the Kentuck. A cross-cut has been run on the vein which had cut one wall and had advanced 30 feet all in ore, and no other wall in sight. Assays show a value of from $50 to $1,200 per ton. A ten-stamp mill of approved pattern has been in operation 60 days, and has thus far produced bullion enough to pay for cost of mill and all running expenses, and a handsome surplus over for future developments and improvements. Bowlder Creek furnishes ample water-power for this mill, and will likewise be utilized as power for the new mill to be erected for the Kentuck. Many other claims have been located in this district which bid fair to develop rich and paying mines. This whole region is well timbered for the needs of many years of mining, and is procured at a very slight cost.

Yellow Jacket District is situated about sixty miles west from Salmon City, and was first prospected for placers in 1869. The principal mines in this district, however, are quartz, free-gold ores, easily reduced by the ordinary stamp-mill process.

The North and South American claims are the most important and best developed. These ledges run parallel, showing croppings 30 to 40 feet in width, and have been traced a distance of two miles. Developments consist of tunnels, shafts, and drifts many hundred feet in length, exposing large bodies of free-gold ore running from $10 to $45 per ton.

The North American extension contains a very large body of ore assaying from $15 to $25 per ton. The country rock is porphyry; the hills low and timbered with pine. Grass and water abound. A ten-stamp mill has been in operation nearly two years, and has produced a large amount of bullion. Experienced miners assert that there is ore enough above ground on the various claims in the district to keep a fifty-stamp mill running for many years.

It is reported that large bodies of silver-lead ore are to be found about 20 miles to the north from this section, but on account of the isolation and distance from supplies, these mines have received no attention from capitalists.

About ten miles from Yellow Jacket is Prairie Basin, in which a number of promising mines have been discovered, among which the Watch-tower, Monument, True Blue, and Bobtail are the principal ones. The Watch-tower is a ten-foot vein carrying both gold and silver, and crops out a distance of 1,200 feet. The Monument crops out 30 feet above ground, showing a strong vein of mineral about 12 feet wide, assaying from $10 to $500. The True Blue is an extension of the Monument, from which two tons of ore were shipped to Winnemucca, Nevada, and gave a yield of $248 per ton. This section has been but very little prospected, and would be an inviting field to the enterprising prospector.

Lemhi District is situated about eight-five miles east of Salmon City, and contains within its limits the famous Viola mine. This is a vast vein of carbonate and galena ore, some sixty feet in width, carrying from forty to seventy per cent lead and from thirty to seventy ounces of silver to the ton. Thousands of tons of this ore are annually extracted and shipped from the mine to Kansas City, Omaha, and Denver; but regardless of the amount of ore extracted, every blow of the pick reveals greater riches. All the workings are in ore, and it is estimated that over 60,000 tons are now in sight, and the end is not yet. This mine has produced nearly half a million dollars for its fortunate owners in a little less than two years. Many other valuable mines are being developed, in the hope that capital may be attracted, and that reduction works will be built, and in that event this district would alone add $500,000 annually to the metal product of Lemhi County. Nicholia is a little town which has been started by the mining company, contains a post-office, hotel, stage-barn, and a number of dwelling-houses occupied by the miners and their families. Population about 100.

Spring Mountain District is reached by a good wagon-road from Salmon City, and distant from that place about seventy-five miles in an easterly direction. The mines of this district are heavy carbonate and galena ores, ranging from 30 to 60 per cent lead and from 45 to 120 ounces in silver. Over 100 claims have been recorded, many of which have been developed and have plenty of ore on the dump ready for the smelter.

The Spring Mountain Mining Company has expended large sums in the development of numerous claims, has built a 30-ton water-jacket smelter, ore-houses, offices, and boarding-houses. A first-class saw-mill produces all the lumber required, and is also owned by the company. All the material for fluxing the ores of this district are at hand, limestone, iron ore, and quartz being abundant. A test run of ore has been made, has given satisfactory returns, and in a short time this promising district will be on a sound producing basis. Spring Mountain is the post-office, with a population of about 100.

Texas District, distant from Salmon City about sixty-five miles, is in many respects similar to the Spring Mountain district—carbonate and galena ores, varying from 40 to 60 per cent lead, and running from 40 to 500 ounces in silver. The veins are strong, well defined, and carry large bodies of ore, which is easily extracted, and can be taken from most of the mine-dumps in wagons. Iron and limestone abound and can be procured for fluxing with but little expense. A twenty-ton smelter and concentrator are in course of erection, and will be completed this season. A fine body of excellent timber is convenient, and a saw-mill is cheaply converting it into lumber of good quality.

Blue Wing or Pahsamari District is situated about sixty miles southeast of Salmon City, overlooking and close to Pahsamari Valley. Being favorably located in a sheltered section of country, with timber and water in abundance all around, a mild climate free from storms and snows, its many promising mines can be worked summer and winter. Forty to fifty claims have been located, and nearly all are more or less developed by tunnels and shafts, showing large bodies of good milling ore of fair grade and comparatively free of base metals. The general character of ores is silver chlorides, running from 50 to 240 ounces in silver to the ton. Thousands of tons of ore are above the surface in the croppings, ready to be blasted or picked down for reduction, the conditions being extremely favorable for cheap extraction and reduction. Like many other districts, this awaits but the magic hand of capital to pour out a continuous stream of precious metals for many years to come, giving profitable employment to many hundreds of miners and laborers, and returning handsome dividends to the fortunate investors.

The Lemhi Indian Reservation, extending from the summit of the main range of the Rockies to the summit of the Salmon River range, and being about 100 square miles in area, besides taking in a very large part of the finest farming and grazing lands in Lemhi Valley, is known to contain as rich mines of gold, silver, copper, lead, and iron as have been discovered anywhere in the county; but being an Indian reservation, the prospector, miner, and farmer are alike excluded therefrom. The mineral lands contained within the reservation should be thrown open for exploration and purchase, as they cannot be a benefit to the Indians. If this were done another mining district would be opened up which would equal if not surpass any of the now famous mining districts of Idaho.

Salmon City District.—Within a radius of seventeen miles of Salmon City, and connected with it by good wagon-roads, are situated many good mines of gold quartz, which will, by reason of the large bodies of ore in sight and above ground, attract the attention of capitalists. These mines are favorably situated for development, and their ores can be cheaply extracted and milled with large profit. Some of the principal of these claims are the Silver Star, Freeman, California, Washoe, Ranger, and El Dorado.

The Silver Star is about fifteen miles north of Salmon City, on Morse Creek, showing as large an outcrop as any mine in Lemhi County. The ore is contained in three large chimneys, and about 12,000 tons are estimated to be above ground ready to be mined. A large amount of ore has been blasted down, and is ready for the mill; very little work has been done below the surface. The ore is a lively, light gray quartz, and carries from $20 to $30 in gold to the ton, and can be mined and milled for $7 per ton. A sufficient quantity of water to run a twenty-stamp steam mill is within 100 feet of the mine. Timber is abundant and easy to obtain. A good wagon-road connects the mine with Salmon City. The mine is patented, and an absolute title can be given.

The Ranger mine is eighteen miles east of Salmon City, is developed, and opened up by shafts, tunnels, and drifts, to the depth of 200 feet; is a strong eighteen-inch vein, and mill runs show $20 to the ton.

The El Dorado, within sight of the Ranger, is a six-foot vein, and mills $10 to the ton, with an unlimited body of ore exposed in all the works. A wire tramway and a first-class twenty-stamp mill have been put up for working the ores of these mines. A wagon-road connects both mines with Salmon City.

The Freeman mine is eighteen miles north of Salmon City, is opened by tunnels and a shaft about seventy feet in depth, showing a vein varying from twelve inches to three feet in width. The ore is free-milling gold quartz, working $20 to the ton, with a large amount on the dumps and exposed in the workings. Fine water-power for all necessary machinery is within half a mile of the mine.

The California is one mile west of the Freeman, and opened by two tunnels run in on the vein, showing ore all the way. The lowest tunnel is in eighty feet; average width of vein is eighteen inches, of good, free-milling gold ore, averaging $21 per ton. Timber is abundant all around these mines.

The Washoe is a strong vein of free-milling gold quartz, about three feet wide, from which assays have been obtained running $40 to the ton. Work has been done on the claim during a number of years.

Many other fine prospects have been found in the surrounding hills, and could be developed into good paying mines, but the poverty of the owners and lack of facility for reduction have prevented and retarded their development.

Salmon City, the county seat, is located at the confluence of the Lemhi with the Salmon River, and was located and laid out in 1867. It is the distributing point and base of supplies for all this section of north-eastern Idaho, has a population of 500, and is a thrifty, well-built town, containing hotels, stores, warehouses, and many dwelling-houses. A brick church has recently been completed at a cost of $3,500. A large, commodious school-house, costing $4,000, and affording ample educational facilities for present and future needs, has also been placed at the disposal of the people. The various secret and benevolent societies are in a flourishing condition, owning the buildings in which they meet. A fine bridge spans Salmon River at this place. The people are, as a general rule, industrious, thrifty, intelligent, and enterprising. A daily mail and stage line affords excellent facilities for communication with the railroad, 110 miles distant. Both Salmon and Lemhi rivers afford as good if not better water-power than can be found anywhere in the United States, and this place is a desirable point for investment of capital in manufactures. Salmon City, situated as it is in the center of a rich agricultural, stock-raising, and mining country, surrounded by some of the grandest scenery in the world, with a delightful climate, free from excessive heat in summer and extreme cold and storms in winter, is one of the most desirable places for residence in all the intermountain county.

Junction is fifty miles distant from the county seat, in the midst of a fine dairy and stock-raising community, not far distant from the now famous Viola, Spring Mountain, and Texas mining districts; its population is about 200; altitude 6,329 feet above sea-level. The town is favorably located on the Lemhi River, is well built, containing a fine hotel, stores, and dwelling-houses. This point is favorably located for dairying and stock-raising, many thousands of acres being as yet unoccupied and awaiting the advent of the industrious home-seeker.

Gibbonsville is situated on the north fork of Salmon River, about forty miles north of Salmon City, and is supported by the mines of that section, in the center of which it is located. Population about 100.

The present population of Lemhi County approximates 1,800. The total production of gold and silver from the placer and quartz mines of Lemhi

County since 1867 to date is over $8,700,000, an annual yield of over $500,000. The present year's production will not fall far short of $300,000, and can by the introduction of capital and proper reduction machinery be swelled to $1,500,000 in a very short time. With the Utah and Northern Railway within 100 miles of the Salmon River, a magnificent mining, farming, stock-raising, and dairy country on every hand, Lemhi County offers to the capitalists, manufacturers, miners, prospectors, settlers, and mechanics a field for profitable investment and labor second to no section in the United States. Its immense natural resources and natural advantages will at no distant day bring it to the front rank of any section of this young and growing Territory, the future State of Idaho.

NEZ PERCÉ COUNTY—NORTH IDAHO.

Nez Percé County was originally organized under an act of the legislature of Washington Territory, and embraced the following boundaries: Beginning at the mouth of the Clearwater River, thence up the same to the south fork of the Clearwater; thence with the south fork to the Lo Lo Creek; thence with a southern boundary of Shoshone County to the summit of the Bitter Root Mountains; thence south to the main divide to the waters of the Salmon River, and the south fork of Clearwater to the Snake River; thence with the Snake River to the mouth of the Clearwater, the place of beginning. This organization took place in 1861, one year and four months before the organization of Idaho Territory, and remained with these boundaries till the meeting of the first legislature of Idaho in 1863-4, when the southern boundary was changed so as to extend to Pittsburg Landing. At the meeting of the second legislature, 1834-5, two new counties, Lahtoh and Kootenai, were created, embracing the country north of the Clearwater, extending to the British line, and attached to Nez Percé for judicial purposes. At a subsequent legislature Lahtoh was abolished, and that portion south of the Hangman Creek Mountain made to form a part of Nez Percé County. At another subsequent legislature, that portion of Nez Percé lying south and east of a line drawn from the mouth of Moloney Creek on Salmon River to the mouth of the middle fork of Clearwater was attached to Idaho County. Nez Percé now extends from the Hangman Creek Mountain on the north to the Salmon River on the south, and from the Snake River and the one hundred and seventeenth meridian on the west for the boundaries of Shoshone, and Idaho on the east. Within these boundaries there are nearly nine hundred square miles of Indian reservation, embracing a large portion of the best lands in north Idaho. The present population of the county is not far from 9,000. The chief pursuits of the inhabitants are grain-raising and stock-raising. The eastern portion contains about one third of the area of the county—timbered lands—the remainder of the county consists of prairie lands and cañons of the streams. The prominent streams are the Clearwater, Potlatch Creek, a tributary thereto, Lapwai Creek, also a tributary, and the north and south Palouse rivers, tributary to the Snake River in Washington Territory. The general course of these rivers is from east to west, and they flow from the timbered lands on the east. The Clearwater is navigable for steamboats of light draft from the eastern boundaries of the county to the western. The Palouse River is only navigable for timber and lumber for about two months in each year. There is considerable use made of these rivers for lumbering purposes. With an expenditure of $50,000 the Clearwater can be made navigable at all seasons of the year, except when obstructed by ice for two or three months in the winter. The climate of the country is generally very mild; snow seldom falls in any part of the county more than one or two feet in any year, and except in the higher altitudes remains on the ground not more than two months. Sufficient rain falls to furnish all necessary moisture for the crops. We never have had since the organization of the county a failure of crops by reason of drought, although some years the yield in the crops has been greater than others, in consequence of more moisture. All kinds of hardy fruits are grown in the county, while on the lowlands, along the Clearwater, the finest of peaches and grapes are grown in abundance.

The average product of the wheat crop for the present year has been over thirty bushels per acre; the barley crop, about sixty; the oat crop, seventy; the flax crop, twenty-two. Instances of sixty bushels per acre have been raised in wheat, and eighty in barley, and one hundred and ten in oats, and thirty-two bushels in flax. Vegetables of all kinds have a very prolific growth. In some instances potatoes have been produced whose weight has been six and seven pounds each. Squashes have been raised the present season whose weight was from one hundred and thirty-five to one hundred and fifty pounds each. In the north-eastern portion of the county there are placer gold mines which have been worked for several years to profit, and recently there are other gold mines discovered farther east which now contain about two hundred population, where reliable reports give a yield of about $5 per day per man. There are organized in the county one independent school district, embracing the city of Lewiston and a small area of country adjacent, and other districts in the county. In this independent district, schools are taught nine months each year, in the other districts three months at least, and in some of them four and five months each year. In this independent district there are two school-houses: the one of the city of Lewiston proper built and furnished at a cost of about $13,000; in the other and outside of the city, at a cost of about $1,000. This district is under the management of five supervisors, one superintendent, and five teachers, aggregating a monthly salary of $355. In this district there are two hundred and eighty-two scholars, according to the last census, between the ages of five and twenty-one years, with about two hundred in regular attendance upon the public school, besides a collegiate institute, embracing about thirty scholars, under the control of the Methodist society; a Catholic sisters' school, just organized, embracing twenty pupils; a parochial Episcopal school, embracing ten scholars in regular attendance. The county contains, besides the city of Lewiston, five towns where there are trading posts, namely: Moscow, Viola, Chambers, Genesee, and Julietta. The most important of these is Moscow, containing a population of about eight hundred, with ten or twelve trading houses. Lewiston has about thirty trading houses; it has two good hotels, with several restaurants, and numerous saloons; it has a court-house and jail; it has five churches, where worship is maintained nearly every sabbath; it has numerous mechanical workshops for the different trades, and a resident population of about 1,800. The city is situated at the junction of the Snake and Clearwater rivers; steamboats on the Snake River reach this point twice per week, from the terminus of the Oregon Railroad and Navigation railroad at Riparia, a distance of seventy miles below Lewiston. The climate of Lewiston is milder than in any portion of the North-west. The thermometer in winter seldom goes below zero, but averages from twenty-six to fifty-four above zero. The heat in summer occasionally reaches to one hundred degrees above zero. It is considered one of the healthiest towns in the North-west, contagious diseases seldom obtaining any foothold in the town; although more than five hundred miles from the sea, the altitude of the place is less than eight hundred feet above the level of the sea. The other towns in the county, excepting Julietta, have an altitude of considerably over two thousand feet above the level of the sea, and the great bulk of the agricultural lands are situated over two thousand feet above the level of the sea; nevertheless, all the cereals, and vegetables, and fruits except the peach, are grown there with ease, and in great profusion. Lewiston was first settled in 1861; the town was located that year in consequence of the discovery of important gold mines, lying east of the Nez Percé County in Shoshone and Idaho counties, and for many years it was the trading emporium for all these mines.

Some fifteen hundred or two thousand pack-animals were, during every season except the winter, constantly employed in conveying goods and supplies to the mines east. As these mines began to diminish in their yield, so did the demand for transportation gradually diminish, and the people of Lewiston either deserted the place or changed their occupation to trade with the agricultural portion of the population, which gradually assumed large proportions in the surrounding country as the value and product of the lands became known. It is now a prominent shipping point for agricultural products which are sent to the Pacific as transportation facilities are furnished.

The population of the place is no greater than it was in 1861-2, but then it was merely transient; now it is permanent. At first the people mostly lived and did business in tents and small shanties; now they have many fine residences and shops and stores, which give the town an appearance of prosperity and happiness. Three daily, two tri-weekly mails, and one weekly mail, arrive at Lewiston.

Moscow, the second town in size, has a growth of only about six years. It is situated 27 miles north of Lewiston, in the midst of a fine agricultural country, and has a very prosperous trade with the farmers. There are five flouring-mills in the county: two at Lewiston, one at Moscow, one at Julietta, and one at Viola. The mills at Lewiston and at Moscow manufacture flour for a foreign market, besides manufacturing for home consumption. The assessable property of the county for the present year is $2,050,546, upon which there is levied a tax of seventeen mills on the dollar on that portion which is outside of the city of Lewiston, and eleven mills on that which is inside; that which is inside has an addition of six mills on the dollar as a city tax, and that which is in Lewiston independent school district has an additional tax of ten mills upon the dollar for school purposes. This seventeen-mill tax includes both county and territorial purposes, also the eleven-mill tax includes county and territorial purposes. Give this county cheap means of transportation of its surplus products to Portland, and no county in the territory has greater elements of prosperity than Nez Percé County.

ONEIDA COUNTY.

Oneida County, which disputes with Alturas the claim to possessing the largest area of any of Idaho's counties, is situated in the south-eastern portion of the territory. For over two hundred miles within its boundaries the Utah and Northern Railroad runs in a northerly direction. The Oregon Short Line crosses it from east to west. It is chiefly as an agricultural region that Oneida lays its claim to pre-eminence. In the neighborhood of Oxford and Malad Valley all the most important kinds of cereals and garden vegetables are raised. Wheat, oats, potatoes, cabbages, turnips, pease, and small fruits are successfully cultivated. The county itself is larger than some Eastern States, and throughout her borders may be found opportunities for almost any kind of an investment. It is at present attracting especial attention as a stock country. The stock ranges along Snake River cannot be surpassed. There are at the present writing probably not over 50,000 head of stock in the county, though the ranges are capable of sustaining many times that amount for years to come.

Malad City is the county seat, has a population of 1,000, and is the supply point for an extensive farming country. Franklin, near the head of Cache Valley, is the southernmost town in Idaho, dating its origin as far back as 1860. Oxford is the headquarters of the United States land-office for the district.

At the point where the Oregon Short Line and the Utah and Northern railways unite at Port Neuf is a place long noted in the West because of the associations and incidents connected with the stage lines of the past. Port Neuf Valley was, in the days of staging between Salt Lake and Montana, an oasis in the desert country at which travelers were glad to stop. The Harkness ranch was known to all travelers. The location is a most excellent one, because of the rich bottom-lands, and the fine stream of pure water. Port Neuf River heads off to the north-east, and has many pretty falls. These falls are formed by dams across the stream, the dams being simply a deposit of matter held in solution, which has built up very thin walls almost as firm as iron. The whole valley for forty or fifty miles abounds with this class of formation, skirted by fields of land. Mr. H. O. Harkness has a ranch extending along the river, where the soil is the best and easiest cultivated and irrigated. He has 400 acres of meadow-land, yielding large crops, and he cultivated the past year 100 acres in cereals, producing 4,000 bushels of small grain and 1,000 bushels of potatoes. His hay crop was over 300 tons, while most of his meadow-lands were pastured. He has about 7,500 cattle, 500 calves, and a large herd of horses and mules. Being a great admirer of fine stock, he has entered largely into the breeding of such, and has met with grand success. During the summer his ranch gives employment to about twenty men, and half that number during winter. His ranch and stock business is a sample of what Idaho farming can produce when managed properly.

The Harkness House, located near the McCammon depot, is a fine structure, lately completed. It is a two-story house, 30 by 132 feet, in which are twenty-four rooms for guests, and eleven other rooms, such as dining and cook rooms, office, parlors, etc., all of which are nicely furnished. A porch extends the full length of the front. A wing 22 by 32 feet is used as a store and post-office. A good stock of general merchandise is kept for sale, and exchanged for live-stock, produce, etc. A boarding and sale stable forms a prominent feature. This is 32 by 70 feet, two stories high, the first being used for stabling horses, while the upper floor has a capacity for the storage of thirty-five tons of hay on one side and 6,000 bushels of grain on the other, with a wagon-way between. Loaded wagons are hauled up to the upper floor by means of a railway operated by pulleys and horse-power. The river runs close to the hotel, and just below it are two very pretty falls, formed by a division of the water by an island. These falls are about sixteen feet high.

With such excellent hotel accommodations, pleasant surroundings, nice drives, etc., this is a delightful place to visit in the summer, and two railroads passing through make the place easily accessible.

Soda Springs.—To the people of Utah and Idaho Soda Springs has been long and favorably known, but because of the lack of transportation facilities, and until the completion of the Oregon Short Line Railway, it has only within a year or two been brought into prominence beyond the limit named. The town is situated on the Oregon Short Line Railway, 146 miles west of Granger, the junction of the main line of the Union Pacific, and 68 miles east of Pocotello, the junction of the Utah and Northern Railway with the first-named road.

It takes its name from the many fine mineral springs in its immediate vicinity, among them the famous Hooper and Ninety Per Cent, and because of the already ascertained medicinal properties of their waters, in connection with magnificent climate and scenery, good hunting and trout-fishing in forest and stream near by, will in the near future make Soda the most noted health and pleasure resort in the west, if not in the whole country. As to the comparative merits of the waters with those of other famous springs, we take the liberty of publishing an extract from a private letter recently received from a prominent physician. He says: "I was born and raised not far from Saratoga, have seen White Sulphur and most of the best springs in this country at least, and I must say that those at Soda Springs beat them all away out of sight."

The principal chemical ingredients of the waters are iron, sulphur, and magnesia, but all known and designated by old settlers by the name of Soda Springs.

The waters of many of the springs are sparkling, effervescent, and exceedingly pleasant to the taste, and the famous Hooper beautiful to look upon. This spring is located one and a half miles north of the Oregon Short Line depot, and about twenty feet from Soda Creek. From this spring about 600 inches of the most wholesome and pleasant-tasting soda-water flows all the year round. This water is about sixty per cent soda, and about four feet east of it is an ammonia spring, which boils up almost to the surface of the ground, and from which ammonia gases escape, which inhaled at the surface prove a sure cure for catarrh and headache. In this same group, and within a radius of twenty feet, are to be found a warm and cold mud spring, and a clear, pure, cold-water spring in addition to the two described above, the first-named being the only one which overflows its banks. They are now owned by the Oregon Short Line Railway Company and E. T. Williams.

Two miles north-east from the Hooper is located the Formation Spring, so named because of the wonderfully fantastic formation of the bed of its overflow, which by continually damming itself and changing its course, has exposed to the view of the pleasure-seeker about twenty acres of petrified brush, leaves, grass, moss, weeds, etc., and innumerable caves and grottoes of unknown depth and extent. The water of this spring is strongly impregnated with lime.

The spring which next attracts the attention of the visitor is the Ninety Per Cent, located one and a half miles north-west of town, and is owned by David Wright. This spring, as its name denotes, is ninety per cent soda, a trifle too strong to imbibe in its natural state, but with the additions of a little sugar and lemon or other flavoring, makes a most delicious beverage.

Taking a south-westerly course from the Ninety Per Cent one mile, the Gas Fountain is reached. This consists of a large jet of gas escaping from a crevice in the rocks with a noise similar to steam escaping from a cylinder.

In the town of Soda Springs there are two more warm springs, both located on the summit of mounds nearly 100 feet high, which have been formed by the sediment of their own overflow. Both of these springs furnish excellent facilities for bathing.

But the spring most noted for its curative qualities, though probably not so pleasant to the taste, is owned by E. T. Williams, and is situated in the lot on which is his large hotel. But to show how completely surrounded we are by the beauties of nature, I must not omit mentioning that wonder of wonders—Swan Lake; for here has Nature outdone herself in her display of the picturesque and sublime. This lake is over 1,000 feet above the valley of Bear River, and located eight miles south-east of Soda. It is about 200 yards in diameter, is nearly round, and of unknown depth. Its rim is of lime formation and shaped like an inverted basin; the water so clear that the bottom can be seen where it is known to be forty feet deep. The bottom, when it can be seen, is covered with petrified logs, brush, etc., and affords a very pleasing sight. The property is owned by William M. White.

The climate, especially during the summer and fall months, is very salubrious, the altitude being 5,833 feet above the level of the sea, and the scenery magnificent beyond description. It is in the midst of this wonderful wonderland.

The town contains a population of about 500. All branches of business are represented, including four stores carrying general merchandise, three hotels, and the immediate construction of a fourth of commodious proportions is in contemplation. An extensive saw and planing mill is now in operation, turning out daily large quantities of lumber.

The railway company have in course of construction round-houses and machine-shops, intending as soon as completed to make Soda the end of a division.

There is one newspaper published in the town—the *Idaho Herald*—a new enterprise, having issued its first publication on the 12th day of April, 1884.

Within an area of twenty-five miles exist many natural curiosities, immense parks of soda formations, extinct volcanoes, huge piles of lava-rock, with great yawning chasms extending into the earth to an unknown depth, large caves and caverns with stalactites, some of them immense, pendent from their roofs and sides, formed by the passing of water containing calcareous particles through the pores and fissures of the rocks above; boiling springs, lakes away up in the mountain-tops, numerous petrifactions, with Bear River, the Port Neuf, Soda Creek, the Blackfoot, and other mountain streams in close proximity, affording fine trout-fishing; abundance of wild game, including several species of grouse, wild duck, and geese in the hills and valleys.

It is but a few hours' ride by rail to the great Soshone Falls—Idaho's Niagara, the grounds surrounding which were purchased last summer by a company of wealthy Omaha and Montana gentlemen, whose intention it is to make all the necessary improvements early in the present season, by the construction of a hotel and facilities to enable visitors to obtain perfect views of this grand and wonderful work of nature.

Soda is also on the direct route by rail to the best and only scenic route into the National Park, *via* Utah & Northern and Beaver Cañon.

The hotel accommodations are ample. A number of gentlemen of Salt Lake, Omaha, and other cities have already erected cottages for occupancy during the summer and fall months. Many others contemplate following their example the coming season.

RESOURCES OF IDAHO.   115

In addition to the foregoing, it is not improbable that Soda will before long loom up as a mining section. Very recent discoveries have been made; good prospects found within a short distance of copper and galena ores, carrying both gold and silver, and in one instance exceedingly rich in the precious metals.

Being thus centrally located, with the facilities afforded those who would seek pleasure, sight-seeing, and health to reach all the different points of interest, Soda Spa has already become a desirable location for a summer residence.

The new town of Pocatello, located at the junction of the Utah & Northern and western division of the Oregon Short Line, promises to become of much importance should the land be placed in market.

Pocatello is on the Ross Fork Indian Reservation, and the road is here with its town and station by treaty with the Indians and the sanction of the government. The railroad company have forty acres of land, and have made extensive improvements.

The Pocatello House is 40 by 140 feet, and two stories high, with a basement 33 by 70 feet. On the first floor are located the express, baggage, ticket agent's, telegraph, and other railway offices, two large waiting-rooms, hotel office, dining-rooms, pantry, kitchen, etc., while above are eighteen rooms for guests, besides some rooms occupied by railway officials.

The railway buildings here consist of an eight-stall round-house, a large oil and store room, a platform 400 feet long, a transfer platform and offices, a 1,000-ton ice-house, and fifteen houses for employees, which are large, substantial two-story frame structures.

All the transfer business for the two roads is now done here. This business is extensive and employs a large force of check-clerks, transfer-men, etc.

If the road or some one else owned here land sufficient for making a town, and would sell lots at low rates, this place would soon have a boom, but the road has not as much land as is needed, and the Indians propose to hold on to the land. A large amount of grading has been done in the yards here, preparatory to erecting more buildings, putting in side-tracks, etc.

The location is a pretty one, and the lands can be easily irrigated by taking water from the Port Neuf, a fine stream which passes close to the town on its way to Snake River.

The soil of this part of the plain is good, and only needs water to render it very productive and excellent farming land. Ross's Fork is a swift-running stream 20 or 30 feet wide, and affords sufficient water to irrigate several thousand acres of land.

Blackfoot is the supply point of an extensive stock-raising country. It is also the present railroad station for the Salmon River mines, distant 150 miles.

At Eagle Rock the Snake River comes roaring and rushing over its rocky bed through a steep, narrow cañon. In the neighborhood are some extensive farming lands. Thirteen years ago, while still several hundred miles from the nearest railroad, Professor Cyrus Thomas visited this section. In his report he speaks of the broad, level bottom-lands at this place as being composed of a rich, sandy loam, that needed but the addition of water to render it most excellent farming land. This bottom on the east side is some six or eight miles wide, and stands at a very moderate height above the ordinary water-level of the river. It is flanked on the east by a terrace some fifteen or twenty feet above the bottom. The Professor estimates the average volume of water the river sends down at this place as three feet deep by 400 feet wide, running at the rate of four feet per second, making 4,800 cubic feet per second. This amount of water will irrigate nearly a thousand square miles of land sufficiently for ordinary crops, such as cereals. And as the general level is not far above the average water-level, the canals need not be of very great length, and therefore the water that returns to the channel can be used again and again, thus increasing the area that may be rendered productive by it.

These conclusions have been fully justified by facts during the past few years. Eagle Rock is now one of the most thriving railroad towns in Idaho. It is the end of a railroad division, and the railroad shops give employment to several hundred men. It is the home of one of the most enterprising journals in the Territory, the *Idaho Register*. An intelligent correspondent from there writes:

"Four hundred car-loads of small grain! That is not much for a country as big as this, but it is a beginning. Next year there will be more. More than 500 settlers have located ranches this year. All that has been raised is wanted for seed, and that will not give us half enough. No flour has been made in this country as yet. It is all freighted up from Cache Valley; from there we also get some of our butter, eggs, etc. Two years ago we imported everything. One year from now we will have a surplus to furnish the mining camps, which are right here in our midst.

"The valley about Eagle Rock is well watered. The canal company alone have made more than sixty miles of water-way. In a distance of about ten miles above Eagle Rock the canal has four different outlets into the river. This canal covers 50,000 acres of land. Half of this sixty miles of waterway has been added the past year. The land is free—open to all at government price—and it is good; 40 bushels of wheat, 50 to 70 of oats to the acre. There is no better country for farming and none better for selling farm products.

"The Snake River gravel mines are simply immense. Three men this year working together took out over $4,000 each. Next year they will make $3,000 to the man. Everything is ready for them to shovel in the dirt next spring, as soon as the gravel thaws. Last spring they had everything to prepare. It was then an experiment; it is now a certainty. This year we had two claims running; next year there will probably be 200; certainly some thousands of men are to find profitable employment in the Snake River gravel beds for some generations to come. A New York company are making a canal below town; an Idaho company another.

"Two large mining companies have been organized, respectively in St. Paul and Chicago, to work mining claims some four miles above town. Individuals and groups of two or three have staked off claims for miles along the river-bank. Some have recorded; many have not. There will be lively skirmishing for possession next spring.

"For what is up the river in the Teton country we are waiting. Ore was brought down in November that assayed $10,000 to the ton. The rock is manganese—looks like much of the rock about Butte. Has the source of all the Snake River gold been found?

"The town of Eagle Rock is improving and the population steadily increasing."

Beaver Cañon Station is noted for being the point from which to reach the National Park, 90 miles east. Bassett Brothers have placed a line of hacks on the road to the Park, and last season many people went in that way, and all unite in saying that it is the best route of any. The route is so easy and attractive that the Utah and Northern Company, it is said, will probably build a branch road to Marshall Basin soon, and make this, as it should be, the great route of travel to Wonderland.

Mining.—Apart from the placer mines of Snake River, the mining interests of Oneida have not been largely developed. The principal mining district is Cariboo, distant about 35 miles from Soda Springs, the nearest railroad station, and with which it is connected by wagon-road.

Robinson, Oneida, and Silver Rook claims are on the east side of the mountain. On the west side is the Northern Light, which has been developed a considerable distance, and is in a body of ore 12 feet thick, averaging $25 per ton free gold.

The IXL is a vein showing four and a half feet, averaging $30 to the ton, free gold. Has two openings, with large body of ore in sight, assaying $12.50 to the ton. At the west end of Northern Light is the Lone Star, owned by Hiram House, with a body of ore twelve feet thick. There are three openings, all assaying well in free gold. On the north side is the House; on the east side the Grey Eagle and Union; on the west side the Mayflower. Of the surrounding mines, the Boston is said to be the richest in the district, with plenty of wood and water to work it for years to come. The country in the neighborhood is a beautiful valley, with good soil and plenty of grass. The valley is fast settling up.

Considerable excitement has been caused recently by the discovery of good float rock on Snake River, above Eagle Rock. This float assays about $180.87, chiefly gold. The location is on what is known as Fall Creek, which heads in the immediate neighborhood of the head of Cariboo Creek. It is claimed that this is the same lode, and only about ten miles distant from the Cariboo mines, for which $60,000 has just been offered by the Ontario Company. The ledge is about twelve feet wide, and crops out in many places. The formation of the country is porphyry and granite.

Oneida Salt-works.—About sixty miles north-east of Soda Springs, in a small side valley which opens into Salt Creek, near what is known as the Old Lander Emigrant Road, leading from South Pass to Oregon, are the famous salt springs of Oneida County. There are several springs. No pumping is required, but the water is run through wooden pipes into large galvanized iron pans, in which the salt is made by boiling the water. The water is as cold as ordinary spring water, and is perfectly clear, showing how completely the saline matter is held in solution. The salt is shoveled out once in thirty minutes, and after draining twenty-five hours is thence thrown into the drying-house, there to remain until sacked and ready for shipping. The supply of water would warrant 2,500 pounds per day. There is another small spring near by, which yields water enough for 2,000 pounds of salt per day for a portion of the year. The owners began to supply the market in 1866 at five cents per pound.

Following is an analysis of the Oneida salt made by Dr. Piggott of Baltimore. It shows a higher percentage of pure salt than the celebrated Onondaga brand of Syracuse, while neither Liverpool, Turk's Island, nor Saginaw salt approaches it in purity, or is as white, clear, or soluble in liquids.

Chloride of sodium (pure salt)	97.79
Sulphate of soda	1.54
Chloride of calcium	.67
Sulphate of magnesia	Trace
	100.00

The increasing demand for salt from the smelting works of Idaho and Montana makes the Oneida salt-works of inestimable value.

Game.—The sportsman can find plenty to occupy his attention in Oneida County. The tributaries of the Snake all abound in fish, ducks, and geese. Wild fowl are abundant in all her creeks and sloughs. According to a tradition mentioned by Professor Haydn, Market Lake received its name from the following circumstances: Formerly at a certain season of the year buffalo, deer, antelope, and other species of game were accustomed to congregate here, probably on account of saline matter deposited; and the hunters when they found game scarce in other sections would remark to each other, "Let us go to market." Antelope are still found in some portions of the county.

Lakes.—Among the attractive features in the shape of natural scenery, Henry Lake deserves more than a passing notice. It is situated in the northeastern part of the county, at an altitude of 6,443 feet, and is two miles wide by five miles long. Peaks of the Rocky Mountains rise abruptly for 3,000 feet from close to its shores. Its surface is dotted with islands, and indented with graceful tongues of land rich in foliage. It is especially beautiful in October, when its rivulets are blooming with the leafage of willow, box-elder, sumac, aspen, and other shrubbery, whose gray autumnal tints form a strange contrast with the dark green of the deep pine forests.

Ten miles north-west of Henry is Cliff Lake, which is three miles long by half a mile wide, and in whose azure depths 1,400 feet of line has failed to reach bottom. It is almost completely surrounded by vertical basaltic cliffs. A conical pine-covered island rests upon its bosom. "Henry Lake and surroundings," says a writer, "are well worthy a two or three days' halt upon the part of those who delight in the mountaineering, hunting, fishing, and sailing, or desire rest; and were such scenes grouped anywhere except at the gate of Wonderland, they would be heralded far and wide as attractions worthy a jaunt across the continent."

The first occupation by white men of what is embraced within the present limits of Oneida County dates back many years. As early as 1834 old Fort

Hall was erected on the south side of Snake River near the mouth of the Port Neuf. It was established by Mr. Nathaniel J. Wyeth, who was compelled by stress of circumstances two years later to sell it to the Hudson's Bay Company.

As above narrated, Franklin was established in 1860. The actual development of the county, however, has been within the past seven years. The following statement of its assessed valuation during that period will give a tolerably accurate idea of its material development:

	Assessed Valuation.	Property-tax payers.
1878	$628,201 00	688
1879	717,943 00	795
1880	878,722 00	870
1881	1,211,452 50	1,180
1882	1,401,410 00	1,308
1883	2,101,072 00	1,412
1884	2,380,832 00	1,629

OWYHEE COUNTY.

This is one of the historic counties of Idaho. It is situated in the southwestern portion of the Territory; is bounded on the north by Ada and Alturas counties; on the east by Cassia County; on the south by the State of Nevada; and on the west by the State of Oregon. Its area is 8,130 square miles, being somewhat larger than the State of Massachusetts.

Mining.—As related in the chapter on mining, the mines of Owyhee were among the earliest to arouse an interest in quartz mining. In this region is situated the celebrated Poorman Mine, whose first shipment of one hundred tons brought a return of $90,000. Fifteen tons shipped to Newark, N. J., shortly after yielded $75,000. What was called its second and third class ore yielded an average of $230 per ton, in a lot consisting of 2,382 tons. Its yield produced some of the richest specimens of ruby and native silver ever mined. A specimen of this ruby about two feet square and sixty per cent pure silver, received a special gold medal at the Paris Exposition. The Golden Chariot, Leviathan, South Chariot, Oro Fino, Home Resort, Silver Chord, and others in the vicinity received awards at the Philadelphia Centennial. In the Owyhee Treasury there is a two-foot vein of free gold ore averaging $45 per ton, an eighty-pound lot averaging $6.30 per pound. A 43-pound lot yielded about $50 per pound. The Morning Star has produced about $1,000,000, one lot of one hundred tons yielding an average of $1,000 per ton. The Elmore, with a twenty-stamp mill, yielded $300,000 in a thirty days' run. Other mines, such as the Owyhee, Stormy Hill, and the Webfoot, have each a record that will compare favorably with any of those mentioned. The county has been one of the most productive in the Territory, but has never entirely recovered from the blow it received through the suspension of the Bank of California in 1875, which resulted in the withdrawal from the field of a number of the large companies.

The chief districts are the War Eagle and Florida Mountains, near Silver City; Wagontown, north-west of the same place; Flint, south-east, and South Mountain, thirty miles south, of Silver City. The mines are as rich as they ever were, but being expensive to work, considerable capital is required to develop them properly and profitably.

The following is an extract from the latest published report of the mines of this section (1883):

On War Eagle Mountain, the Poorman mine, which in times past was second to no mine in Idaho, was operated part of the year and considerable ore extracted, which was worked at the War Eagle Mill.

The Glenbrook and Clearbrook mines are situated north of the Poorman; have been worked for several years. The ore is easily mined, and mills about $30 per ton.

The Silver Chord is located south of the Poorman, was formerly operated by an Eastern company, and subsequently by a San Francisco company, with success.

The Belle Peck mine has been prospected by Sands & Co., with a fair chance of finding another ore body.

The Ruth mine is west of the Belle Peck on the ridge. A tunnel has been run on the ledge nearly six hundred feet and some good ore encountered.

At the Richardson mine, north-east of the Poorman, the ledge is small but the ore is exceptionally rich.

The Rattling Jack mine, on the ledge known as the Columbia and Oro Fino, has encountered good ore in a drift on the ledge. Much trouble was experienced from a heavy flow of water, and work was abandoned in sinking a winze, which had progressed twenty-five feet, until machinery could be erected to control the water.

The War Eagle mine has been opened to a depth of over six hundred feet and a long chute of ore exposed.

The Stormy Hill mine is situated south of the War Eagle mine, and is thought to be on the same ledge. A shaft was sunk about two hundred feet deep and drifts started both ways. The ledge is of good size and uniform richness. About one hundred and thirty tons were extracted, ninety of which were milled with an average yield of about $40 to the ton.

The San Juan mine, east of the War Eagle, was worked under a lease and some rich ore taken out.

The Whisky mine is one of the oldest locations on War Eagle Mountain, and the lessees raised some good ore during the season.

In the Webster mine the vein is small but very rich. Work was steadily prosecuted by the owners with success.

The Crane and Driggs mine, but a short distance east of the Golden Chariot, was opened by a tunnel which cut the ledge at a considerable depth. In drifting upon it a body of ore of great richness was encountered. The Red Jacket mine, which was formerly worked by the Red Jacket Company, was operated under a lease, and the lessees took out considerable rich ore that had been left standing in the old workings.

The Lady Washington mine lies north-east of the Red Jacket. A shaft was sunk from where the tunnel cuts the ledge, which ran in rich ore, but little was taken out, as the work was for development.

Florida Mountain.—The Empire State mine is on the west side of the mountain, overlooking Blue Gulch. The country rock on the surface is much broken up, but as depth is attained it becomes more solid, and the walls of the ledges in consequence are better defined. A drift is being run on the vein to connect with the old shaft and winze. They are within a short distance of the winze, and have encountered rich ore in the face of the drift.

The Black Jack mine is north-east of the Empire State. Fair milling ore was taken out, and from the indications it is supposed that a rich ore chute had been struck.

The Starlight is north of the Black Jack, and is doubtless on the same vein. A drift is being run with a width of ore, in the face, of 18 inches of high-grade gold-bearing quartz. In running a cross-cut to tap the ledge, two well-defined veins of low-grade ore were found, one of them being 8 to 10 feet wide.

The Boonville mine, also north of the Black Jack, was worked by A. J. Sands, who also milled the ore taken out.

The Leviathan, south of the Empire State, is supposed to be on the same ledge as the latter. It is an old location and produced considerable ore, which yielded gold of a high degree of fineness.

The Walter and Miller mine is on the east side of Florida Mountain, overlooking Silver City. The vein is about 2 feet in width, and a shaft has been sunk upwards of 100 feet; the ledge is well opened with tunnels also. Mill runs of the ore, at the War Eagle mill, were reported as being quite satisfactory.

With the exception of the Golden Chariot, which was worked for a short time by an incorporated company, all the mines of War Eagle and Florida Mountains were operated by private enterprise.

At Wagontown, north-west of Silver City, the Webfoot was worked with a small force by Jones and Adams. The ledge has held out in width, and better ore was extracted than ever before. A considerable amount of ore is on the dump, awaiting improvement in the condition of the roads in order that it can be hauled to the mill.

The Last Chance is situated near the Webfoot, and is supposed to be on the same vein. A ledge of about 2 feet in width showing good milling ore was exposed in doing assessment work.

The Garfield is a new location half a mile west of the Webfoot. The ledge is about 18 inches in width, the ore being rich in silver.

On the Wilson ledge a tunnel was run to cut the ledge, but it had not been reached by the close of the year. The vein is large and yields a low-grade free-milling ore. The upper tunnel struck the ledge at a depth of 50 feet.

Flint District, south-east of Silver City, is an old mining district, in which many of the principal mines had been abandoned for upwards of ten years. During the past year a number of these mines were relocated and mining operations recommenced. The Rising Star mine was formerly worked to a depth of 300 feet, with a strong vein and good ore. The Rising Sun Company, which operated the mine some years ago, also ran a tunnel on the ledge, but for some unexplained reason left the ore standing and abandoned their mine. Messrs. Warnkee and Sommercamp, who have been at work the past year, extracted ore from this tunnel that yields from $100 to $200 per ton.

The Perseverance was never worked by an incorporated company. It has a strong vein, from which considerable good ore has been taken and is now on the dump.

In Twilight Gulch, the Twilight mine is regarded as one of the best mines in the district. In early days very rich ore was produced, and the vein is a large one. The Astor is south of the Twilight, and produces good ore. The south side is a contact between granite and porphyry. The ledge pitches to the east, and a shaft was started to strike it, but work was stopped before that had been accomplished. The ore is good, and if the mine was properly opened it would pay. Mammoth district is 4 miles east of Flint district, and was organized about the same time. Its ores resemble those of the latter. They are somewhat refractory and require roasting.

The Mammoth ledge, which is one of the largest in the county, has been reopened with fair prospects. The ore assays from $10 to $800 to the ton, and the quantity is large, as the ledge is upwards of 40 feet in width. There are other ledges in this district which when opened up will be likely to prove remunerative.

Stock-raising and Agriculture.—The pre-eminence that once characterized Owyhee as a mining county is now gradually giving way to the cattle interest.

On the ranges of Snake River, Bruneau, Reynolds, Catherine, Castle, Sinker, Cow, and Sucker creeks, and Pleasant Valley, cattle feed and fatten on the nutritious bunch-grass and white sage. On Sucker, Reynolds, and Catherine creeks are extensive sheep-ranges. There are in the county at present estimated to be 50,000 head of cattle, 30,000 head of sheep, and 10,000 head of horses.

Mr. M. Hyde of Silver City is the owner of about 15,000 head of cattle and several hundred horses. He is also the owner of 2,000 acres of farming and pasture land in the county.

The testimony of butchers, stock-buyers, and drovers is that the cattle of Owyhee, "raised on those high prairies and hills, seldom fed in yards, never housed, and nourished on those native grasses, attain a perfection of form and largeness of bone and muscle, and a degree of strength, vigor, and nerve, rarely seen and never exceeded by animals of the same class and breed in any other locality East or West."

In the bottom-lands of all the creeks named are fine agricultural areas.

Bruneau Valley is rapidly settling up with farmers and stock-raisers, and already shows an almost continuous line of ranches nearly to the head waters.

Its remoteness from market has hitherto somewhat retarded its development, but this obstacle is being overcome by railroad construction along the valley of Snake River. The valley is capable of supporting a large agricultural population. It would not surprise us to find this before many years to be among the wealthiest agricultural sections of the Territory.

Along many of the creeks fruit orchards have been raised with success. Apples of the finest varieties are raised along Reynolds Creek; and grapes and peaches said to be equal if not superior to those of Boisé Valley are raised along Sinker Creek. Cereals and grains of all kinds grow in abundance in all the valleys named, and especially along Catherine and Castle creeks in eastern Owyhee, and through Pleasant Valley in western Owyhee.

Silver City is the county seat and chief town in the county. Like all mining towns, it is subject to alternate periods of prosperity and depression. A weekly newspaper, the *Avalanche*, one of the oldest in the Territory, is published there.

There are lodges of Freemasons and Odd Fellows, and a chapter of Royal Arch Masons. There are two good schools.

A Large Horse-ranch.—The Oregon Horse and Land Company have ranches located in Lost Valley, or the old Le Bard ranch; one at the mouth of Sucker Creek, near the Snake River; one at three forks of the Sucker (the Dave Shea ranch); also the old McCusick ranch, on Owyhee Creek. The range occupied is 85 by 150 miles in Idaho and Oregon. The stock of horses owned were originally well-selected Oregon mares, which have since been bred to Norman Percheron horses, and to-day the average of the entire band is probably not exceeded on the coast. They are the largest horse-owners in the United States, having over 8,000 head of fine, large Oregon horses. The present season they purchased eleven stallions from the celebrated breeding farm of M. W. Dunham, Wayne, Illinois. Besides the above they added six Percherons from the Marshal Ney horse, owned in Oregon. They have in use about 200 stallions on their ranches. During the past season their shipments to Eastern markets were twenty-five car-loads, and their purchases this season amounted to 3,000 head. The company began business about one year ago, succeeding one or two individuals owning ranches and bands of horses. Last year they purchased 5,000 head, and have rapidly come to the front as the leading horse-owners of Idaho and the Pacific Coast.

SHOSHONE COUNTY.

In 1861 this county was organized as a tributary to Washington Territory, and continued so until the formation of Idaho, and it was then organized as Shoshone County of Idaho Territory, February 4, 1864. As already related, gold deposits were discovered in Shoshone County in 1860, by Captain Pierce, from whom the present county seat, Pierce City, was named. The prospects proved to be very remunerative, and in a short time were ascertained to be extensive. Oro Fino, Oro Grande, Rhodes, and Cow creeks, with their numerous tributaries, were all found to produce gold in very fair paying quantities. The camp soon acquired a famous reputation as the Oro Fino mines, and for fifteen years supported a population of two thousand, during which time a large amount of gold-dust was shipped weekly from the camp.

The agricultural lands of the county are not extensive, by far the greater portion of its large area being strictly mineral, rugged and mountainous, mostly covered with dense forests of pine, fir, and tamarack, and thick undergrowth.

It is for this reason principally that the county is in its present backward condition, as so many other portions of the Territory have offered easier access to their mineral deposits. But in the course of time the ax of the pioneer and adventurous miner will hew its way to the undiscovered treasures.

There are, however, some known localities in the county where agricultural pursuits are followed with success and profit. The Weippe Plain, extending from the Clearwater along the northern slope of the Lolo Fork of said river for a distance of at least thirty miles, offers as seductive opportunities for agricultural pursuits as may be found in northern Idaho. A number of ranches have been located upon this plain for several years past, and are at present in a flourishing and prosperous condition, with still room left for many more with equal, if not more favorable, positions and locality.

9

Mining.—That portion of Shoshone County lying between the Bitter Root Range and the spur of the same range known as the Cœur d'Alene but two years past was an unknown wilderness. To-day the Cœur d'Alene has become famous throughout the continent, and known perhaps wherever the English language is spoken, for the richness and extent of its mineral resources. In contemplating the fact we may confidently predict a prosperous future for Shoshone.

Cœur d'Alene Mines.—"The name Cœur d'Alene," says Mr. E. V. Smalley, writing in the *Century* magazine for October, 1884, "means heart of an awl, or awl-hearted, and was bestowed by the early French trappers upon the tribe of Indians inhabiting the shores of the lake on the western side of the mountains. The tradition is that the trappers found these Indians so inhospitable, and so close in their fur-bartering operations, that they declared that their hearts were no bigger than the point of a shoemaker's awl, so the name stuck, first to the tribe, then to the lake, then to the river, which is the lake's principal affluent, and to the mountain it drains, and lately it has been applied to everything connected with the new mining camp." This is a commonly accepted derivation of the name, which unfortunately loses its interest from the fact that it is probably entirely erroneous. Since the expression has come into such publicity during the past year, much discussion has been raised concerning its true origin and meaning. Mr. Joseph Paine, United States Indian interpreter at Fort Cœur d'Alene, relieves the reputation of the aborigines in the following much more natural explanation:

"CŒUR D'ALENE, IDAHO, October 5, 1885.

"JAMES L. ONDERDONK, Esq., Boisé City, Idaho:

"DEAR SIR—Answering your communication of the 3d instant, I have to say as follows: During the time of the Hudson's Bay Company the present Mullan road was an Indian and trappers' trail. Near where now stands the old Catholic mission on said road is a short but very steep hill. Indians and trappers on coming to this hill would dismount from their horses, and walking beside their animals, would climb the hill. On reaching the top all would be 'out of breath' or 'winded,' and would have to stop to rest. This fact gave the name to the country round about of 'Cœur d'Alene,' meaning short of breath, or panting. When the priests came to this country they found this name given to this part of the country, and choosing the beautiful spot where now stands the old mission, gave the name of Cœur d'Alene, supposing it to be in the heart of the country which has now become the name of a small tribe of Indians, as well as a lake, river, and range of mountains."

Probably the best way to reach the Cœur d'Alene mines at present is either from Thompson's Falls or Trout Creek. Both of these points are way-stations in Montana on the Northern Pacific. From either of these points it is a day's ride on horseback over the mountains. By far the pleasantest mode of egress is by canoe down the Cœur d'Alene River to the old mission, where is the landing for the steamboats which navigate the rest of the river, and across the lake to Fort Cœur d'Alene. Stages run from this point over fine level roads to Rathdrum on the Northern Pacific, distant eleven miles.

The best-developed and most valuable claim in the district is the Gillette, now owned by Messrs. Porter & Henderson. It is located a short distance below Murray. During our last visit in October last forty men were employed, thirty as miners. The claim was yielding at the rate of an ounce per day per man. A number of handsome nuggets have been extracted.

The following description of the Cœur d'Alene region has been prepared for this work by Rev. W. D. Shippen of Murray:

Gold! The very name excites man's most active thoughts of acquisition, his most earnest spirit of enterprise, and prompts him to the most exhaustive and hazardous pursuits for the discovery and development of the rich treasures of the rocks and gulches of the mountains. The announcement of the discovery of accessible fields of rich mineral deposits is but the watch-word for a mining stampede, in which excited multitudes of eager searchers for the hidden treasures join and press through every opposing barrier, endure every toil, privation, and hardship, and face every danger. Experiences of the severest character seem only to incite "old timers" to the boldest and foremost rush to newly discovered gold-fields. They are the first to come, the best to stay, and the last to grumble; strong in faith, active in pursuit, and most patient in endurance, they teach the pilgrim lessons of prospecting enterprise, and lead the faltering tender-foot to achievements of the richest discoveries and developments of the precious treasures of the great mineral belts.

The first discovery of gold in paying quantities in Cœur d'Alene was made on Pritchard Creek, near to and east of where the town of Murray is now rapidly growing into extensive proportions and notable business importance. The discovery was made in the summer of 1880 by three old prospectors, M. Gillett, A. J. Pritchard, and R. T. Horn. The first pan of dirt that gave promise of the existence of gold here in paying quantities was washed out by Mr. Gillett, and was taken from rim-rock, on what is now known as the Gillett or Discovery Claim. These prospectors then took out about $45 of coarse gold here in one day, and the discovery was first made public by Mr. Pritchard, hence the name of the stream, Pritchard Creek. Soon after the discovery the party went out, and Mr. Pritchard spent the winter of 1880-1 at Evolution in securing means to support him while further prospecting this district during the summer and fall of 1881, in which season he found gold in paying quantities at all the points prospected for several miles on Pritchard Creek. In 1882 he made known these discoveries by letter to some friends, whom he requested to keep the matter secret and join him in the spring of 1883 with a suitable outfit of tools, clothing, and provisions for the prospecting season. His friends were not sufficiently quiet, and the news getting abroad, he was confronted in the spring of 1883 by an eager multitude, who were unprepared with either tools, clothing, or food sufficient to go into the mountains on which the snow yet lay several feet deep. Yet these eager searchers for gold insisted on being shown the discovered grounds where it could be obtained. As threats of hanging were made if Mr. Pritchard did not lead the way, he finally guided them to the place of discovery, but the waters being too high, bed-rock could not be reached, and most of the stampeders left the diggings, strongly denouncing Mr. Pritchard and the country. Those who remained till the waters were gone down made search and found gold in satisfactory amounts to reward their patient endurance and efforts. The stampede now set in from all directions. Claims were taken all along Pritchard and Eagle creeks for miles, until in the spring of 1884 it was almost impossible to get even a small fraction on either of these main streams. But it was ascertained that the wash gravel on the mountains was very rich, and it was not long before the Old Channel was located in ten and twenty acre claims, and the whole country for miles was so staked and blazed as to make confusion doubly confounded to a novice of a prospector in search of a claim. Many farmers from Oregon and from Washington Territory having come in and taken large claims for themselves and friends, and having in many cases very imperfectly marked their boundaries, soon found their claims relocated by those who were determined to share in the rich grounds at all hazards. Then commenced the course of litigation for the rights of claimants, which drew its tedious length along till July or August, retarding development and checking business of every kind. To find the grounds so occupied in large lots as to prevent the opportunity of getting even a fraction of these gold-fields was so exasperating as to create an intense feeling in some towards the original locators; and as many of the claims were located in the names of parties who were never in the district, the jumping of claims became quite extensive, and many of the richest grounds were relocated, among which was the noted Widow Claim, and some others located originally by Mr. Pritchard in the name of some engaging and engageable widows, between whom and himself there was doubtless a mutual admiration, he being a widower at the time of the location of these mines. Some of these matronly ladies were in Eagle City at the term of court at which the title to these claims was settled, only to hear a decision given adverse to their golden hopes, and to retire, leaving the claims in possession of the "jumpers," who are familiarly known in all Cœur d'Alene as the "orphans," or the "widows' boys." They are working these rich grounds with great success, and obtain very gratifying yields at every clean-up. We should here say that it is difficult to learn the exact amounts taken from different claims, as the proprietors do not wish to publish all the results of their mining work, and it is about as impertinent to ask them to tell the yield from a claim as it is to ask men of other pursuits what profits they are realizing. We may, however, give some account of different claims on Pritchard Creek, such as were willingly furnished us. Going down Pritchard Creek west from Marray, we first come to—

The Finnell Fraction, which has two shafts down to bed-rock, about fifteen feet in depth, a drain-ditch of about 200 feet, and the owners are drifting to strike the shafts and get coarse gold in paying quantities at every clean-up.

The Wilson and Clagget claim has shallow bed-rock; runs two strings of sluices with a force of seven men, and its yield is very satisfactory to the owners.

Idaho Bar is owned by G. B. Ives and John Silverthorn. It lies in form of a V along the north side of Pritchard Creek. It contains about fifteen acres. The bed-rock is shallow. They run three strings of sluices, work ten men, and average about $7 per day to the man.

The original discovery belongs to John McAleer & Company; is a ten-acre claim; bed-rock from four to six feet deep; has one drain ditch six hundred feet long and one eight hundred feet long; has two strings of sluice boxes and ten men. They are putting in a large wheel and pump. The gold is mostly fine, but some nuggets have been found in it worth $9 each. The diggings pay $8 per day to the man.

The Last Chance claim is divided among about a dozen partners, all of them industrious and enterprising. The main yields of the claim are of coarse gold, and it has furnished some ten-ounce nuggets. It has two strings of sluices and twenty-two men, and pays $8 per day to the man.

The O. K. claim has two strings of sluices; works fifteen men; 1½ ounces to the man per day. The gold is coarse, and has furnished some twelve-ounce nuggets and many smaller ones. The company have taken out nearly $9,000 from it.

The Frank Grove claim is just opening, works four men, and yields fine gold.

The McGuire claim belongs to Ballou, Warden & Gove, who are sinking a shaft, from which they raise all the water effectually with a pump, worked by a sixteen horse-power engine. The shaft is twenty-three feet deep and not yet to bed-rock. It is situated near the center of Pritchard Gulch, about three fourths of a mile east of Eagle City, on the Murray road.

There are a number of claims on the gulch between Eagle and Murray which are just being opened, but cannot be effectually worked without the aid of machinery. On all of the claims here mentioned, as well as most on this gulch, the immense growth of timber is a great hinderance to the opening and working of the mines. The stupendous cedars, pines, and other large growths have to be undermined, and often fall in the ditches, and must be cut and split up, and sometimes have to be blown to pieces with powder in order to be made movable. Especially is this the case with their ponderous stumps and roots, some of which, while in a body, weigh tons, and cannot be moved till blown to pieces.

The Widow claim lies at the mouth of Gold Run and at the east end of Murray, on Pritchard Gulch, and is being very successfully worked by its owners, the "widows' boys," or "orphans," whose title was settled at the session of Shoshone County Court, held in Eagle City, in July and August, 1884. The claim is very rich, and yields a large daily average to the man.

The Butte boys from Butte City, Montana, and several other companies, are working good claims on this gulch between Murray and Littlefield, where Dr. Littlefield is taking out good pay from his rich claims at and below the mouth of Butte Creek, but the exact output of gold from his grounds is not made public. But few claims are being worked between Littlefield and Raven, three miles above on this gulch.

A great amount of prospecting has been done on Eagle Creek, both above and below Eagle City, but with no satisfactory results except on the claim of Dr. Campbell, about one mile above the confluence of Eagle Creek with the north fork of Cœur d'Alene River. This claim has been very expensive to open, but is said to be paying this season. Gold has been discovered on both the east and north forks of Eagle Creek and on some of their tributaries, but has not been obtained in paying quantities. The same disadvantages of mining exist on these streams as on Pritchard Creek as to a superabundance of timber and water. Besides these main gulches, there are numerous rich claims found in the side gulches.

The Webfoot claim, on the famous Dream Gulch, is so called because it was discovered by Oregon men. It received the name of Dream Gulch on account of a mysterious dream by which one of its chief discoverers was directed to the first rich strikes that were made on it. This gulch runs into Pritchard Creek from the north about one mile west of Murray, and is one of the largest tributaries of that stream between Eagle City and Murray. The gold is coarse, and is a little mixed with quartz. The company have taken out about $36,000 from this claim, all of which came from a very small spot of ground comparatively. A portion of this gold was in very large nuggets, one of which weighed 19¾ ounces. Several of the owners sold a one-eighth interest each for $8,000. The property is considered a very valuable one, and large yields are still expected from it. It has already made several of its owners, who were formerly in moderate circumstances, quite well off, and its liberal yields have been well bestowed on men who are industrious, temperate, and economical, and will use their means as good citizens.

Alder Gulch enters Pritchard Creek at the west end of the town of Murray, coming in also from the north, and is nearly as large as Dream Gulch and furnishes more water. There are some rich claims on this stream, but the bedrock is deep, making it more expensive to mine. Campbell, Pease & Co. have taken some nice nuggets and some coarse gold from their claim, which is well up towards the head of the gulch.

Dry Gulch has one claim on it, from which several good nuggets and a considerable quantity of coarse gold have been taken. A half interest in this claim was sold by its discoverer, W. H. Freeman, to banker William Hawkins for $10,000. There are several other good claims on this gulch, but they have not been developed yet so as to pay.

Buckskin and Missoula Gulches between Dream and Alder also have some good claims on them that will yield richly when sufficient supplies of water are brought on them.

Gold Run Gulch comes in at the east end of Murray, entering Pritchard Creek also from the north. Some very coarse gold and several good-sized nuggets have been taken from this gulch. Judge W. H. Clagget and Johnny Miller are opening a bar claim just at the mouth of this gulch, which prospects very rich. Above this, and between it and Butte Creek, which enters Pritchard Gulch at Littlefield, come in from the north, Cougar, Wesp, and Ruder gulches, from all of which good prospects have been taken, and on all which locations have been made from their mouths to their sources. From them much treasure will be taken when a sufficient supply of water can be obtained.

Butte Gulch, which also comes in from the north, joins Pritchard Creek at the town of Littlefield. It also is very rich, and is claimed from mouth to source. It is at the mouth of and immediately below this that the rich claims of Dr. Littlefield are located, which are being so successfully worked by him.

Bear Gulch comes into Pritchard Creek at the little mining town of Raven. It prospects very rich, is all located, and has more water than any other side gulch we have named, but for some reason its rich grounds have not been as fully developed as its advantages and richness would seem to demand of those who have laid claims on it. It is only a question of time, however, till it will contribute its full share to the rich treasures given from the wealthy gulches on the north side of Pritchard Creek between Eagle City and Raven. There are a number of small ravines on this side of Pritchard Gulch between Bear and Summit, but none mined to any notable extent.

Granite Creek enters Pritchard Gulch from the south just above Raven and the mouth of Bear. Just below it, and on the same side of Pritchard, some rich bar diggings have been opened, and a ditch from Granite Creek brought on to them. There are no paying placers on Granite Creek, but there are some rich quartz discoveries near its source in the mountains. It affords a good stream of water all the year, and has a very rapid fall, and flows very swiftly.

Tiger Gulch comes in from the south, nearly opposite Murray. Some good prospects have been found on it, and claims have been taken up almost to its source, but as yet none of them is paying. Tiger and Granite are the only gulches that are of any size or note coming in from the south between Eagle City and Sullivan. In a mere sketch at this early period of the partial development of the rich grounds on either side of Pritchard Creek it is impossible to give more than a dim glance or cautious hint at the immense treasure that is yet to be washed from the golden sands of these wealthy side streams. It only requires that the abundant waters of the main streams be brought upon these mineral gardens, and the cleansing waves will wrench from their rocky coffers hundreds of thousands of dollars of bright gold, to increase the riches of Idaho, and add a tribute to the nation's wealth—compelling the public to recognize the intrinsic importance of this portion of the territory, and drawing hundreds of men and tons of machinery to this great mineral belt for its development.

The Old Channel Wash.—Not the least among the mining interests of Cœur d'Alene are the rich deposits of gold found in the Old Channel Wash on the mountains extending from above Bear Creek to Eagle City, and along the mountains on Eagle Creek for some distance towards the north fork of Cœur d'Alene River, its entire length being over twenty miles, estimated by some at thirty miles. The mining records of Cœur d'Alene district show that the first location on this rich channel was made by A. F. Parker, editor of the Cœur d'Alene *Eagle*, published at Eagle City. His discovery was made and recorded in October, 1883, and during that fall and the following winter this Old Channel on the mountains along Pritchard and Eagle creeks was so covered with claims as to render it almost impossible to get any of it in the spring of 1884 without relocating grounds that were already claimed. One of the first of these Old Channel claims was opened by Reese Bros. and Palmer, on Alder Hill, on the north side of the mountains, near Murray. These gentlemen obtained rich pannings by carrying the dirt from the hill to the creek to wash out the gold, but they have since brought a small sluice head of water onto the diggings, by which they can secure much more satisfactory results. The first day's wash of a small amount of gravel yielded a clean-up of $18. The gold shows a bright, clear, yellow appearance, and is smoothly washed. Just opposite this claim on the east side of Alder, on the hill north of Murray, is the Freeman fraction on this old wash, from which Mr. Freeman carries the dirt in sacks some distance down the mountain to water and washes out of it from $3 to $6 per day of yellow coarse gold. The first time Mrs. Freeman, wife of the owner, visited this claim, she picked up from the bed-rock an ounce nugget which she preserves as a memento of her first visit to this camp and this mine. Back & Co. also mined from their Old Wash claim, on the north side of the mountain at Raven, coarse gold to the amount of $8 per day to the man. The yield of these several claims, of such uniform height from the creek bed, and such a distance apart, shows a uniform richness of the gravel on this Old Channel, as well as the great similarity of the character of the gold taken from it at different points. It is a fact worthy of note that this Wash Channel lies almost altogther on the north side of the main Pritchard Gulch. Though at and below Osborne, and about a mile above Eagle, it diverges to the south side, where some rich prospects have been found on the mountains, and several claims have been located.

Eagle City is situated near the junction of Eagle and Pritchard creeks, and between the two streams. The site is a beautiful one for a town, the two principal streets, Eagle and Pritchard, forming almost a complete angle at the foot of the mountain—Eagle street stretching up the valley of Eagle Creek to the north, and Pritchard street extending up the valley of Pritchard creek to the east. In the early part of the year 1884, Eagle City gave promise of becoming the metropolis of the Cœur d'Alene. Town lots were laid out and taken up for fully three fourths of a mile along each valley, and were rated very high. Extensive improvements were rapidly made, expensive business houses were erected, and there was a general rush of business of all kinds common to a stampede mining camp. But as the richest mines being opened were more contiguous to Murray, four miles east of Eagle, up Pritchard Creek, business began early in the season to center in that rival burg, which soon began to lead, and before midsummer had largely absorbed the business interests and trade of the Cœur d'Alene, so that Eagle City is now almost deserted.

Murray is now the business center of this mining region; many substantial business houses have been erected here, fire-proof cellars provided, in which tons of goods are stored for the trade of the country, and a number of very comfortable dwellings have been built, and a commodious hospital is being erected for the care of the sick, a public school has been established, a good bank has been opened, and a live newspaper, the *Idaho Sun*, is published tri-weekly. Every branch of business is carried on in the spirit of genuine business enterprise. The medical and legal professions are well represented, and Murray seems favored with all the elements that contribute to the permanent prosperity of a mining town. The people of this great mining district are of no ordinary class, but are of more than average intelligence, who see first the great resources of the West, and with comprehension and earnest spirit of enterprise seize and appropriate them as the rightful inheritance of the industrious and self-sacrificing citizens of this free domain for themselves, their heirs, and their country.

Beaver Creek runs about parallel with Pritchard Creek, and empties into the north fork of Cœur d'Alene River about seven miles below where Pritchard Creek enters that stream. It heads high up in the mountains from which Granite Creek flows into Pritchard Creek. There are some very rich discoveries of quartz leads as well as placer deposits on this stream, from which it is becoming very attractive as a mining region, called Beaver district. The placers are generally deep on this creek, and have to be mined mostly by drifting. Reports of rich strikes in this district are frequent, and the bank at Murray is receiving numerous deposits of considerable quantities of beautiful coarse gold from these diggings, which are becoming noted as among the richest in the Cœur d'Alene. In this district is the little camp of

Carbon Center, so named on account of the large deposits of carboniferous ores found in that vicinity. Among these we mention the Silver Tip and the Sunset lodes; the latter being an extension of the former, and the two consisting of a mineral body that appears to be almost a mountain of ore. The same character of quartz is found in large bodies on Cañon Creek, several miles east from these leads, and is supposed to be but an extension of the same veins. Going down Beaver from Carbon a distance of three miles to the Ingram gardens, thence bearing south-west two and a half miles up a gulch to the summit, thence down a gulch to the south and west to the south fork of Cœur d'Alene River, and entering the old Mullan road half a mile above Evolution, is one of the most natural routes for a wagon-road that can be found in all this mountain region, owing to its easy grade through a low pass. It will doubtless in time become a great public thoroughfare to the mines. This route takes us to the region of

Nigger Prairie.—This name is given to a small grassy opening in the timber on the old Mullan road. It was so named from having been occupied by a negro man as an eating and feeding station several years ago, and who it is said was killed by an Indian, and left dead on the premises, and was found and buried by white men. This clothes its history with a somewhat romantic sadness.

The Quartz Mines of this locality are very numerous, and almost fabulously rich. From Mr. Carl Trowbridge we learned that the Hunter district was organized on the 4th day of September, 1884.

The Earl and Potts leads assay 1,000 ounces in silver per ton, and the Hunter lode is a large vein of 400-ounce rock.

The James G. Blaine is almost a mountain of ore, which assays $12 in gold per ton, and carries a trace of silver. It is owned by Mr. Carl Trowbridge, who regards it as a very rich strike.

The Silver Wave shows very rich in silver, and is five feet and a half wide.

The Napoleon is fifteen feet wide, is an iron and silver lead, and is very rich. It is owned by Thomas Noland, who prizes it very highly.

The Columbia is a well-defined vein twelve feet wide, very rich in silver, and is owned by Frank Bal.

Leads of the above description are very numerous in the Hunter district, where fully one hundred quartz locations have been made and recorded. The most intelligent and experienced mining men who have visited this part of Cœur d'Alene express the belief that in a few years this will become one of the most prosperous quartz-mining portions of Idaho.

At Nigger Prairie, the center of the Hunter district, Messrs. Marr & Good have laid off a town site, which the miners named Marrgood in honor of the enterprising proprietors. Several miners of this district will winter here, and several at each of the other camps in the district—Camp Noland, three miles west, Placerville, six miles west, Chloride Hill, three miles north, and French Boys, three miles east. In all about fifty men will stay in the district during the winter. Game of all kinds is plenty, the winters are mild, and the miners know to hunt, and will live well.

Mountain lakes nestle in the very tops of the Rockies, like a bevy of miniature seas, at the heads of Granite and Pritchard creeks on the north side, and at the sources of Beaver and Cañon creeks on the south side of the range, among the peaks in which these streams all take their rise.

These lakes vary in size from twenty to a hundred acres in area. They are all as clear as crystal, glistening in the sunlight by day, and reflecting the very image of the moon and stars by night. Their waters are always fresh and cold; from all of them flow beautiful streams down the mountain gorges—in places leaping and plunging in roaring cataracts over steep, rocky walls from ten to thirty feet high—romping and rollicking down the stony stairways of their mountain home. They make the piney forests resonant with the music of their merry laugh by day and their solemn song by night. They are fourteen in number, in a radius of from five to seven miles. Fish abound in some of them, as well as in all of the streams that flow from them. Game of all kinds is plentiful in the forests all around, and this is destined to become one of the most delightful and attractive pleasure resorts for sportsmen in the Rocky Mountains. When wagon and coach roads are built to Murray and other prominent mining camps in the Cœur d'Alene, and capital and machinery are brought to bear to lift the mineral treasures from these gulches, or pound and smelt them from the rocks, and the wealth of these rich deposits is more fully known, recognized, and sought after, and population comes with all its developing energies and refining influence—then this land, so despised and denounced by some, grossly misrepresented by others, will blossom as the rose: so rich are its mines, so fertile its soil, so plentiful and refreshing its waters, so abundant its timbers, so grand its mountains, so beautiful its lakes, and so sublime its scenery. It will be to those who dwell in it like Mt. Zion was to the ancient Jew, "beautiful for situation, and the joy of the whole earth."

In addition to the quartz locations mentioned by Mr. Shippen may be mentioned the prospects on what is called the Cœur d'Alene chloride belt, situate about eight miles from Eagle City, on the west fork of Eagle Creek.

Chief of these are the Margaret, Oregonian, Webfoot, Tribune, Emily, May, and Coolidge. The ore from these ledges shows up a yellow chloride that is very rich in silver, the lowest figures from a half-dozen assays being $51 in silver, while the highest has reached $1,300 of silver to the ton. The ore is also rich in gold, and being of the free-milling variety, can be easily and cheaply worked. Dr. W. Lang Chapman and Dr. E. O. Smith of Portland, Oregon, are the owners of these ledges, and they have done considerable development work on the Margaret, which makes a better showing for the depth attained than any other quartz property in the camp. The Margaret was bonded some time since for $30,000, and we learn that a half-interest in the mine was disposed of to Portland capitalists for $25,000.

The forks of the Eagle are described as a veritable network of massive quartz veins, such as the Mammoth, Silver Belle, Pan Handle, Golden Eagle, and countless others, while to the eastward of the North Fork is the Gray Eagle, already incorporated for $100,000.

Then there are also the Skookum belt of quartz ledges, three miles up Pritchard Creek, and the New Comstock with its extensions, an equal distance below town. None of these ledges are on the same belt as the famous Mother Lode, or the Fannie, or the Carbon Center group.

Nearly all of these have been discovered since May 1, 1884.

The Mother Lode is one of the most singular formations ever unearthed in quartz lead. There is an immensely rich slab of gold quartz right in the bed of the creek. It is apparently a quartz dike, which crosses Pritchard Creek at right angles but parallel with the bed-rock formation. The piece which was open to inspection is thickly splashed with gold, containing several rich veins. The estimates of the gold in sight are said to have been as various as the men who made the estimates. The mine is now (November, 1884) bonded for $130,000, with privilege of driving a tunnel 75 feet along the ledge and sinking 25 feet. The tunnel is now in 70 feet, and for this distance, as we are assured, it reveals the same wonderful wealth that first brought the lode into prominence. It is said that the original discovery was only a bowlder, being so thickly spattered with gold that it was deemed impossible that any ledge could carry such rock. It now seems to be certain that it is a well-defined, true fissure vein, and will be absurdly cheap at the price specified in the bond.

The Fannie mine on Trail Creek shows a four-foot vein of galena, with a three-inch stratum of gold-bearing quartz on the hanging wall that is "literally held together by stringers of gold." A five-stamp battery is to be erected next spring to reduce the ore from this mine.

William H. Chambers, Esq., assayer, of Eagle City, has kindly furnished me with the following abstract of assays made by Timmons & Chambers, Eagle, Idaho:

Margaret lode, situated six miles above Eagle, on Eagle Creek, six-foot fissure vein, silver $55, gold $51.

Gray Eagle mine, situated three miles from Eagle, on Eagle Creek, four-foot vein, galena, silver 55 ounces.

Mother lode, five and one half miles above Eagle, on Pritchard Creek, eight-foot vein, gold quartz, 14 ounces gold.

Montana lode, situated four miles from Eagle, two-foot vein, galena, 21 ounces silver.

Kate Burnette, Golden Chest, and Golden Gate, all in Reader Gulch; average per ton, $30 gold.

Virginia lode, situated three miles above Eagle, twenty-foot fissure vein; average assay from vein, $40 gold, free-milling gold quartz, owned by W. D. Waite, Eagle, Idaho.

Skukum lode, situated on Pritchard Creek, two miles above Eagle; gold quartz, $14 gold.

Bullion and Monarch mines, carbonate ores, four-foot veins, 40 to 60 ounces silver sulphuret ores.

Lucky Baldwin, situated in Dream Gulch, two-foot vein; gold quartz, $25 gold.

Dream ledge, Dream Gulch, four-foot vein, $8 gold.

The Sunset group, six miles from Eagle, Beaver district, comprising eight distinct ledges. Galena and carbonate ores, average 40 to 60 ounces silver.

The Jack Waite property, situated twelve miles above Eagle, on the east fork of Eagle Creek, copper and galena ore, twenty-foot fissure vein. Average from 40 to 160 ounces silver.

EAGLE, IDAHO, Sept. 30, 1884.

HON. J. L. ONDERDONK.

DEAR SIR—In submitting the above abstract from my assay memorandum, I will add that I cannot vouch for the description of the above properties only as they have been given me by the owners, excepting as to the ores assayed by me. Without exception, the properties named in the above abstract have had but little or no work done on them to demonstrate whether the veins are of a permanent character or not. The outlook for the camp I consider very encouraging, and all we need is capital to unearth our golden treasures, and we will demonstrate to the croakers that we have the banner mines of the Pacific slope. I have included in abstract but a few of the many quartz properties in our camp. Very truly yours,

W. H. CHAMBERS.

Judge William H. Claggett, writing from Murray, under date of September 22, 1884, gives the following candid statement of the true situation of the Cœur d'Alene mines:

"Before the claims on these tributaries could be opened for work, the water supply from the melting of the snow failed, and the high water in the main gulch discouraged, if it did not wholly prevent, any systematic attempt to open the claims. Then, just when everybody was getting ready to work, the entire camp found itself involved in litigation. Suits were begun in the district court to recover possession of nearly every claim in the camp. This litigation absolutely paralyzed development down to the 6th day of August, when the court adjourned. The result of the trials was to leave the claims in the hands of those who were called the 'jumpers,' and for the purposes of development, the 6th day of August last was the beginning of the life of the camp. Everything of any consequence in the shape of placer mining has been done since that date, which makes the camp at this time, to all practical intents and purposes, less than two months old. There being no water in the tributaries with which to mine, the development has been confined to the main gulch, commencing about two miles above Eagle and running up the gulch a distance of about seven miles. The gulch itself is more like a mountain basin than anything else. It is from 40 to 120 rods wide, and on the north side, having a general parallel course with it, there are several old river-beds or channels having a vertical elevation above the gulch of from 75 to 300 feet, through which intersecting ravines have cut, and the main gulch is mostly supplied with gold washed down from these old river-beds. This 'old wash,' as it is commonly called, has been traced for a distance of thirty miles. Thousands of acres of it have been located. In the absence of water to work it, it has thus far been only slightly prospected by shafts and tunnels, the miners waiting for some one with sufficient capital to bring water upon the hills.

"Messrs. Walsh & Hubbel, old and experienced placer miners from California, are now digging a ditch for this purpose, and when this and other ditches are completed, the Cœur d'Alene region will be an eye-opener to those who imagine that there is nothing there. Men are now packing gravel in sacks from the sides of the mountain upon their backs to water, and making from $25 to $50 per week. When a sufficient number of mining ditches shall be dug, the whole aspect of things will be changed. The water being taken from the main gulch will enable the gulch miners to work to better advantage. Troubled as they are with a superfluity of water, hydraulicking the hill ground will make available the immense resources of wealth which it contains, while the muddy water, turned back into the main gulch, will puddle the bed of Pritchard Creek, so that the gulch claims can be successfully opened in the deep ground. Three or four days before leaving home I went over the entire camp where mining has been carried on, and found that less than four acres of bed-rock had been cleaned up, all told. This shows a yield of over $40,000 to the acre. The present output of gold is not less than 1,000, nor more than 1,500, ounces of dust per week. Several of the claim-owners ship their dust directly to Helena, and my estimate is based upon my knowledge as to what these claims yield, the quantity of dust purchased weekly by the banks, and taken in by a few of the merchants. It is a mistake to suppose that Pritchard Gulch comprises the entire gold-field. On Trail Gulch several claims are opened, and are proved to be rich, while there is as much to show that Beaver Creek is rich as Pritchard Gulch itself showed last spring. There are two great wants to be supplied: first, a number of mining ditches to carry water upon the old wash; and second, a practicable wagon-road into the mines, over which mining machinery can be hauled and coaches travel."

As both these wants will in all probability be supplied next season, we may look for a record from Cœur d'Alene in the future which will more than realize the golden dreams said to have given the name to one of the richest gulches.

WASHINGTON COUNTY.

This county was organized February 20, 1879, from portions of Ada and Idaho counties. It is situated in western Idaho, being bounded on the north by Idaho County, on the east by Idaho and Boisé counties, on the south by Ada County, and on the west by the State of Oregon. Its area is 3,000 square miles.

The county has been especially favored by nature, as agriculture, stock-raising, and mining can each be followed successfully. Weiser Valley, Indian Valley, Middle Valley, and Mann's Creek are rapidly filling up with a prosperous farming population. Fruits, cereals, and all kinds of vegetables grow in abundance.

As an indication of the growth of the county during the past five years may be mentioned the fact that in 1879 the assessed valuation of the entire county was $161,945, and there were 163 property-tax payers. In 1884 the assessed valuation had increased to $627,978.75, and the number of tax-payers to 509; and yet the real development of the county has scarcely begun. Late in the autumn of 1884 the Oregon Short Line was completed to within her borders, and her county seat, Weiser City, now enjoys the distinction of being an important station on a great transcontinental railroad.

We are entering upon a new era in the history of western Idaho. The period of the overland stage-coach is nearly past, and the railroad and telegraph are here. The pioneer may step into an elegant Pullman sleeping-car at Weiser and journey along without fatigue across the continent. In three to five days he may return to his childhood home in Iowa, Missouri, Illinois, or even Maine. The news may be received by wire of the rise and fall of commercial values in London, New York, or any other of the world's great markets, within an hour after they are called. The returns of the late election were received here nearly as soon as they were known in Chicago. Our merchants receive their freight as cheaply and as soon as they do at Ogden or Salt Lake City, Utah. Our horses, beef, wool, and other productions may be shipped to Boston, New York, Omaha, and Chicago at as low rates as the same articles were shipped from Wyoming Territory ten years ago. Our mines are enabled by the railway to ship their ores to Omaha, Salt Lake City, and San Francisco at comparatively low rates. For these and other reasons, with which we are all familiar, we are now entering upon a new era, and we must all now aim to adjust ourselves and our affairs to the new order of things. The farmer must turn his attention to raising horses, cattle, or sheep, instead of raising grain and vegetables. With the great natural grazing lands on every side, and the unequaled natural facilities for raising stock, the town of Weiser will grow into importance. Washington County is to-day claimed to be the banner county of the whole Territory, either in agricultural, grazing, or mineral lands. This county has some of the finest farms, fruits, grains, vegetables, horses, cattle, sheep, fish, timber, and it can show some of the most valuable mines.

For several years prospecting has been going on along the eastern side of Snake River in what is generally known as the Weiser country. Washington, Heath, and Mineral districts show some of the finest prospects in the west.

The Washington District is about twenty-five miles north-west from Weiser City, and about four miles east of Snake River. The district is about ten miles long and three miles wide, extending north-east and south-west from Fourth of July Camp to Rock Creek.

The formation of the district is porphyry, and is said to bear considerable resemblance to the Comstock district in Nevada. The Black Maria, Muldoon, and Daniel Boone are among the principal mines thus far located. The croppings vary in width from ten to fifty feet. The Black Maria has been opened by a shaft six by eight feet for a distance of 100 feet or more, on an incline of 40°, all in ore. Several hundred tons of ore have been extracted. It is free milling, and increases in richness as it increases in depth. The vein is regular in formation, and can be traced the whole extent of the location.

The vein of the Daniel Boone is smaller than that of the Black Maria, but is exceedingly rich.

The **Heath District** is about fifty miles north of Weiser. They are all large quartz ledges, carrying silver chlorides and copper. The Belmont, Greenhorn, and Philadelphia are prominent locations in this district. The first named has been worked successfully for several years. The region is well timbered and watered, and with its accessibility to railroads will doubtless be thoroughly explored during the coming season.

Mineral is now making regular bullion shipments. The richness of the mines has already been proved.

Ruthburg District is in the hands of determined men, who are exposing at this writing thousands of tons of ore.

Last, but not least, comes the Seven Devil country. This copper district will roll out thousands of tons of copper at no distant day, and, as is well known, the ores carry a fair per cent of gold and silver.

The late discoveries made in what is known as the Seven Devil Mountains, situate some seventy-five miles north of Weiser, continue to excite the attention of mining men. There are a great many veins in the district, carrying copper, gold, and silver. The copper runs as high as sixty per cent of the ores, with $12 in gold and $15 in silver. Weiser is the natural outfitting point to these mines. It has a good wagon-road to within a short distance of the mines. There is abundance of timber for smelting purposes on the ground. The veins are wide and well defined, lying between granite and lime. The prospectors are still at work, and at every blast they are uncovering more ore. They come to Weiser, secure a fresh supply of provisions, and return without any unnecessary delay. Some of them will spend the winter at the mines. Great outcrops of peacock copper, ten and twenty feet wide, are found. It is a great camp; free gold is found with the copper, as well as several ounces in silver. The natural facilities for reducing these ores upon the ground are unequaled. The timber is simply inexhaustible, plenty of lime and iron, and an abundance of water. This is beyond a question of doubt the coming country. The spring will witness a great stampede of legitimate prospectors into the Seven Devil range.

The placer mines of Snake River, in this county, are growing in importance every year. The golden sands of that majestic river will be utilized at no distant day. There are large tracts of placer ground in the vicinity of the Seven Devil mines. This ground is said to pay two and three dollars per day to the man. Next spring we may expect this ground to be opened and give employment to a large number of men.

Weiser City is the county seat and chief town of the county. It is the last town on the Oregon Short Line before crossing into Oregon, and appears to have a bright future before it. It is located on a pretty site on the north side of Weiser River, some distance before its confluence with Snake River. The mountains skirting the valley are not high, and afford good stock-ranges, while the soil of the broad valley is so rich, and lies so favorable for irrigation and cultivation, as to make this a most desirable country for farming, fruit-raising, and stock-ranches. Heretofore the chief industry has been that of stock-raising, and the country is well supplied with cattle and horses. The ranges are not confined alone to this side of the Snake, but extend across into Oregon, up the Malheur and other valleys which come down from the west; south-west to Snake River opposite this place, and which by means of ferry send trade here. Weiser has grown rapidly this year, and there are many good substantial buildings. It is healthy, and the climate is all that could be desired. It is the natural point for outfitting for the Seven Devil country, for Ruthburg, for Mineral, for Salmon Meadows, and Warrens. It is the natural manufacturing point for this county, either for lumber, flour, or woolen mills. It has valuable water-power for running machinery that will be utilized at no distant day, we hope. The valley adjacent may be made to blossom as the rose when all our water facilities are properly distributed. Mineral will always trade here—the cattle, horse, and wool growers of this county must come here to the railroad.

The people must have several large houses of general merchandise to enable them to buy their goods at living prices.

The valley above Weiser City produced large crops this season, the yield of grain being above the average. This valley is rapidly settling up. The canal which takes water from Weiser River and conveys it to irrigate lands of the valley, is nearing completion and will cover a large area. Here it is so high on the hills as to give some forty or fifty feet fall for use in the town, and it is proposed to put in pipes for a system of water-works.

CHAPTER VII.—IDAHO INDIANS.

The native wild tribes of Idaho are now of chiefly historic interest. The existing remnants are confined to reservations, and are rapidly learning the arts of peace and civilization. There are four Indian agencies situated wholly within the limits of the Territory. According to the latest official reports, the registrations on these reservations were, in 1883, as follows:

Cœur d'Alene, Kootenai County, Pend d'Oreilles and Kootenais, 600.
Nez Percé (Fort Lapwai), Nez Percé County, Nez Percés, 1,250.
Lemhi, Lemhi County, Shoshones, Bannocks, and Sheepeaters, 800.
Fort Hall, Ross's Fork, Oneida County, Bannocks, 471, Shoshones, 1,085.

The Indians inhabiting the most northern portions of Idaho were the Kootenais, who dwelt in British Columbia and the extreme northern portion of Idaho, the Pend d'Oreilles, who dwelt about the lake of the same name, and for from fifty to seventy-five miles above and below the lake on Clarke's Fork; and the Cœur d'Alenes, who dwelt on Cœur d'Alene Lake and its tributaries. The Pend d'Oreilles and Cœur d'Alenes belonged to the Salish family, which dwelt south of the Shushwaps, between the forty-ninth and forty-seventh parallels, and on the Columbia and its tributaries. The remnants of these last-named Indians now in Idaho are on the Cœur d'Alene reservation. Mr. Joseph Paine, United States Indian interpreter at Fort Cœur d'Alene, informs me that the Cœur d'Alenes had three settlements in north Idaho, one at the old mission, one at the mouth of Cœur d'Alene River, and one at the site of the present Fort Cœur d'Alene. The origin of the name is discussed in the article on Shoshone County. They number at present about two hundred and fifty, all converted to the Roman Catholic religion. Most of them have farms in severalty, own houses, cattle, sheep, wagons, mowers, reapers, and all necessary and improved agricultural implements, raise large crops of wheat, oats, patatoes, hay, etc.; they own droves of hogs, and are to-day probably as prosperous and peaceful a tribe as can be found west of the Rocky Mountains. This tribe are self-supporting, and have never asked or received aid from the United States, and have never been at war with the white men. They have schools under the direction of the Roman Catholic nuns, and many of their young people are acquiring a fair knowledge of the English language.

The Sahaptin family, like the Salish just described, belongs to the inland tribes of the Columbia group. They inhabited the region between the Cascade and Bitter Root mountains, and the forty-fifth and forty-seventh parallels. Of its nations, the Nez Percés or Sahaptins proper dwelt on the Clearwater and its branches, and on the Snake about the forks. Ross, in his work entitled "Fur Hunters," says they derive their name from the custom of boring their noses to receive a white shell, like the fluke of an anchor. Most writers follow Ross in taking for granted that these Indians were so named from some habit of piercing their noses, though there is no tradition of anything of the sort. According to others it is a word tortured from *nez prés*, meaning flat nose, which was given them by the old French Canadian trappers in early days.

Mr. H. H. Bancroft, to whose work on the Native Races of the Pacific Coast I am indebted for many of the items in the following pages, states that in bodily strength the Sahaptin Indians are inferior to the whites, but superior, as might be expected from their habits, to the more indolent fish-eaters on the Pacific. The Nez Percés and Cayuses are considered the best specimens, while in the north the Kootenais seem to be superior to the other Shushwap nations. The Salish are assigned by Wilkes and Hale an intermediate place in physical attributes between the coast and mountain tribes, being in stature and proportion superior to the Chinooks, but inferior to the Nez Percés. Inland a higher order of face is observed than on the coast. The cheek-bones are still high, the forehead is rather low, the face long, the eyes black, rarely oblique, the nose prominent, and frequently aquiline, the lips thin, the teeth white and regular, but generally much worn. The general expression of the features is stern, often melancholy, but not as a rule harsh or repulsive. Dignified, fine-looking men, and handsome young women, have been remarked in nearly all the tribes, but here again the Sahaptins bear off the palm. The complexion is of decidedly coppery hue. The hair is generally coarse and worn long. The beard is very thin, and its growth is carefully prevented by plucking. Methods adopted by other tribes to create deformities of the head are comparatively unknown among the Nez Percés, who are generally better clad than some of their neighboring tribes. They build houses of straw and mats in the form of the roof of a house. Lewis and Clarke's narrative refers to one of these as one hundred and fifty feet long and about fifteen wide, closed at the ends and having a number of doors on each side.

War and hunting were their chief occupation, but they were and are not infrequently compelled to resort to roots, and berries, and mosses. The favorite roots are the camas, couse, and bitter root, and the natives to obtain these make regular migrations as for game or fish. The women are generally much more kindly treated among the Nez Percés and Pend d'Oreilles than among the generality of aboriginal tribes.

In their personal habits, as well as the care of their lodges, the Nez Percés and Kootenais are mentioned as neat and cleanly. De Smet, however, represents the Pend d'Oreille women as untidy, even for savages. "The inland families," says Bancroft, "cannot be called a warlike race." They seldom resort to arms, yet when fighting becomes necessary, the Cayuses, Nez Percés, Flatheads, and Kootenais are notably brave warriors for defense or vengeance against a foreign foe. The two former waged both defensive and aggressive warfare against the Snakes of the south, while the latter joined their arms against their common foes, the Blackfeet. Departure on a warlike expedition is preceded by ceremonies, including councils of the wise, great, and old, smoking the pipe, harangues by the chiefs, dances, and a general review or display of equestrian feats and manœuvers of battle. After battle they smoke the customary pipe of peace with the enemy, and renew their protestations of eternal friendship. In the matter of marriage, the standard of a wife's qualifications is her capacity for work.

The Nez Percés have more and better stock than other nations. Individuals often own large bands of horses. The Kootenais are the most northern tribe who are accustomed to the horse. It is supposed that these animals were introduced among the northern tribes by Shoshones from the south, the last named being connected with the Comanches, who obtained horses from the Spaniards during the sixteenth century. The rights of property are duly respected, but it is said that among the Salish nations on the death of the father his relatives would not scruple in the least to seize the most valuable property, regardless of the rights of the children who are too young to take care of themselves. With the Pend d'Oreilles, when reduced to severe straits, it was not uncommon to bury the very old and very young alive, because, they said, "these cannot take care of themselves, and they had better die." On approaching his majority, the young Pend d'Oreille would be sent to a high mountain where he would have to remain until he dreamed of some animal, bird, or fish, which was to be thereafter his medicine. A claw, tooth, or feather of such animal was thereafter to be worn as his charm. The howling of certain beasts, especially of the medicine-wolf, was supposed to forebode evil. Among the Nez Percés it was the custom to overcome the spirit of fatigue, or *mawish* as it was called, by a certain ceremony which was supposed to confer great powers of endurance. This ceremony was repeated yearly from the age of eighteen to forty, and the performance would last three to seven days. It consisted of thrusting willow sticks down the throat into the stomach, a succession of hot and cold baths, and fasting.

Medicine-men are supposed to acquire wonderful powers by retiring to the mountains and conferring with the medicine-wolf, after which they become invulnerable, and bullets fired at them flatten on their breast. They have a superstitious fear of having their portraits taken. Steam baths or sweat-houses are used for the purpose of purification in their religious rites. These sweat-houses usually consist of a hole in the ground from three to eight feet deep, and about fifteen feet in diameter, with a small hole for entrance, which is closed up after the bather enters. A fire is built in this retreat by means of which stones are heated. In this oven-like receptacle, heated to a suffocating temperature, the naked native wallows in the steam and mud, singing, yelling, and praying, and at last rushes out dripping with perspiration, and plunges into the nearest stream.

The good qualities of the Kootenais and Nez Percés have been commended by all having acquaintance with them. "Honest, just, and often charitable; ordinarily cold and reserved, but on occasions social and almost gay; quick-tempered and almost revengeful under what they consider injustice, but readily appeased by kind treatment; cruel only to captive enemies, stoical in the endurance of torture; devotedly attached to home and family—these natives probably come as near as it is permitted to flesh and blood savages to the noble red man of the forest sometimes met in romance."

The Nez Percés now on the reservation in Nez Percé County at Fort Lapwai belong to the treaty Indians as opposed to the non-treaty Nez Percés who, under Joseph, were banished to Indian territory. The difficulties arising from the obstinacy of the non-treaties have been sufficiently detailed in the first chapter. The Nez Percés now in Idaho have ever been stanch friends of the whites; they are brave, but industrious and peaceable. They number about 1,250. With the exception of the agricultural implements issued to them by the government, they can be justly termed self-supporting. Their means of support are agriculture and stock-raising. Each year witnesses decided advancements. According to Indian Agent Charles E. Monteith, last year these Indians cultivated 5,050 acres of land, being an increase of 550 over the preceding year. They have now 7,300 acres under fence. Last year they raised 35,000 bushels of wheat, 5,000 bushels of corn, 6,000 bushels of oats and barley, 10,850 bushels of vegetables, and 200 tons of hay. Among other results of their labor were 200 pounds of butter, 73,000 feet of lumber sawed, 450 cords of wood cut, 225 rods of fencing made, and $400 worth of furs sold. They possess 14,000 head of horses, 23 mules, 3,800 cattle, 875 swine, and 3,000 domestic fowls.

The children are said to be advancing nearly as rapidly in their school-room studies as average white children, and show a remarkable aptitude in all kinds of farm and garden work. Seventy-five children received instructions in the various branches of industry and book knowledge. The department has recently instituted a measure to compel the children to attend school by withholding government aid from those who refuse to send their children when called upon by the agent.

At the suggestion of Mr. Monteith, a code of laws has been adopted by these Indians in council, and the result has been most satisfactory. Cases of drunkenness have been reduced two thirds. These laws are directed against not only drunkenness, but theft, interference in school matters, assault, wife-beating, and graver offenses.

Laws of the Nez Perces.—The following were adopted by the Nez Percés at the suggestion of the early missionaries as their laws:

ART. 1. Whoever willfully takes life shall be hanged.
ART. 2. Whoever burns a dwelling-house shall be hanged.
ART. 3. Whoever burns an out-building shall be imprisoned six months, receive fifty lashes, and pay all damages.

Art. 4. Whoever carelessly burns a house or any property shall pay damages.

Art. 5. If any one enter a dwelling without permission of the occupants, the chiefs shall punish him as they think proper. Public rooms are excepted.

Art. 6. If any one steal, he shall pay back twofold; and if it be the value of a beaver skin or less, he shall receive twenty-five lashes; and if the value be over a beaver skin, he shall pay back twofold, and receive fifty lashes.

Art. 7. If any one take a horse and ride it without permission, or take any article and use it without liberty, he shall pay for the use of it, and receive from twenty to fifty lashes, as the chiefs shall direct.

Art. 8. If any one enter a field and injure the crops, or throw down the fence so cattle and horses go in and do damage, he shall pay all damages, and receive twenty-five lashes for every offense.

Art. 9. Those only may keep dogs who travel or live among the game; if a dog kill a lamb, calf, or any domestic animal, the owner shall pay the damages and kill the dog.

Art. 10. If an Indian raise a gun or other weapon against a white man, it shall be reported to the chiefs, and they shall punish it. If a white man do the same to an Indian, it shall be reported to Dr. White, and he shall punish and redress it.

Art. 11. If an Indian break these laws, he shall be punished by his chiefs; if a white man break them, he shall be reported to the agent, and punished at his instance.

The Lemhi Indians are composed of Shoshones, Bannocks, and Sheepeaters. There are about 800 in all. Mr. John Harries, agent, thus characterizes them: The Shoshone or Snake Indians are fairly honest, peaceable and intelligent. The Bannocks possess more of the sly cunning and innate restlessness of disposition than would appear to be good for them or agreeable to their nearest neighbors. The Sheepeaters are naturally quieter and less demonstrative than either, and therefore seem more inclined to take life easy. The Shoshone element largely predominates, and doubtless in a short time will absorb the other two, to the advantage of all.

The Shoshone family is generally included in the California group of native tribes. Their territory formerly spread over south-eastern Oregon and southern Idaho, extending into Utah, Arizona, and eastern Idaho. They are divided into several tribes, of which the Bannocks were originally one. The word "Shoshone" means "Snake Indian," though Ross is authority for the assertion that it means "inland."

The Snakes are better dressed than the tribes farther south, and make some pretensions to ornamentation. Their clothing is generally made of the skins of larger game, ornamented with beads, shells, fringes, feathers, and pieces of brilliant-colored cloth. Their dwellings are also superior to those of the Utahs, though consisting chiefly of skins thrown over long poles leaning against each other in the form of a circle. A hole is left in the top for a chimney. Another one in the bottom, about three feet high, is used as a door, and closed by placing a skin against it. The poorer Shoshones live on pine-nuts, roots, berries, insects, rats, mice, and rabbits. Those living in Idaho, however, are generally are supplied with plenty of fish and game. In their native wild condition they can hardly be called a cleanly race. Their characteristic weapon is the *poggamoggon*. "It consists of a heavy stone, sometimes wrapped in leather, attached by a sinew thong about two inches in length to the end of a stout, leather-covered handle measuring nearly two feet. A loop fastened to the end held in the hand prevents the warrior from losing the weapon in the fight, and allows him to hold the club in readiness while he uses the bow and arrow."

The Snakes had a limited knowledge of pottery, and made very good vessels from baked clay. Some of these were in the form of jars, with narrow necks and stoppers. They possessed little knowledge of the use of boats beyond crude and clumsy logs made of branches and rushes, generally preferring to swim the streams. Dried fish, horses, skins, and furs were their currency. No trade was indulged in unless preceded by a solemn smoke. Among the Idaho Snakes four and five beaver-skins were sold for a knife or an awl.

Horses were held at the value of an ax. "A ship of seventy-four guns might have been loaded with provision, such as dried buffalo, bought with buttons and rings." The standard of values was absurdly confused. The utility of an article was a matter of no consideration. A beaver-skin could be bought with a brass ring, but a necklace of bears' claws could not be bought for a dozen such rings. Axes, knives, ammunition, beads, buttons, and rings were most in demand. For clothing they had little or no use; a blanket was worth no more than a knife, and a yard of fine cloth was worth less than a pot of vermilion. They had no established laws. Like all other Indians, they are natural gamblers, and take to "poker" with an aptitude that is astonishing. They are skillful riders, and possess good horses. "The Snakes have been considered," says Ross, "as rather a dull and degraded people, weak in intellect and wanting in courage. And this opinion is very probable to a casual observer at first sight, or when seen in small numbers, for their apparent timidity, grave and reserved habits, give them an air of stupidity. An intimate knowledge of the Snake character will, however, place them on an equal footing with that of other kindred nations, both in respect to their mental faculties and moral attributes." "The Shoshones of Idaho," says a writer in the *California Farmer*, "are highly intelligent and lively, the most virtuous and unsophisticated of all the Indians of the United States."

The Bannocks are naturally a brave and warlike race. They inhabited the country between Fort Boisé and Fort Hall. As the name implies, it was given to those Indians who dug and lived on roots. At least, so says Johnston, in Schoolcraft's *Archives*.

The Sheepeaters, like the Bannocks, are doubtless an offshoot of the Snake or Shoshone Indians. The Tookarikkas, or Sheepeaters, occupied the Salmon River country, the upper part of Snake River valley, and the mountains near Boisé Basin. They belong to the genuine Snakes. Other inferior bands were the Hokandikas, or Salt Lake Diggers, who lived in the neighborhood of Salt Lake, and Aggitikkas, or Salmon-eaters, who occupied the region around Salmon Falls, on Snake River. The Bannocks are far inferior to the Shoshones or Snakes proper.

Though the Lemhi Reservation is situated at an altitude of 5,500 feet, agriculture has been pursued with fair success. Thirty Indian families have now little patches of oats and garden stuff. The Indians raised last year about 2,000 bushels of oats, 40 bushels of potatoes, 50 bushels of turnips, 5 bushels of onions, and 20 bushels of other small vegetables. The quantity produced on the agency farm was small, as it was the first year's crop.

These Lemhi Indians are greatly improving in habits of industry. Besides cultivating their little garden patches, many of them have been engaged in cutting rails, fencing, and ditching. They hauled over 40,000 pounds of freight last season from the railroad to the agency, a distance of seventy miles. "The possession of wagons," says Mr. Harries, "by some Indians, is materially helping to lift what is literally a heavy burden off the backs of the squaws in the matter of the hauling of the firewood." Some difficulty has been encountered in educating the children, as there is a superstition among them that "if the Indian children learn to read and write they will die." This feeling has such a strong hold upon the mothers particularly, that hitherto it has been difficult to overcome the prejudice against education. With the improvidence characteristic of the race, moreover, the rations issued to the lodges on Saturday seldom last beyond Monday or Tuesday, so that unless the children are fed at the school, they are not likely to have much to eat the biggest part of the week. Indians are not superior to the generality of human nature, and naturally encounter some difficulty in studying on an empty stomach. It is intended to overcome these obstacles by establishing a boarding-school, where the physical as well as intellectual wants of the children will be properly cared for.

The Indians stationed at the Fort Hall agency are both Bannocks and Shoshones. The latter are industrious, good-natured, and quiet. The Bannocks are more restless and roving. Of the 471 Bannocks registered there, 240 last year were engaged in farming; while of the 1,083 Shoshones, fully

950 were so engaged. The crops raised were wheat, oats, barley, potatoes, and other root crops.

According to the last report of Dr. A. S. Cook, agent at Fort Hall, the crops raised last year were as follows :

240 acres of	wheat		4,200	bushels
330 "	" oats		9,600	"
55 "	" barley		1,500	"
45 "	" potatoes		3,000	"
16 "	" turnips		1,000	"
606 acres.			19,300	"

There is an Indian school at this agency, which is proving a success. The military buildings and property at Fort Hall, having been transferred to the Interior Department, are hereafter to be used for an industrial school. Workshops will be opened as fast as they can be made practicable. The Indians take great interest in these shops, and it is believed that they will be a very successful feature in the agency. These Indians, according to Dr. Cook, are making steady advancement in agricultural and civilized pursuits. This is noticeable to all who come in contact with them, and they are manifesting an increased desire to conform to the customs of civilized life. They have commenced to acquire property for themselves. They purchased three mowing-machines, six hay-rakes, and two wagons this year; four more mowing-machines and two hay-rakes have been purchased, making seven mowers and eight hay-rakes owned by Indians. As they show so much inclination to industry and civilized pursuits, it is believed that if a quarter-section of land should be allotted to each head of a family, and some assistance be given them to commence its cultivation, the reservation could then be thrown open to settlers, thus bringing the Indians into civilized communities. "I believe," says Dr. Cook, "that they would improve more from observation and necessity, and sooner become self-sustaining, than by the present method."

Sign-language.—The use of sign-language exists to a greater or less degree among Idaho Indians as among most tribes. Thus the tribal sign of the Pend d'Oreilles is made by holding both fists as if grasping a paddle, vertically downward and working a canoe. Two strokes are made on each side of the body from the side backward. The tribal sign of the Nez Percés is made by closing the right hand, leaving the index straight, but flexed at right angles with the palm, then passing it horizontally to the left, by and under the nose. That of the Shoshone or Snake Indians is the right hand horizontal, flat, palm downward, advanced to the front by a motion to represent the crawling of a snake. For that of the Bannocks, make a whistling sound "phew" (beginning at a high note and ending about an octave lower); then draw the extended index finger across the throat from left to right, and out to nearly arm's length. They used to cut the throats of their prisoners.

Major Haworth states that the Bannocks made the following sign for themselves: brush the flat right hand backward over the forehead as if forcing back the hair. This represents the manner of wearing the tuft of hair backward from the forehead. He also states that the Shoshones make the same sign for the Bannocks as for themselves.

It is not difficult to understand how readily ideas may be conveyed by signs and gestures. Thus the Shoshone sign for *rain* is made by holding the hand or hands at the height of and before the shoulder, fingers pendent, palm down, then pushing it downward a short distance. That for *to weep* is made by holding the hand as in *rain*, and the gesture made from the eye downward over the cheek, back of the fingers nearly touching the face.

Brave or *strong-hearted* is made by the Shoshone and Bannock Indians by merely placing the clenched fist to the breast, the latter having allusion to the heart, the clenching of the hand to strength, vigor, or force.

As a good example illustrative of the universality of sign-language, may be mentioned the conversation which took place at Washington in 1880 between Tendoy, chief of the Shoshone and Bannock Indians of Lemhi reservation, Idaho, and Huerito, one of the Apache chiefs from New Mexico, in the presence of Dr. W. J. Hoffman. Neither of these Indians *spoke* any language known to the other, had lived over a thousand miles apart, and had never met or heard of one another before.

Huerito—Who are you?
Tendoy—Shoshone Chief.
Huerito—How old are you?
Tendoy—Fifty-six.
Huerito—Very well. Are there any buffalo in your country?
Tendoy—Yes; many black buffalo. Did you hear anything from the Secretary? If so tell me.
Huerito—He told me that in four days I would go to my country.
Tendoy—In two days I go to my country just as you go to yours. I go to mine where there is a great deal of snow, and we shall see each other no more.

Here was an intelligent dialogue carried on by two savages, strangers to each other, without a word spoken on either side. Thus to make the last answer as Tendoy did, place the flat hands horizontally, about two feet apart, move them quickly in an upward curve toward one another until the right lies across the left, meaning *night*, repeat this sign, two *nights*, literally, *two sleeps hence;* point toward the individual addressed with the right hand, *you;* and in a continuous movement pass the hand to the right, *i. e.,* toward the south, nearly to arm's length, *go;* then throw the fist edgwise toward the ground at that distance, *your country;* then touch the breast with the tips of the left fingers, *I;* move the hand slowly toward the left, *i. e.,* toward the north to arm's length, *go to;* and throw the clenched hand toward the ground, *my country.* Make the sign of *rain* as already described, then place the flat hands to the left of the body about two feet from the ground, *deep;* literally, *deep rain, snow.* Raise the hands about a foot, *very deep, much;* place the hands before the body, about twelve inches apart, palms down, with forefinger only extended and pointing toward one another; push toward and from one another several times, *see each other;* then hold the flat right hand in front of the breast pointing forward, palm to the left, and throw it once on its back toward the right, *not, no more.*

In the first chapter of this work a brief synopsis was given of the Indian troubles which so long retarded the development of Idaho. All danger from that source has now been removed forever. The feeble remnants of once powerful tribes have settled down to the prosaic arts of peace. The great increase of white population, the construction of railroad and telegraph lines, the rapid diminution of their own numbers, all preclude the possibility of Indian outbreaks in the future. Yet we should be grossly lacking in appreciation if we should overlook the struggles and hardships endured by the early settler, in combating these treacherous foes, and rendering the land safe as it now is beyond the shadow of peril. Surely, when the true history of heroism is written, the story of our north-western pioneers should receive proper recognition.

CHAPTER VIII.—MISCELLANEOUS.

SCHOOLS.

The cause of education is keeping pace with the material development of the Territory. There are at present 238 school districts and a school population (between five and twenty-one years of age) of 13,140. The school system consists of a territorial superintendent, county superintendents, and district trustees.

The general school law provides that all moneys accruing from the sale of all lands heretofore given, or which may hereafter be given, by the Congress of the United States for school purposes in said Territory, and all moneys that may hereafter be given and appropriated by the Congress of the United States for school purposes, unless the same by special provision shall be appropriated for the establishment of a university or other high-school, together with any moneys by legacy or otherwise donated for educational purposes, and appropriated for the general fund, and all moneys accruing to the Territory from unclaimed moneys from the estates of deceased persons, shall be set apart and shall constitute an irreducible and indivisible Territorial General School Fund, the interest only accruing from which shall be appropriated to the respective counties of the Territory in the manner hereinafter specified and directed.

For the purpose of establishing and maintaining public schools in the several counties of the Territory, it is the duty of the county commissioners of each county, at the time of levying the taxes for county and territorial purposes, to levy a tax of not less than two mills nor more than eight mills on each and every dollar of taxable property in their respective counties for school purposes.

The proceeds of fines and forfeitures, and certain licenses, also go to the county school fund.

Boisé City and Lewiston each constitute an independent school district. Each has a graded school in every way creditable to the Territory. For more particular information concerning these graded schools, the reader is referred to the articles on Ada and Nez Percé counties. Religious, sectarian, and political doctrines are expressly forbidden to be taught.

Teachers' salaries vary according to locality and character of the school. In agricultural sections they range from $50 to $75 per month; in mining regions, from $60 to $125; and in the larger towns, from $65 to $150 per month.

The schools generally are better than could be naturally expected in so new a country. Great care is exercised in the selection of teachers, and the home-seeker coming to Idaho may be sure of finding abundant educational facilities in the elementary and graded schools of the Territory.

By the Act of February 18, 1881, Congress granted to the Territory of Idaho seventy-two sections of public lands for school purposes, under certain restrictions. These, with the 3,000,000 acres of school lands (sixteenth and thirty-sixth sections) allowed under the general law, will undoubtedly at some future day form the basis of a sound, substantial school system.

CHURCHES.

All the leading churches and denominations are well represented.

Episcopalians.—Idaho and Utah constitute one missionary diocese, under the charge of Bishop D. S. Tuttle of Salt Lake City. There are in Idaho at present seven parishes, as follows: Boisé City, St. Michael's; Silver City, St. James; Idaho City, St. Mark's; Lewiston, Nativity; Blackfoot, Holy Innocents; Bellevue, St. Paul's; Hailey, Emanuel; Ketchum, St. Mark's. Value of church property, $4,000.

Methodist.—There are 10 Methodist church buildings, 7 parsonages, 15 ministers in regular work, and a membership of 650. There are 2 church schools, Columbia River Conference Academy at Grangeville, Idaho County, and the Lewiston Collegiate Institute at Lewiston. Rev. W. A. Hall is the principal of the former, Rev. Levi Tarr, A. M., president of the latter. These schools are in a prosperous condition. Value of church property, exclusive of schools, $35,500.

Presbyterians.—Churches, 7; schools, 5; church membership, 500; scholars, 400; ministers, 4; teachers, 10. Church and school property, $20,000.

Baptists.—Churches, 5; namely, at Boisé City, Mann's Creek, Middleton, Payette, and Weiser. Membership, 139.

Roman Catholics have parishes in the chief settlements.

The Church of Latter-day Saints numbers a large following in southeastern Idaho.

SOCIETIES.

Masonic.—Grand Lodge of Idaho instituted December 17, 1867. Lodges under the jurisdiction of the Grand Lodge of Idaho, A. F. & A. M.

No.	Name.	Location.	Membership, 1883.
1	Idaho	Idaho City	43
2	Boisé	Boisé City	68
3	Placer	Placerville	27
7	Shoshone	Boisé City	37
9	Mt. Idaho	Mt. Idaho	52
10	Nez Percé	Lewiston	55
11	Lemhi	Salmon City	35
12	Alturas	Rocky Bar	24
13	Silver City	Silver City	55
14	Cassia	Albion	20
15	St. John	Bellevue	22
16	Hailey	Hailey	—
12			438

R. A. M.—Royal Arch Masons have chapters at the following places: Idaho, No. 1, Idaho City; Cyrus, No. 2, Silver City; Boisé, No. 3, Boisé City; Lewiston, No. 4, Lewiston; Alturas, No. 5, Hailey.

Knights Templar.—Idaho Commandery, No. 1, Boisé City.

Odd Fellows.—Grand Lodge of Idaho instituted November 13, 1883. Lodges under jurisdiction of Grand Lodge of Idaho, I. O. O. F.

No.	Name.	Location.	Membership.	Value of Property.
1	Pioneer	Idaho City	31	$3,000
2	Owyhee	Silver City	55	2,000
3	Ada	Boisé City	59	5,000
4	Excelsior	Centreville	20	1,800
5	Rocky Mountain	Salmon City	23	3,000
6	Covenant	Placerville	21	2,000
7	Mt. Idaho	Mt. Idaho	16	1,000
8	Lewiston	Lewiston	40	1,500
9	Bellevue	Bellevue	35	1,000
10	Caldwell	Caldwell	20	500
	Total		320	$20,800

Encampment.—Idaho Encampment, No. 1, Boisé City; membership, 38.

Grand Army of the Republic, under the Department of Utah, including Utah, Idaho, and Montana. G. A. R. Posts in Idaho:

James A. Garfield	No. 4	Bellevue.
A. Guernsey	No. 5	Lewiston.
McPherson	No. 7	Salmon City.
Patrick Collins	No. 11	Boisé City.

United Workmen.—Under the Grand Lodge of Nevada. Lodges of A. O. U. W. in Idaho:

No.	Name.	Location.
1	Hailey	Hailey.
2	Ketchum	Ketchum.
3	Bullion	Bullion.
4	Shoshone	Shoshone.
5	Idaho	Boisé City.
6	Teton	Eagle Rock.
7	Gate City	Bellevue.

NEWSPAPERS.

Daily.

*Wood River Times	Hailey, Alturas County.
*News Miner	Hailey, Alturas County.
*Inter-Idaho	Hailey, Alturas County.

Tri-Weekly.

*Statesman	Boisé City, Ada County.
Sun	Murray, Shoshone County.
*Keystone	Ketchum, Alturas County.

Semi-Weekly.

*World	Idaho City, Boisé County.
Democrat	Boisé City, Ada County.

Weekly.

Republican	Boisé City, Ada County.
Tribune	Caldwell, Ada County.
Chronicle	Bellevue, Alturas County.
Journal	Shoshone, Alturas County.
Democrat	Paris, Bear Lake County.
Messenger	Challis, Custer County.
Press	Houston, Custer County.
Courier	Rathdrum, Kootenai County.
Teller	Lewiston, Nez Percé County.
Nez Percé News	Lewiston, Nez Percé County.
Mirror	Moscow, Nez Percé County.
Register	Eagle Rock, Oneida County.
Herald	Soda Springs, Oneida County.
Avalanche	Silver City, Owyhee County.
Leader	Weiser City, Washington County.

*Also Weekly.

U. S. LAND-OFFICES.

Land-offices have been located as follows: Boisé City, Ada County; Lewiston, Nez Percé County; Oxford, Oneida County; and Hailey, Alturas County. The Cœur d'Alene land-office was recently established, but is not yet in active operation.

RAILROADS.

The railroad system of Idaho has been sufficiently described in the first chapter. For the information of those desiring to visit Idaho, we subjoin the following tables of distances taken from the latest railway schedules.

Union Pacific Railway.—Oregon Short Line, trains daily. Emigrant passengers carried on express trains.

WESTWARD.				
Day of the Week.	No. 1 Oregon Express.	Distance from Omaha.	STATIONS.	Population.
Sunday	P. M. 8 25	0	............Omaha............Ar	50,000
Tuesday....	A. M. 11 00	876	............Granger............	
"	11 36	891	............Nutria............	
"	P. M. 12 39	918	............Ham's Fork............	
"	12 46	920	............Twin Creek............	
"	12 59	925	............Fossil............	
"	1 50	947	............Beckwith............	
"	2 45	959	......Cokeville, Wyoming.........	50
"	3 09	968	............Border............	
"	3 25	974	......Nuphar, Idaho...........	
"	4 25	991	............Montpelier............	100
"	5 01	1005	............Novene............	
"	5 41	1020	............Stock Yards............	
"	5 45	1021	............Soda Springs............	500
"	6 30	1038	............Squaw Creek............	50
"	7 11	1053	............Lava............	
"	7 50	1067	............McCammon............	50
"	8 19	1078	............Inkom............	
"	8 50 9 25	1090	Ar............Pocatello............Lv Lv............Pocatello............Ar	100
"	9 40	1099	............Michaud............	
"	10 20	1115	............American Falls............	100
"	11 00	1132	............Wapi............	
"	11 38	1148	............Minidoka............	
Wednesday	A. M. 12 18	1165	............Kimama............	
"	2 00	1197	............Shoshone*............	500
"	2 39	1213	............Toponis............	
"	3 49	1241	............King Hill............	
"	4 50	1261	............Medbury............	
"	5 40	1279	............Mountain Home............	50
"	6 43	1305	............Bisuka............	
"	7 30	1324	............Kuna†............	50
"	8 35	1343	............Caldwell............	400
"	9 15	1358	............Parma............	
"	10 05	1370	............Ontario............	100
"	10 12	1378	............Payette............	100
"	10 50	1391	............Weiser............	700
"	11 35	1407	............Old's Ferry............	
"	Noon	1416	Ar............Huntington............Lv	

*Connects with Wood River branch.
†Connects with daily stages for Boisé, Idaho, and Silver cities.

Wood River Branch.

Miles.	Stations.
0	Shoshone.
14	Pina.
30	Tikura.
37	Picabo.
52	Bellevue.
57	Hailey.
64	Gimlet.
69	Ketchum.

Utah and Northern Railway.

Distance from Ogden.		Population.	Elevation.
......	Ogden, Utah	8,000	4,294
78	Franklin, Idaho	1,000	4,510
90	Battle Creek	....	4,407
101	Oxford	500	4,771
125	Arimo	300	4,656
132	McCammon*	....	....
154	Pocatello†	100	4,402
166	Ross Fork	....	....
179	Blackfoot‡	300	4,512
205	Eagle Rock	600	4,720
222	Market Lake	....	4,780
243	Camas	50	....
272	Beaver Cañon	500	6,035
300	Spring Hill	100	6,106
323	Red Rock§	100	5,610
454	Garrison‖	....	....

* Daily stage to Malad, 36 miles.
† Connects with Oregon Short Line for the west.
‡ Connects with daily stages for Arco, Houston, Lost River, Challis, Bayhorse, Bonanza, and Yankee Fork.
§ Connects with daily stages for Salmon City and Lemhi mines.
‖ Connects with Northern Pacific.

Rates of Fare from Omaha.

TO—	1st Class.	2d Class.	Emigrant.	Distance from Omaha.
Beaver Cañon	$63 40	$42 50	....	1,390
Bellevue	66 80	52 80	$45 00	1,248
Blackfoot	55 95	41 95	....	1,115
Boisé City	74 80	60 80	47 00	1,330
Caldwell	74 30	60 30	45 00	1,343
Challis	78 95	61 95	....	1,265
Eagle Rock	58 00	42 50	....	1,141
Hailey	67 20	53 20	45 00	1,254
Idaho City	79 80	65 80	52 00	1,375
Ketchum	68 20	54 20	45 00	1,266
Kuna	72 80	58 80	45 00	1,324
Lewiston	92 85	77 40	49 00	.....
Pocatello	54 00	40 00	....	1,090
Salmon City	79 45	54 50	....	1,360
Shoshone	62 60	48 60	45 00	1,197
Weiser City	78 45	64 45	45 00	1,391

Northern Pacific.—Distance from St. Paul.

	Miles.
Garrison*	1,206
Thompson's Falls†	1,381
Trout Creek†	1,404
Sand Point	1,467
Rathdrum†	1,509
Walla Walla	1,729

* Junction Utah and Northern Railway   † Outfitting points for Cœur d'Alene.

WAGES IN IDAHO.

Bakers, per month and board	$65 00
Blacksmiths, per day	5 00
Bookkeepers, per month	125 00
Bricklayers, per day	5 00
Butchers, per month and board	65 00
Carpenters, per day	4 00
First cook, per month and board	110 00
Second " " " " "	55 00
Cooks in families, per month and board	30 00
Chambermaids, " " " "	30 00
Clerks, per month	80 00
Dressmakers	70 00
Dairymen, per month and board	25 00
Engineers in mills, per day	4 50
Farm hands, per month and board	25 00
Harness-makers, per day	3 00
Hostlers, per month and board	50 00
Laundresses, " " "	30 00
Laborers, " " "	35 00
Lumbermen, " " "	50 00
Machinists, per day	4 50
Miners, "	3 50
Millers, per month and board	65 00
Millwrights, per day	4 50
Painters, "	4 00
Printers, per week	20 00
Plasterers, per day	6 00
School-teachers, per month	65 00
Servants, per month and board	30 00
Shepherds, " " " "	30 00
Stonemasons, per day	6 00
Teamsters, per month and board	50 00
Waiters, " " " "	55 00

IDAHO ALTITUDES.

Following are elevations of all prominent towns, lakes, valleys, etc., of Idaho, as ascertained by the observations of Prof. Hayden and other explorers:

Place.	Feet.
American Falls	4,320
Atlanta	5,525
Alturas Lake	6,600
Bear River Bridge	5,744
Bennington	5,798
Blackfoot Fork Bridge	4,456
Blackfoot City	4,523
Blackfoot Peak	7,490

RESOURCES OF IDAHO.

Place.	Feet.
Bear Lake	5,900
Black Rock	5,500
Bloomington	5,985
Bonanza City	6,400
Bellevue	5,200
Boisé City	2,800
Big Camas Prairie	4,000
Camas Prairie (North)	3,500
Camas Station	4,722
Clifton	4,893
Cœur d'Alene Mission	2,280
Cottonwood	3,300
Clawson Toll Gate	4,300
Custer Mine	8,400
Craig Mountain	4,080
Custer Mountain	8,760
Caribou Mountain	9,854
Custer City	6,560
Centreville	4,825
Challis	5,400
Dry Creek Station	5,689
Eagle Rock	4,720
Elk Prairie	2,380
Estes Mountain	10,050
Fort Hall	4,783
Fort Lapwai	2,000
Franklin City	4,516
Florida Mountain	7,750
Florence	8,000
Fish Haven	5,932
Forks of Lolo	4,450
Gentile Valley (head)	5,245
Galena City	7,900
Gladiator Mine	9,700
Grand Teton	13,691
Georgetown	5,800
Georgetown Peak	8,646
Henry Lake	6,443
Junction of Lolo and Middle Forks Clearwater	1,304
Junction of South and Middle Forks Clearwater	1,110
Idaho City	4,263
Junction Station	6,329
Jessie Benton Mine	7,600
Jackson Lake	6,806
Ketchum	5,700
Keeney's Station	4,933
Laketown	6,000
Lewiston	680
Little Salmon Meadows	3,500
Lake Pend d'Oreille	1,456
Liberty	6,060
Lake Cœur d'Alene	3,500
Long Valley	3,700
Malade City	4,700
Market Lake	4,795
Montpelier	5,793
Morristown	5,700
Moose Lake	5,600
Mouth of Owyhee River	2,130
Mouth of Port Neuf River	4,522
Mount Idaho City	3,480
Mount Stevens	7,000

Place.	Feet.
Montana Mine	9,500
Meade Mountain	10,540
Mount Preuss	9,979
Marsh Cone	7,663
Malade Mountain	9,220
Oneida Salt Works	6,300
Oneida (town)	5,700
Ovid	5,760
Oxford	4,862
Oliver Call's Bridge	3,304
Paris	5,836
Pleasant Valley Station	6,086
Pocatello Station	4,512
Packer's Bridge	4,500
Paris Peak	9,522
Placerville	5,100
Putnam Mountain	8,933
Quartzburg	5,115
Ross Fork Station	4,394
Red Rock Ranch	4,792
Rock Creek	4,513
Rocky Bar	5,200
Red Fish Lake	6,600
Sawtelle's Peak	9,070
St. Charles	5,932
St. George	5,771
Salmon City	4,030
Salt River Valley	5,800
Soda Springs	5,779
Sweetwater Crossing	1,360
Silver City	6,680
Sawtooth City	7,000
Soda Peak	9,683
Summit, between Challis and Bonanza	9,100
Summit, between Boisé and Idaho	4,815
Summit, between Idaho City and Centerville	4,812
South Mountain City	6,450
Salmon Falls	3,226
Stoner's Station	4,621
Shaw's Mountain Station	3,547
Stierman's Station	3,745
Upper Weiser Valley	3,000
Wood River (average)	4,900
War Eagle Mountain	7,980
Weston	4,600
Yuba City	5,650

INDEX.

CHAPTER I.—HISTORICAL.

	PAGE.
Organization	9
Origin of the Name	10
First Discoverers	11
Indian Depredations	13
Development	19

CHAPTER II.—DESCRIPTIVE.

Mountains	22
Rivers	22
Valleys	23
Climate	24
Natural Scenery	26
Lakes	28

CHAPTER III.—NATIVE TREES, PLANTS, AND ANIMALS.

Timber	29
Wild Fruits	31
Grasses	31
Wild Flowers	31
Native Animals	32

CHAPTER IV.—MINING.

Discovery of Gold	33
Wood River's Record	38
Snake River Placers	39

CHAPTER V.—FARMING AND STOCK-RAISING.

Soils	47
Stock-raising	51
The Reclamation of Desert Lands	53

CHAPTER VI.—COUNTIES OF IDAHO.

	PAGE.
Ada County	54
Alturas County	65
The Great Central Wood River Region	69
Bear Lake County	76
Boisé County	79
Cassia County	81
Custer County	86
Idaho County	94
Kootenai County	98
Lemhi County	101
Nez Percé County—North Idaho	110
Oneida County	112
Owyhee County	118
Shoshone County	121
Washington County	131

CHAPTER VII.—IDAHO INDIANS.

Native Tribes	133	138

CHAPTER VIII.—MISCELLANEOUS.

Schools	139
Churches	140
Societies	141
Newspapers	142
U. S. Land-offices	142
Railroads	143
Wages in Idaho	145
Idaho Altitudes	145

www.ingramcontent.com/pod-product-compliance
Lightning Source LLC
Chambersburg PA
CBHW030345170426
43202CB00010B/1243